Library of Congress Control Number: 2018939919
ISBN: 978-1-7320048-3-2

Printed in China

Designed by Jen Zhao

First Artvoices Art Books Publishing edition 2018

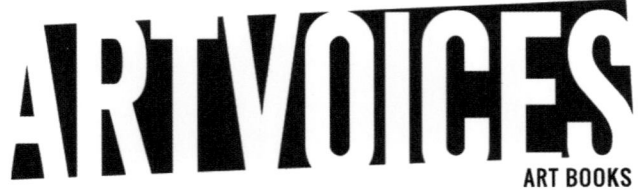

Artvoices Art Books Publishing
www.artvoicesartbooks.com

LORIEN SUÁREZ-KANERVA

COALESCING
GEOMETRIES

DEDICATED TO MY SON KENNY

TABLE OF CONTENTS

Foreword
LORIEN SUÁREZ-KANERVA: MODERNISM NOW
BY PETER FRANK
10

Introduction
LORIEN SUÁREZ. TRANSPOSED GEOMETRIES
BY MILAGROS BELLO, PH.D.
14

Publisher's Note
'IT'S NOT ABOUT A REVOLUTION'
BY TERRENCE SANDERS
20

FIRST PAINTINGS
ESSAY BY JOHN MENDELSOHN
24

LIVING WATER, GUITARRA ALEGRE & RAYUELA SERIES
36

FIRST WHEEL WITHIN A WHEEL ARTWORKS
ESSAY BY JOHN MENDELSOHN
58

WHEEL WITHIN A WHEEL SERIES - 5 YEARS LATER
84

'SIMPLY COMPLEX'
BY EVAN SENN
36

EVOLUTIONARY ABSTRACTION
BY BRITTNI WINKLER
90

REFLECTION: A DYNAMIC ARRANGEMENT OF PARTS AMONGST THE WHOLE
BY LORIEN SUÁREZ-KANERVA
138

AN INSIDE EXAMINATION INTO THE MAKINGS OF THE PROCESS AND PRACTICE
BY LORIEN SUÁREZ-KANERVA
158

GEOMETRIC BOTANICALS
168

OBJECTS OF VIRTÙ: CREATIVITY IN USE
BY LORIEN SUÁREZ-KANERVA
170

ACKNOWLEDGMENTS
183

CV
184

LORIEN SUÁREZ-KANERVA: MODERNISM NOW

BY PETER FRANK

THE MODERNIST THESIS HAS NOT BEEN SWEPT AWAY BY ITS POST-MODERNIST ANTITHESIS.

A "Neo-Modernist" tendency has endured in artistic practice around the world – Western and otherwise – all throughout the many crises of contemporary art. One persistent development bespeaking the persistence of Modernism (certainly in its neo-Modernist guise) can be called "Reconstructivism," returning as it does to the geometric – and fundamentally optical – language(s) of post-Cubist non-objectivity. In her painting Lorien Suárez-Kanerva evinces that post-Cubist heritage, and the Modernist – now neo-Modernist – principles that heritage inheres.

In fact, the whole construct of "heritage" plays a central role in Suárez-Kanerva's practice and self-regard. From the first she has regarded Modernist masters such as Kandinsky and the Delaunays (notably Sonia Delaunay-Terk) as her guiding spirits; their vision, of a visual world invented within but no less out of the natural world and applied to human society, is her vision. Whether impelled by the spiritual, as in the case of Malevich or Hilma af Klint; by logic, as in that of Moholy-Nagy; or by a conflation of the physical and the metaphysical, as in Mondrian or O'Keeffe, Suárez-Kanerva has taken their language(s) of abstraction and their abiding seriousness of purpose as her own. She does not recycle their Modernism, but embraces and transforms it. Her Reconstructivism truly seeks to reconstruct.

Suárez-Kanerva maintains the Modernist spirit by admitting further to a mixed cultural heritage of her own – a very mixed cultural heritage that would more likely tear apart than unify a single artist's practice. Venezuelan on her father's side, Finnish on her mother's, Suárez-Kanerva operates from the access she has felt to two very different peoples – concentrating on what the artistic outputs of those two peoples, as ethnic groups and/or as communities, share with each other. Both Finland and Venezuela have contributed distinctly to Modernism: the European country, gaining its independence after the First World War, had given visual form to its cultural self-expression at this crucial time in Modernist history; while Venezuela, like its South American neighbors, saw a notable surge in avant garde experimentation after the Second World War, a signal moment in late Modernism.

Finland's kansallisromantiikka, in effect Jugendstil pressed into the service of a "romantic nationalism," included a high-precision realism in painting, the angular stylizations and patterning of cutting-edge tapestry production, and, most famously, architectural innovations that anticipated Art Deco. The vibrant examples, then, of Akseli Gallen-Kallela, Eliel Saarinen, and other artist-designer-architects of the independence generation have provided Suárez-Kanerva bold models of formal elaboration. So, in a very different manner, have the influential styles of postwar Finnish and Scandinavian, especially Danish, design (as well as the intrepid example of Swedish painter af Klint).

The Venezuelan impact on Suárez-Kanerva has been more immediate, as it was central to her childhood spent in part in Caracas. She has distinct memories of a cityscape punctuated with sculptures and architectural installations by Jesus Raphael Soto, Carlos Cruz Diez, Alejandro Otero, and other non-objective artists interested in creating a melding of optical and architectural effect. These public works echoed, and often influenced, similar projects throughout the continent (and ultimately the world), and marked their makers as progenitors of the Op Art movement – a movement now remembered for its eye-dazzling artifacts, but marked in its heyday by the aestheticization of social space.

Like these exemplars in 1960s Venezuela and early-1900s Finland, Suárez-Kanerva feels impelled by social and intellectual – and by extension spiritual – forces larger than she; and, like them, she responds to this impulse with an art that is at once standardized and personalized. That is, Suárez-Kanerva's compositions base themselves on highly regulated, often patterned structures, elaborations on arcs and curves as well as straight lines and enclosed forms, generated almost to the point of obsession. This is not to say that Suárez-Kanerva dependably fills her pictures with repeated geometric detail, nor even less that she allows her imagination (much less her color) to be subject to the restraints of a compositional formula. Dense and rhythmic as her works can be, Suárez-Kanerva never allows them to devolve into predictable designs; she always provides some sort of opening in her structure to allow her lines and shapes freedom, even erratic movement. Rather than march across the picture plane, her shapes swell and ebb, advance and withdraw, churn and rest, in a constant play of shape and light. However subtly, she always subsumes the strictures of the grid into the relationships of compositions as fluid as they are poised.

Suárez-Kanerva's main body of Reconstructivist abstraction falls within her rubric of "Wheel Within A Wheel," a title indicative not only of the dominance of rounded forms, but of formal dynamics that are at once restless and perpetual. All her compositions radiate. Yes, they are visually radiant as self-defined images; but they also depend on the sense that one form is giving birth to the next, throwing it off like so many seeds or tendrils yet in a formally refined, even stylized manner, so that the structural quality of these images conjures the mapped interactions of sub-atomic particles as much as of floral or animal sexual energy. Suárez-Kanerva's Wheels Within Wheels speak of generation on all levels of existence.

More recently, the artist has returned to the specifically botanical impulse of her earliest paintings, realizing vivid, curvaceous images, at once languid and forceful, grouped under the title "Geometric Botanicals." Allowing herself reversion to a more simply interpreted source, plants, Suárez-Kanerva seeks to explore the less complicated and daunting metaphors the Wheel Within a Wheel paintings leave behind. Even so, Suárez-Kanerva finds an elaborate world of form and energy in and among her Geometric Botanicals, one that allows her to translate such biological improvisations not just to canvas and paper, but to wearable cloth, as clothing and adornment.

Continually researching science and philosophy for further inspiration, Lorien Suárez-Kanerva displays – and reaffirms – the complex intellectual and spiritual motivations set forth in Modernist discourse, making her, as stated before, something of a neo-Modernist (specifically a Reconstructivist). Modernism demands of its adherents a sophisticated grasp of the universe, as much science as art, and demands as well a deep personal investment in the reconfiguration of that grasp. Some artists manifest this investment as an outpouring of expression; others, as a cultivation of a carefully deduced world view. With her keen sense of ethnic and cognitive multiplicity, Suárez-Kanerva works between these two polarities, seeking rational form for mystical, or at least metaphorical, thought. Her painting, so readily appealing to the eye, is beautiful for a reason.

**PETER FRANK is Associate Editor for Fabrik magazine. He is former critic for Angeleno magazine and the L. A. Weekly, served as Editor for THEmagazine Los Angeles and Visions Art Quarterly, and contributes articles to publications around the world. Frank was born in 1950 in New York, where he received a B.A. and M.A. in art history from Columbia University and was art critic for The Village Voice and the SoHo Weekly News, and moved to Los Angeles in 1988. Frank, who recently served as Senior Curator at the Riverside Art Museum, has organized numerous theme and survey shows for the Solomon R. Guggenheim Museum in New York, the Museo Reina Sofia in Madrid, the Venice Biennale, Documenta, and other venues. Currently Frank is preparing a survey of the artist Tony DeLap for the Laguna [CA] Art Museum. McPherson & Co./Documentext published Frank's Something Else Press: An Annotated Bibliography in 1983. A cycle of poems, The Travelogues, was issued by Sun & Moon Press in 1982. Abbeville Press released New, Used & Improved, an overview of the New York art scene co-written with Michael McKenzie, in 1987. Frank has written many monographs and catalogues on a wide array of modern and contemporary artists. He has taught and lectured extensively throughout North America and Europe.

LORIEN SUÁREZ: TRANSPOSED GEOMETRIES

BY MILAGROS BELLO, PH.D.

LORIEN SUÁREZ CREATES COMPLEX WEBS OF HAND-MADE FRACTALIZED PATTERNS.

She proposes geometric figures in never-ending configurations of infinite iterations. At different scales, and through different "fractured" recurring schemes, the geometric forms progressively augment and multiply in expansive dimensions. Vortexes and vibrant fluids, both tactile and aerial, operate in recursive constructions. Depths, ratios, proportions, scales, and ranges in strong colored stances emerge as relational points of departure. They mimic the cosmic world in imaginary projections of conversing energy waves, multiplying crystals, galactic systems, molecular interfaces, and collisions of particles as forceful form/type model generators.

At first, and attuned with the Mandelbrot model, the artist's work establishes schemes of visual chaos and order, producing multiple organizations in orderly generators and extensive, shaped iterations. Continuous and self-mirrored structures expand or contract in a decentered visual composition. Euclidian "fractalized" and multihued circles, rectangles, and squares, subdivide in vibrant assemblies of variable densities. (1)

The visual morphologies of hard-edge outlines superimpose or revolve one into other in mathematical calculations. The works conform a vision of the universe in its meticulous micro and macro optic constructs. The viewer changes perspective from the rational vertical/horizontal paradigm to a sprawling kinetic perception projecting invisible domains in which materiality dissolves towards intangibility and immanence.

The intricate visual result signals the artist's insight and awareness that plainly reveal her force and strong being. She affirms, "Creating art is in essence a practice of being attentive and focused in the present moment. Creative insights come to light. Over time, intuitive spiritual expressiveness grows." The work comes from a vigorous creativity and a resourceful inventiveness that doesn't need the use of any computer software mediation. It's Suárez's artistic hand over canvas or paper, the painter's sole imprint, that sets the conception of this ingenious imagery.

Endorsing her artistic identity, Suárez asserts: "Art to me is a form of knowledge of the heart. Creative practice brings forth discoveries that outlive their creators, serve the evolution of meaningful understanding, and give birth to a more profound vision of the unfolding of life."

In a further step, the artist goes beyond in the complexity of her geometrical creations. Their self-generated turns and expansions also

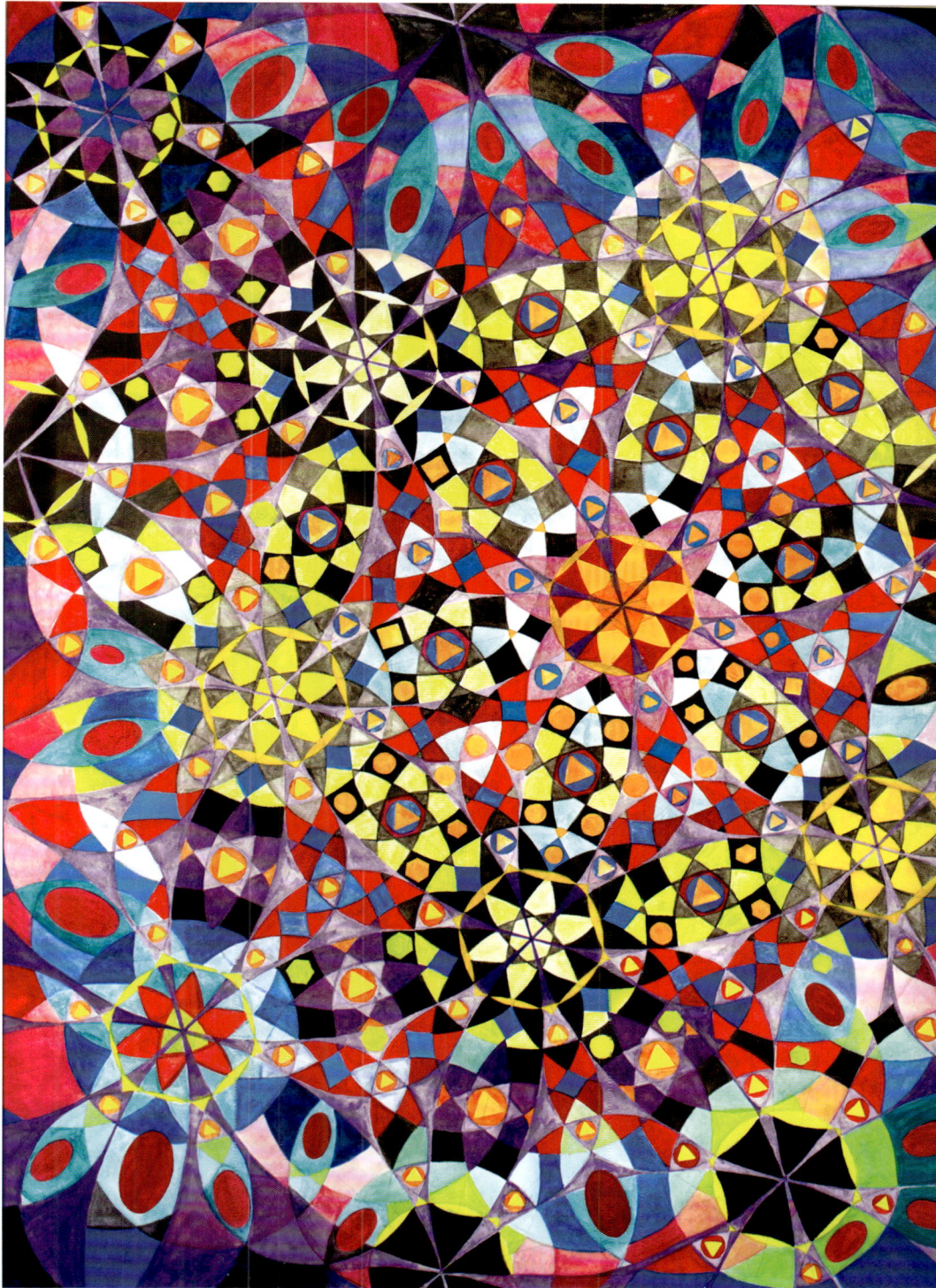

WHEEL WITHIN A WHEEL 16

correlate to jewel-like geometric shapes, such as it is in the "amplituhedron", a geometric object that challenges notions of space and time in quantum physics (2). This refers to a jewel-like multifaceted master geometry that was conceived by physicists Nima Arkani-Hamed (a professor of physics at the Institute for Advanced Study in Princeton, N.J.) and Jaroslav Trnka (a post-doctoral researcher at the California Institute of Technology) to project quantum particles' multidimensional trajectories in the subatomic world. Departing from this parameter, the artist traces comprehensive structures that build up together in many facets and volumes, in a rich interplay of kinematic conglomerates (3). She creates "transposed geometries", altered and swapped, rearranged in sparkled diagrams, in fizzed organizations, in an open system of space, time, and movement.

The work merges two essential elements of visual plasticity appropriated from modernist aesthetics, a potent graphic line of defined contours that strongly delineate and give character to forms, and a chart of colors that desegregate and disseminate into rich tone values and hues. It is at once both a graphic and a painterly approach, reinforcing the "autonomy of means" of the pieces in which the image possesses a "self-sufficient autonomy" (4). The rhythmic lines entwined with luxuriant hues consolidate a compelling visual execution in which any reference to the real is unnecessary.

The Watercolor, *Wheel Within A Wheel 16*, one of Suárez's seminal works from 2003, displays a visual chaos/order of a crystal configuration. Fractal colored forms repeat in augmenting boosting patterns, virally interweaving and magnifying. Numerous geometrical subsidiaries, triangles, circles, and convex polygons proliferate in a lavish arrangement of the aerial composition. Governing circles, positioned in tensional asymmetrical locations,

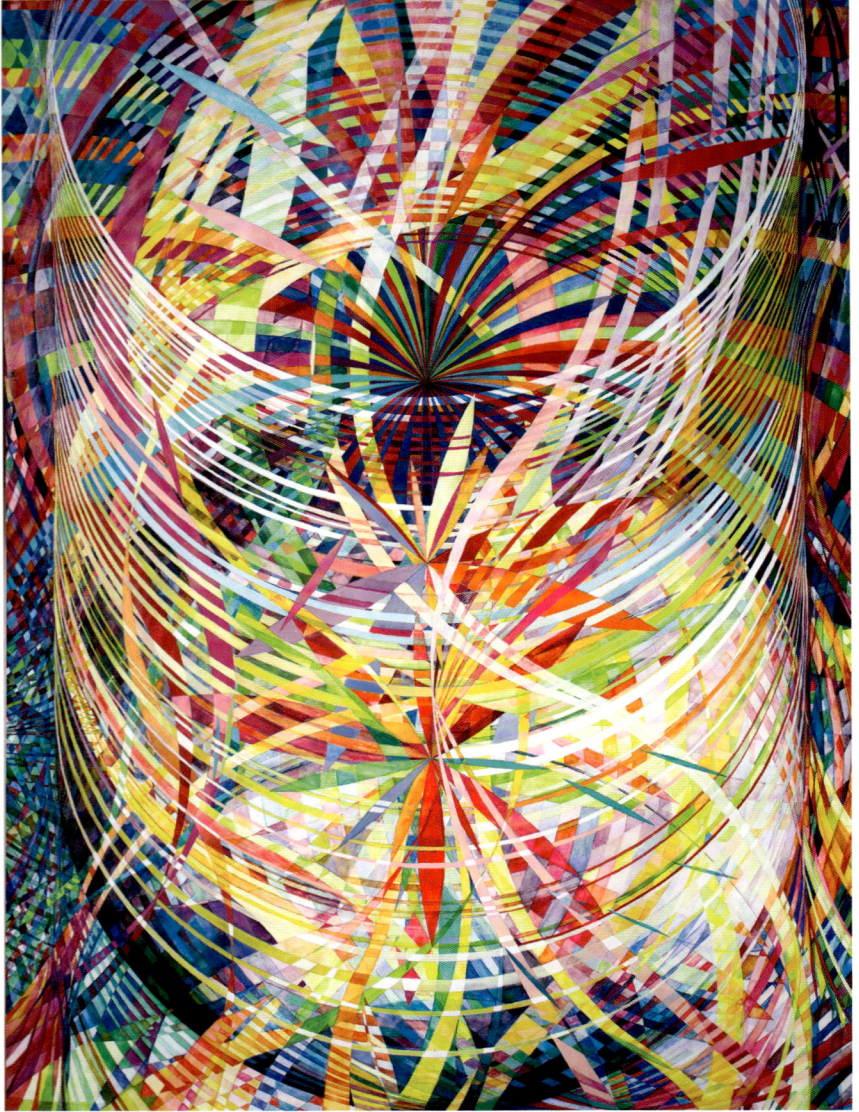

WHEEL WITHIN A WHEEL 50

emerge as dominant form generators. The flowery and elaborate crystal forms wide spread in the hinted space producing powerful optical effects.

The work *Wheel Within A Wheel 50*, a watercolor/gouache (2007), shows a huge spinning spiral rotating ad infinitum in a scattering process. It is a complex formulation of multiple interactions and frequencies, showing high-amplitude

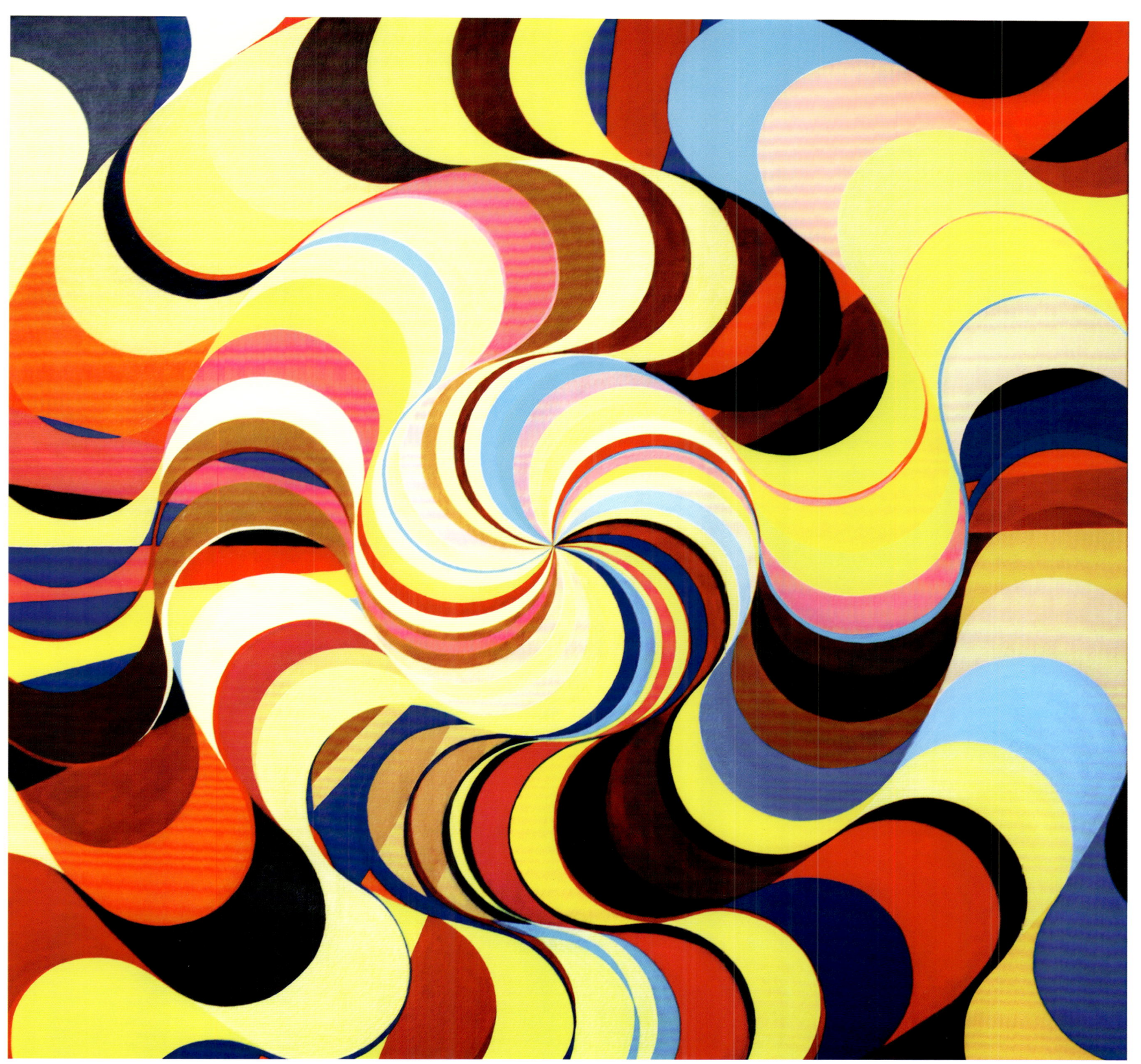

WHEEL WITHIN A WHEEL 114

dimensions that refer to a 3-D quantum graph of moving particles. It is a visual platform for an all-encompassing inward/outward continuum of space-time. At the center of the spiral, there are three core generators, three epicenters of expanding energy, that radially project crisp trajectories, fracturing the planes inside-out and vice versa. The interlacing of colors enhances the kinetic effects, into a hyper recursive panorama of the universe.

The acrylic painting *Wheel Within A Wheel 114 (2017)*, marks as one of the most important canvass in the artist's production. In it, there is a deep immersion into pure pictorialism, and a major emphasis on volume, paint and mass. Expressive layers of glutinous tint appear in fractioned compounds. A bulky snake-like geometry retorts and spirals inside-out in figure/ground illusionistic effects. The negative space disappears into the physical body of the colossal curly geometry. The multihued fragments succeed one another, continuously dissolving into endless torsions as in a sequel of an Escher-like tessellation design.

In summary terms, the artist names the unnamable, and visually articulates the invisible routes of the metaphysics of the cosmos.

4.   Drucker, Johanna. Theorizing Modernism. Visual Art and the Critical Tradition. Columbia   University Press. Col. Interpretations in Art. 1994 ed. p.70

**Dr. Milagros Bello holds a Ph.D. in Sociology of Art, and a French Masters Degree in Art History from Sorbonne University, Paris, France. She presented a Doctoral Thesis in the New Figurative Painting in Latin America, Venezuelan Chapter. Of Venezuelan origin, she immigrated to the USA in 2000 to teach Critical Theories at the Florida International University. Since then she has taught at the Florida Atlantic University, and at the Miami International University of Art and Design. She has curated numerous shows in Latin American Art, and International Art. She is the former Senior Editor of Arte al Dia Magazine. She is an art writer, and had published art articles in Arte al Dia Magazine, and Art Districts magazine. Since 2010 to present she is the director and chief curator of Curator's Voice Art Projects in Miami.

REFERENCES

1.   Taylor, Richard. Fractal Expressionism. Where Art Meets Science. https://blogs.uoregon.edu/richardtaylor/files/2015/12/PollockFractalExpressionism2003-2b1h6rl.pdf

2.   Wolchover, Natalie. A Jewel at the Heart of Quantum Physics. Quanta Magazine. https://www.quantamagazine.org/physicists-discover-geometry-underlying-particle-physics-20130917/

3.   Wolchover, Natalie. Op. cit.

IT'S NOT ABOUT A REVOLUTION

BY TERRENCE SANDERS-SMITH

ARTVOICES ART BOOKS MISSION IS TO INTRODUCE ARTISTS THAT REDEFINE THEIR MEDIUM AS WELL AS PRESERVING A LEGACY FOR MID CAREER AND UNDER RECOGNIZED ARTISTS.

The monographs created are tangible proof of their practice and process for the education of the now and next generations of art curators, critics, and enthusiasts.

As the publisher of Artvoices Art Books I am pleased and very excited to release 'Coalescing Geometries' by Lorien Suárez-Kanerva. This monograph represents new territory for Artvoices Art Books, which primarily focuses on socio-political titles and artists.

Lorien Suárez-Kanerva is a revolutionary artist in her own right, but her visual dialogue is not accusatory and judgmental but approving and inviting. My first impression upon examining her work was to feel and not to uncover. As an art critic, writer and or journalist our first reaction arguably is to deconstruct what lies beneath the aesthetic of the artist intent. Ms. Suárez-Kanerva work touched me on a very personal level where it was ok to let my guard down and enjoy the work, better yet the moment as if I was dreaming awake in a rain forest or a national forest.

Ms. Suárez-Kanerva life work is a respite from the atrocities and inhumanity that takes place Worldwide on a daily basis. A balance so to speak that assists us in maintaining our sanity of a World population that has been systematically desensitized by societies oppressors.

When you study or experience one of the paintings by Suárez-Kanerva you are initially inundated and impressed with her use of color, scale and line. At first glance the paintings appear an optical illusion of a multitude of spheres and color. It's a World of beautiful and wondrous controlled chaos very much like an 'untouched pure oasis'. Historically and in parallel if Op Art artist Bridget Riley and Impressionist Georgia O'Keeffe had a child it would be Lorien Suárez-Kanerva.

Lorien Suárez-Kanerva work at the core reminds us not to lose sight of what's important. Not vanity, superficialities,

material wealth and or power but nature. All humans are part of nature but in our ambitions and greed we sometimes lose focus on what is essential and necessary for our survival as humans and as a planet.

Lorien Suárez-Kanerva unfortunately exists in a sea of artists whose abstraction and or abstract expressionism works remind us of artists who have contributed to the landscape of modern and contemporary art in years or decades past. Ms. Suárez-Kanerva unlike a majority of her contemporaries is passionate, honest, and unaffected by market trends. She is committed to creating work she loves and is in hopes you and I the viewer standing in front of one of her pieces escapes to a place of uninterrupted wondrous beauty.

One of the greatest characteristics and achievements of Lorien Suárez-Kanerva body of work is that like nature it's for everyone to enjoy. You don't need to know art history to enjoy her art. There's something innately simplistic and universal that embodies our collective humanity.

LORIEN SUÁREZ-KANERVA

COALESCING
GEOMETRIES

FIRST PAINTINGS

BY JOHN MENDELSOHN

WHEN WE GET SO CLOSE TO AN EXPERIENCE THAT WE NO LONGER KNOW ITS NAME, IT LOSES SOME OF ITS FIXED IDENTITY, AND WE LOSE SOME OF OURS.

This magical transaction is at the heart of the paintings of Lorien Suárez. She focuses her attention on the forms of growing things, drawing so near that their essential natures begin to emerge clearly. The process is no less mysterious for its painterly directness.

In two contrasting yet related bodies of work, a sense of movement flows through the paintings, both defining form and creating currents of visual energy. In both series, the viewer is immersed in realms of animated color that are both abstract and highly specific. Together, the series constitute a response to the natural world that is personal and passionate, embracing the visible and the emotive as two aspects of a single phenomenon.

One series of paintings is ephemeral, light-filled, and buoyant. Suárez layers translucent acrylic paint in sweeping arcs and branching lines, to suggest the leaves of a palm tree and the play of water. These paintings radiate as if we are looking through atmospheres gently glowing with color. Even with the lightness of their gestural brush strokes, these paintings have a structural clarity, a kind of organic architecture coalescing from fluid space.

A second series of paintings is pulsating, floral, and vivid in color. Here nature is lavish and joyous, ragged and raw. The forms range from flame-like leaves and spiky tendrils to many petaled blossoms. In this work, Suárez acknowledges the influence of Delaunay and Kandinsky, who as young painters were similarly fired by nature's sweet wildness. These paintings vibrate with echoing, wave-like patterns, and with color chords of increasing intensity, red with purple-blue, turquoise with yellow-green.

In the two series, we are presented with seemingly opposed visions, the transcendent and the sensuous. Rather than confronting us with a duality, the painter seems to want us to notice that like spirit and body, these two qualities inhabit a single world that lives equally in nature and in our own true selves.

**John Mendelsohr is a painter based in New York who has written on contemporary art for many publications. He contributed an essay to the recent book, Deborah Remington: A Life in Drawing. His paintings have been exhibited extensively in the U.S. and internationally.

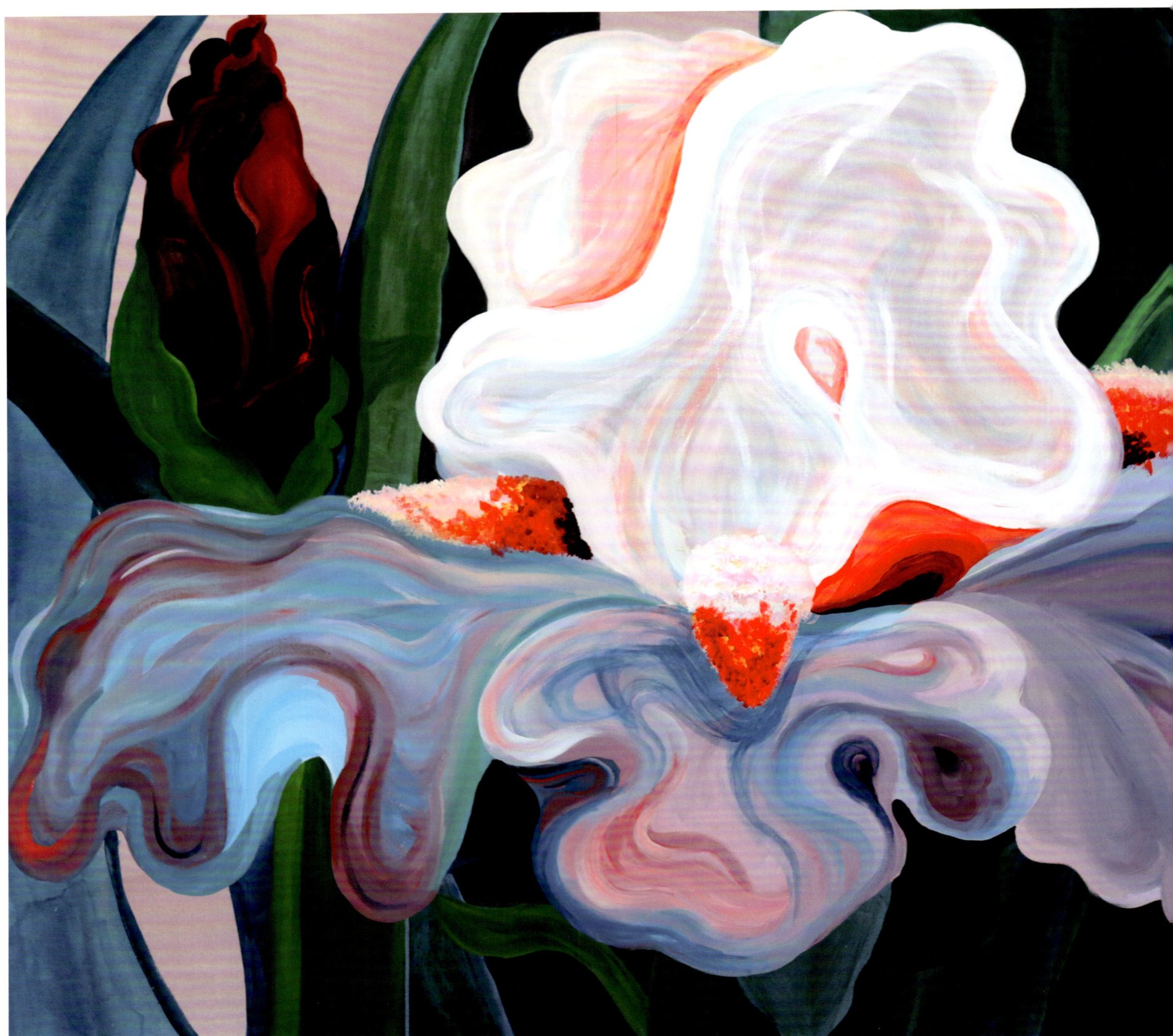

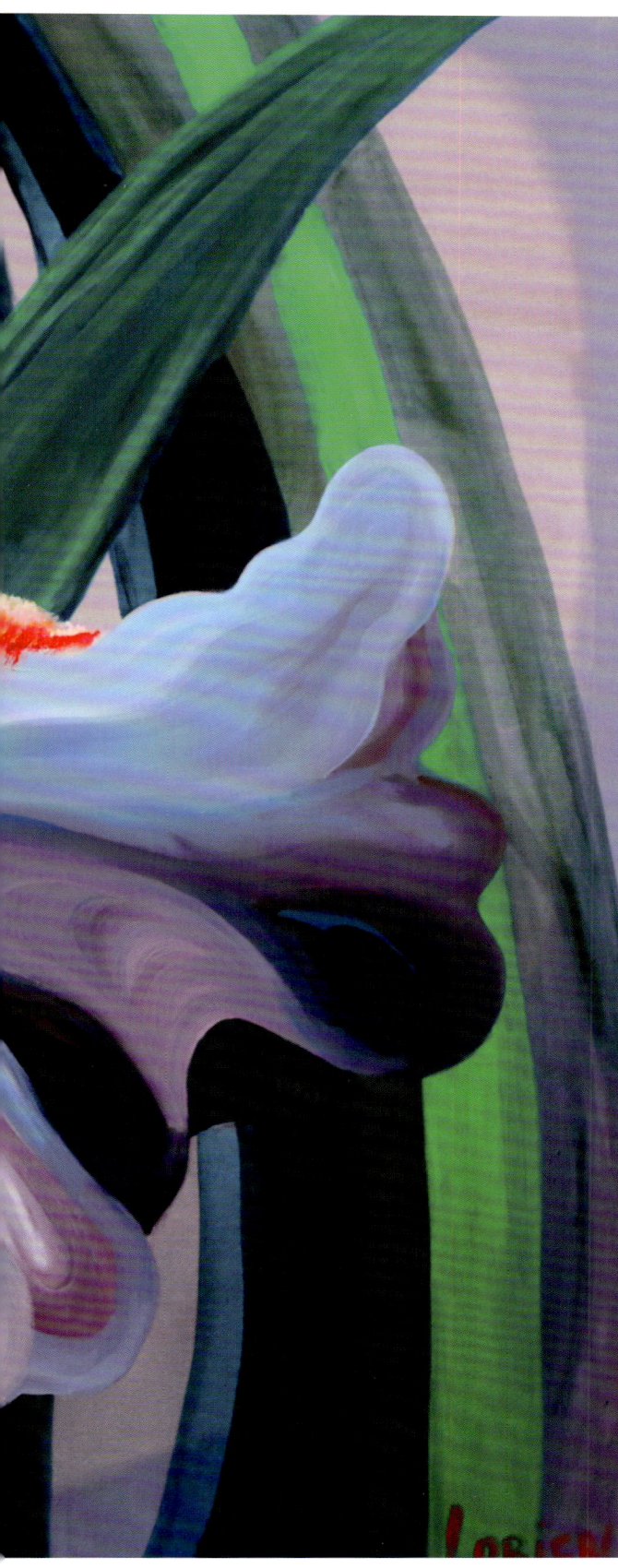

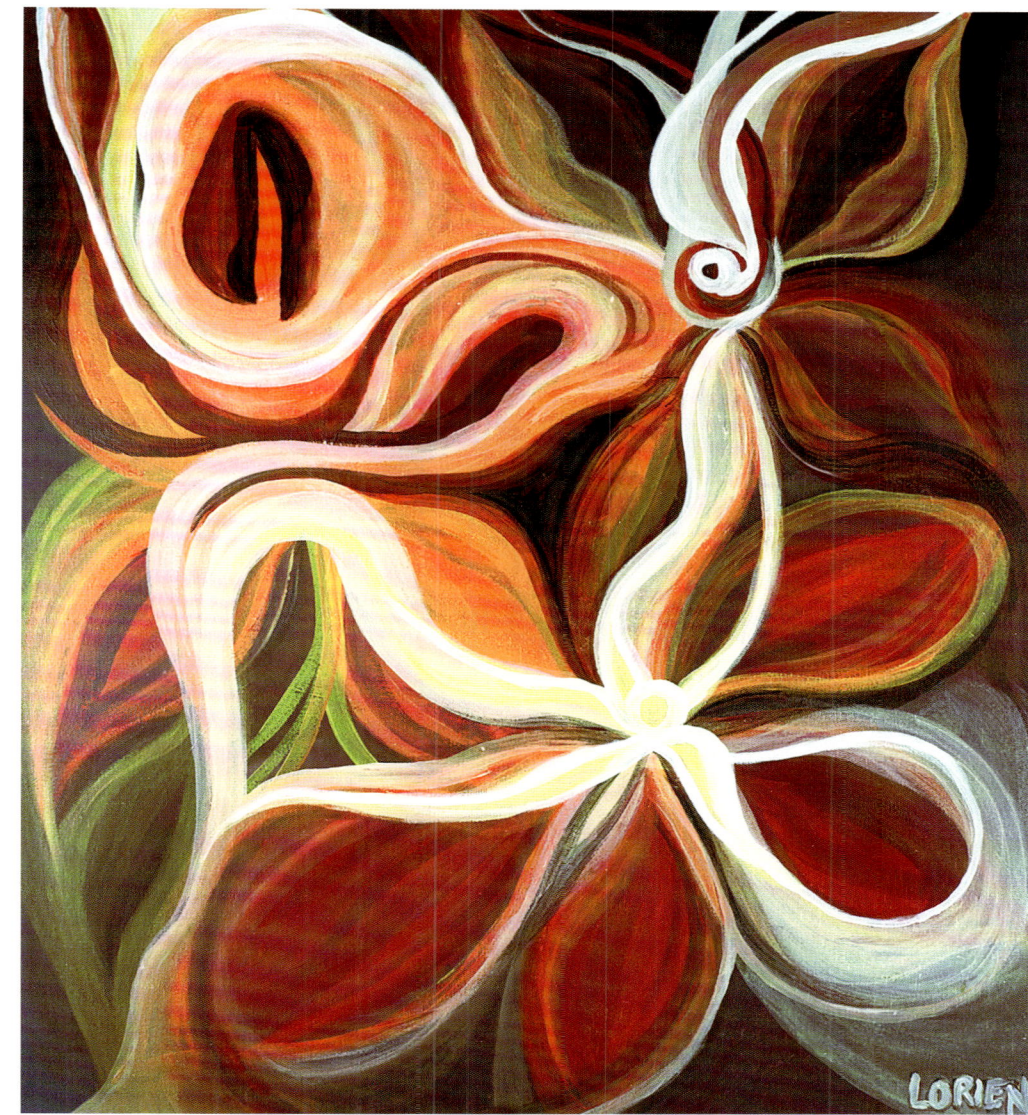

IRIS *(LEFT)*

48 IN X 72 IN , ACRYLIC, 1988

BLOSSOMS

40 IN X 30 IN , ACRYLIC, 1988

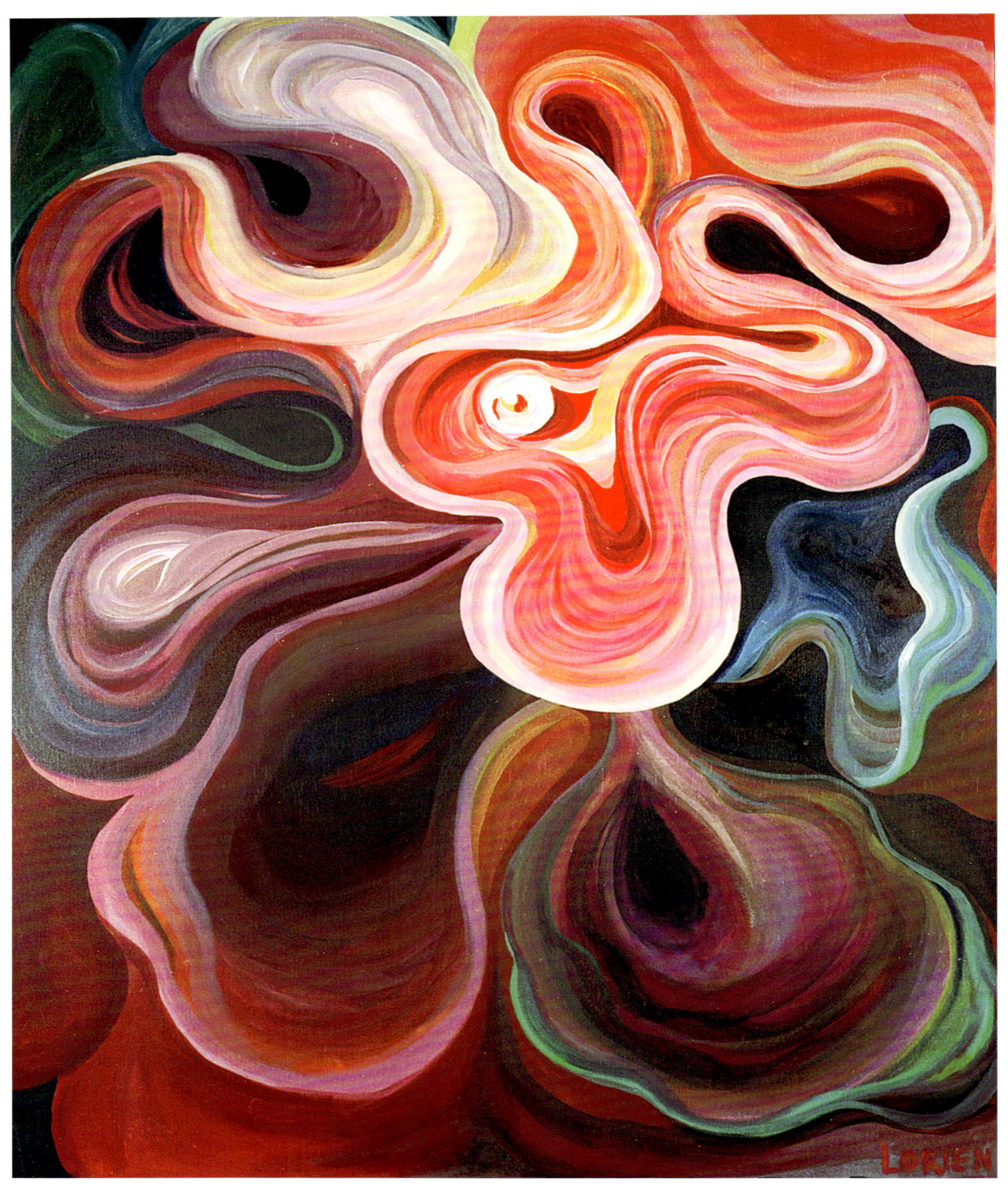

BLOSSOM

48 IN X 36 IN
ACRYLIC, 1987

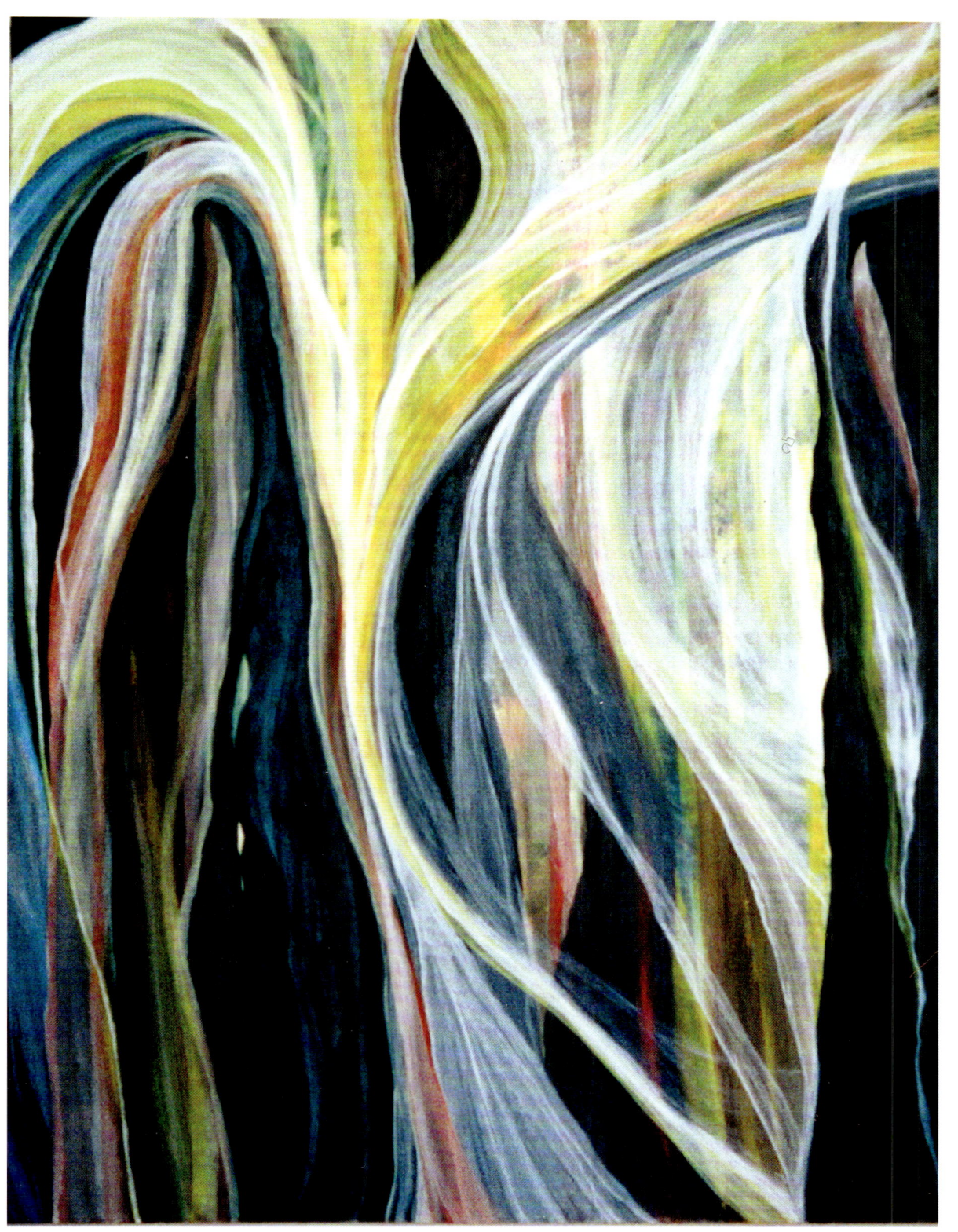

**FOREST LIGHT &
SHADOWS**
48 IN X 36 IN
ACRYLIC, 1988

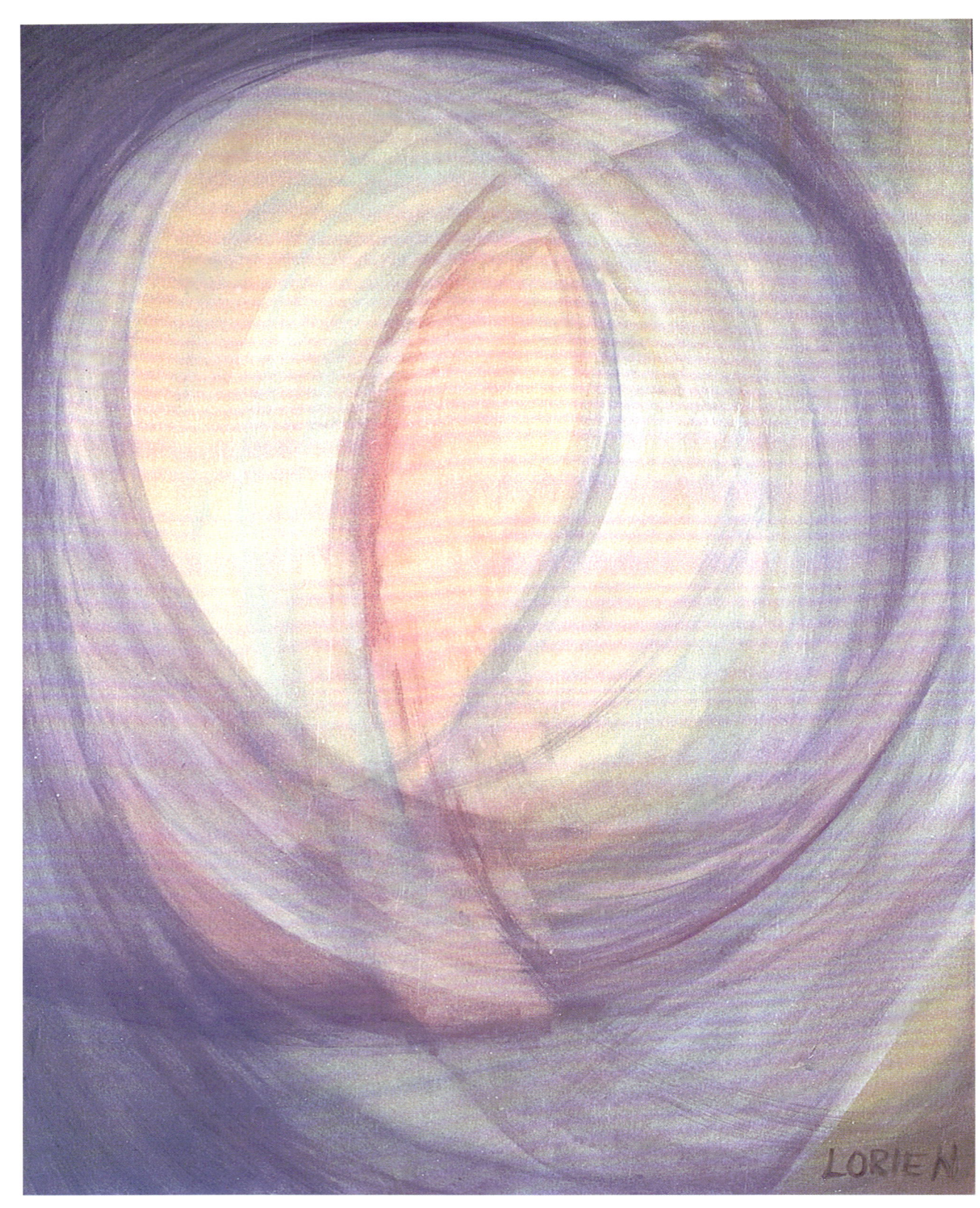

ETHEREAL 1

48 IN X 36 IN
ACRYLIC, 2000

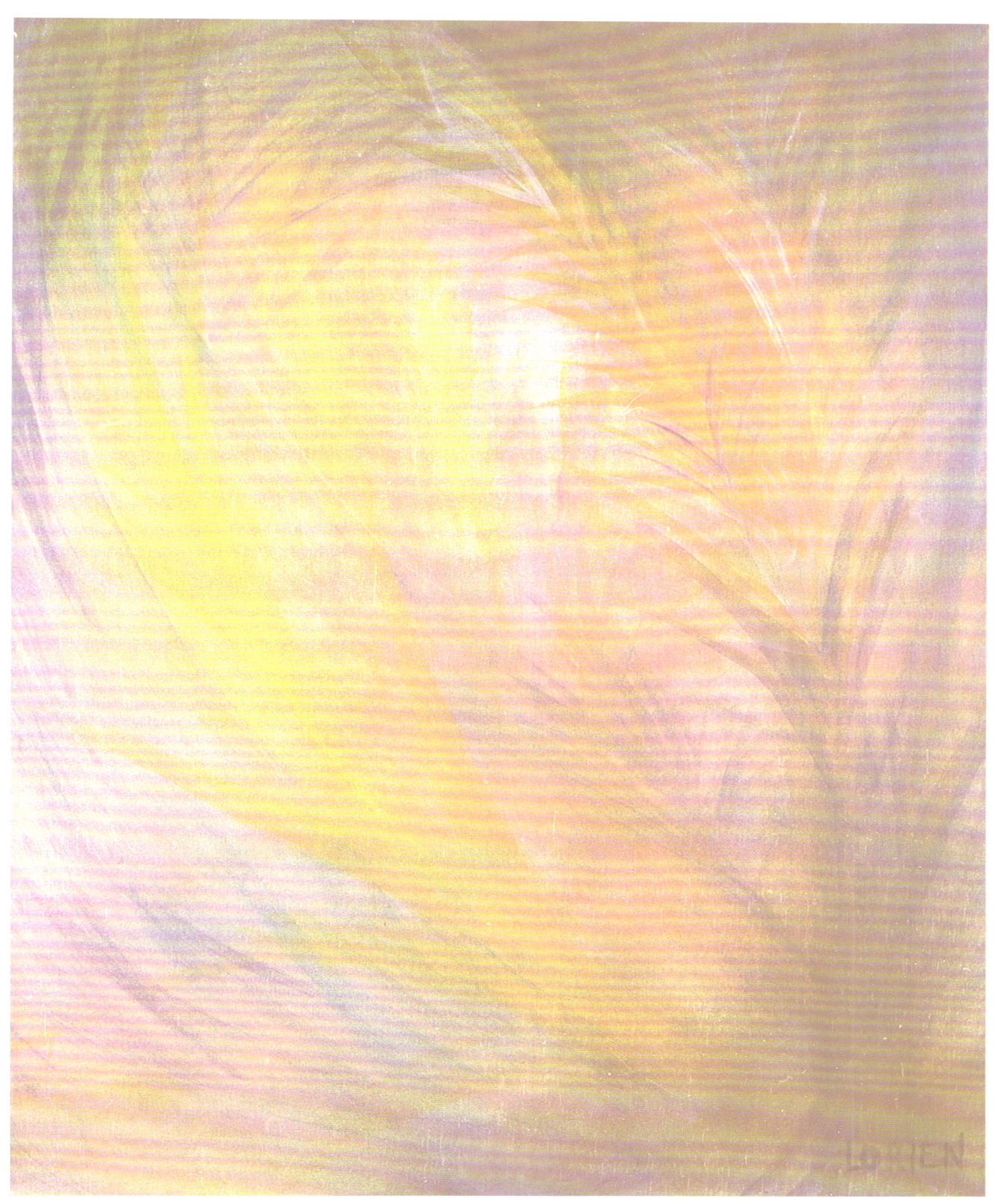

ETHEREAL 2
48 IN X 36 IN
ACRYLIC, 2000

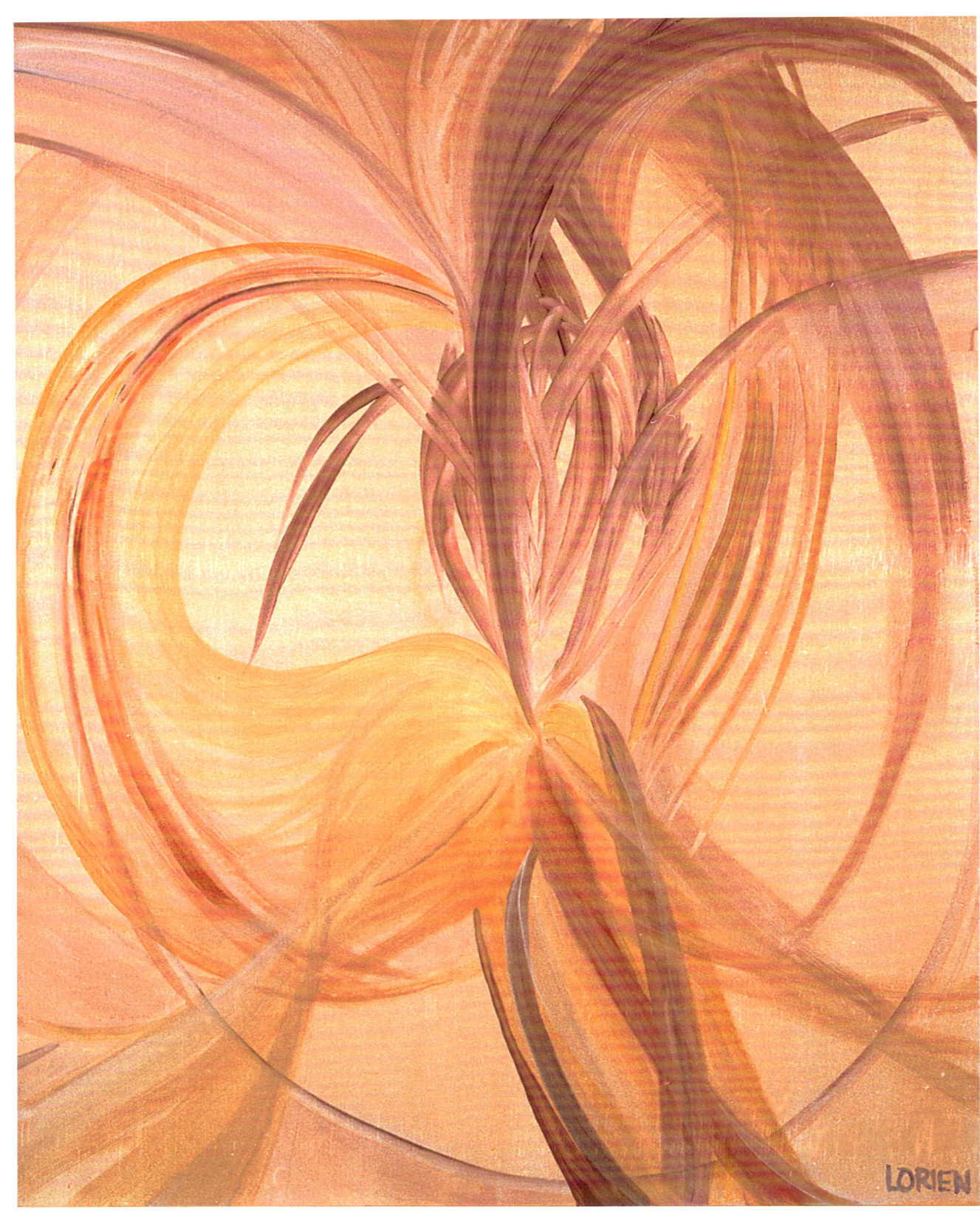

PALM ETHEREAL 3

48 IN X 36 IN
ACRYLIC, 2000

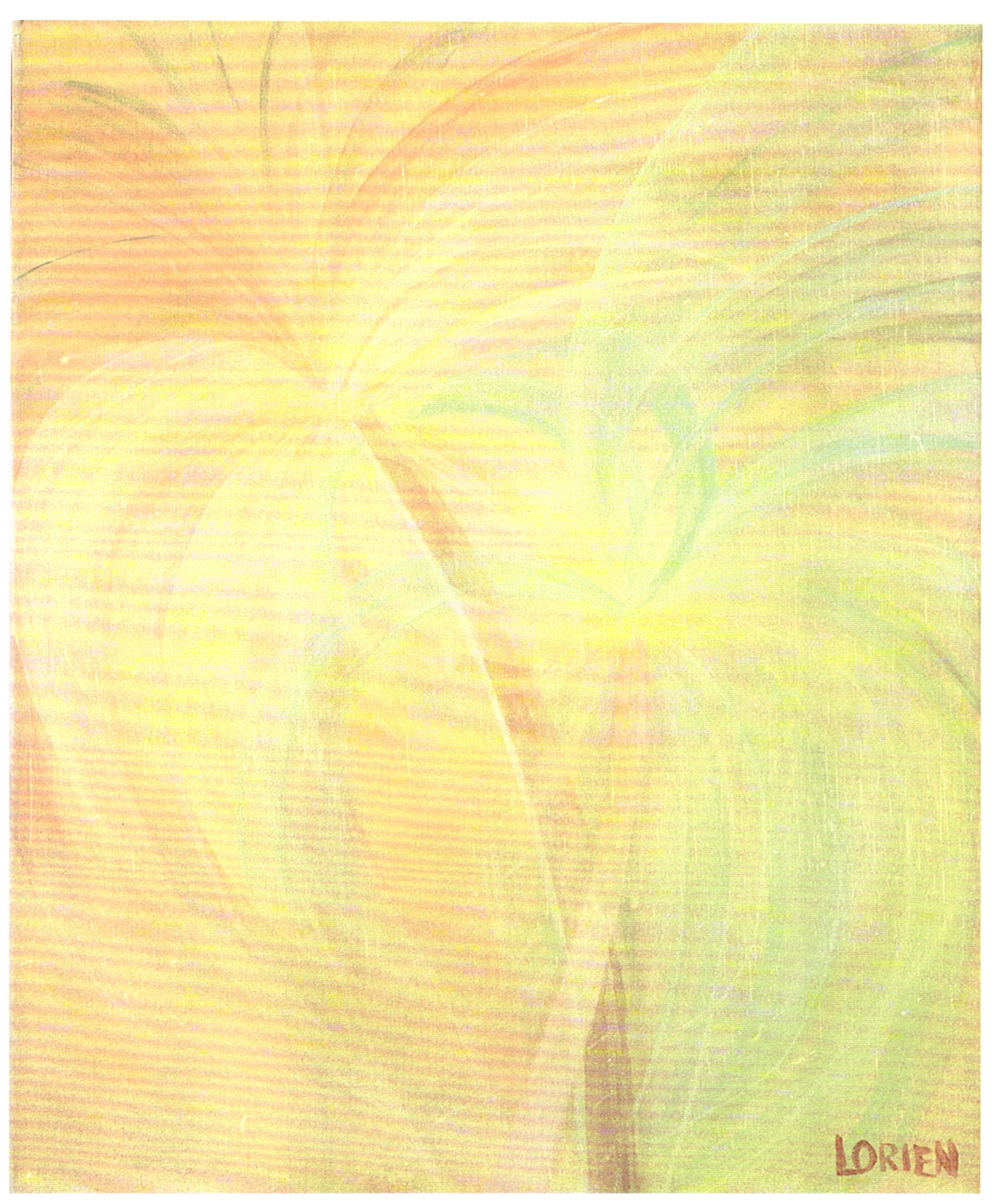

PALMS ETHEREAL 4
20 IN X 16 IN
ACRYLIC, 2000

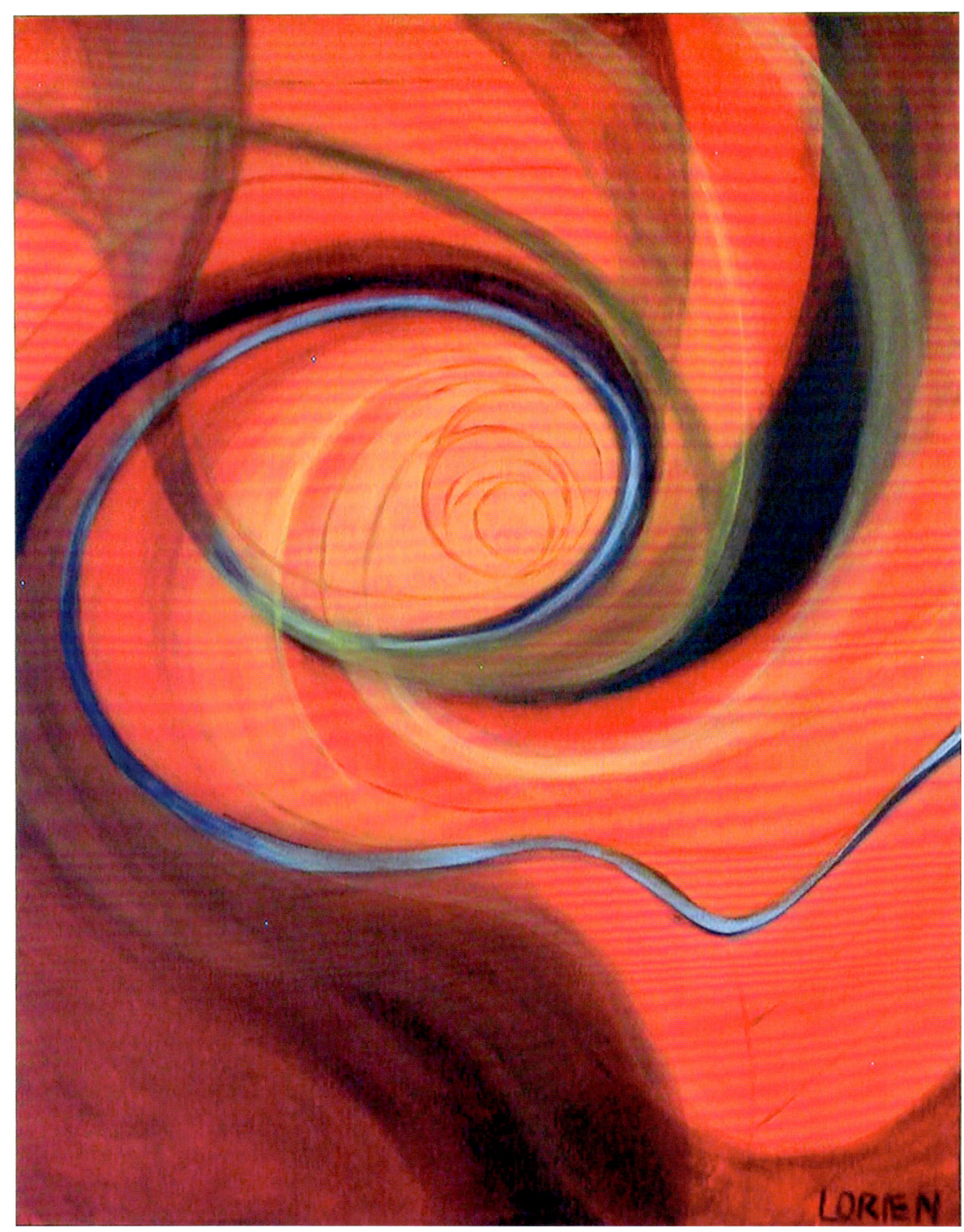

SPIRAL

48 IN X 36 IN
ACRYLIC, 2002

SAILS *(RIGHT)*

24 IN X 20 IN
ACRYLIC, 2002

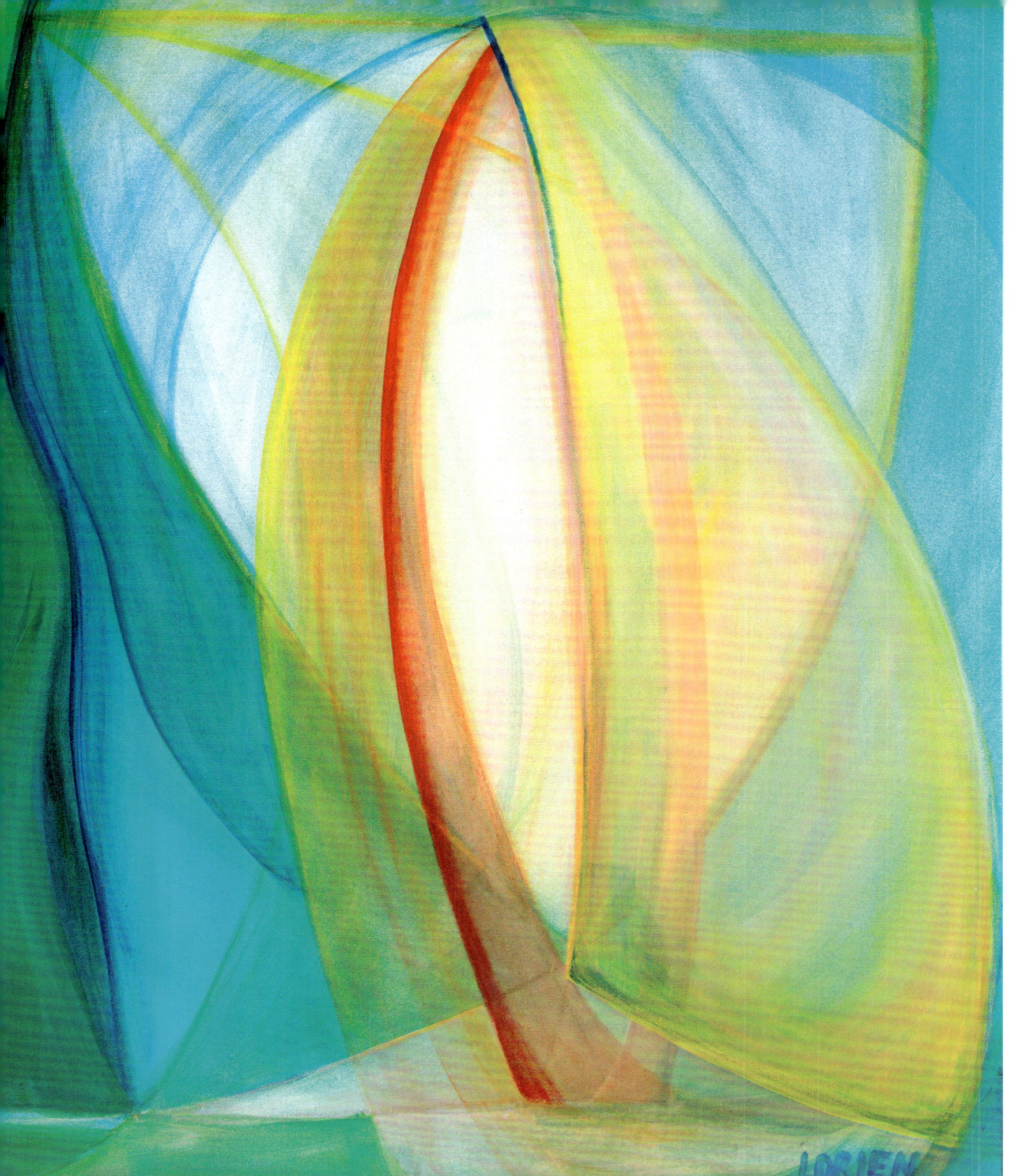

GUITARRA ALEGRE, LIVING WATER & RAYUELA

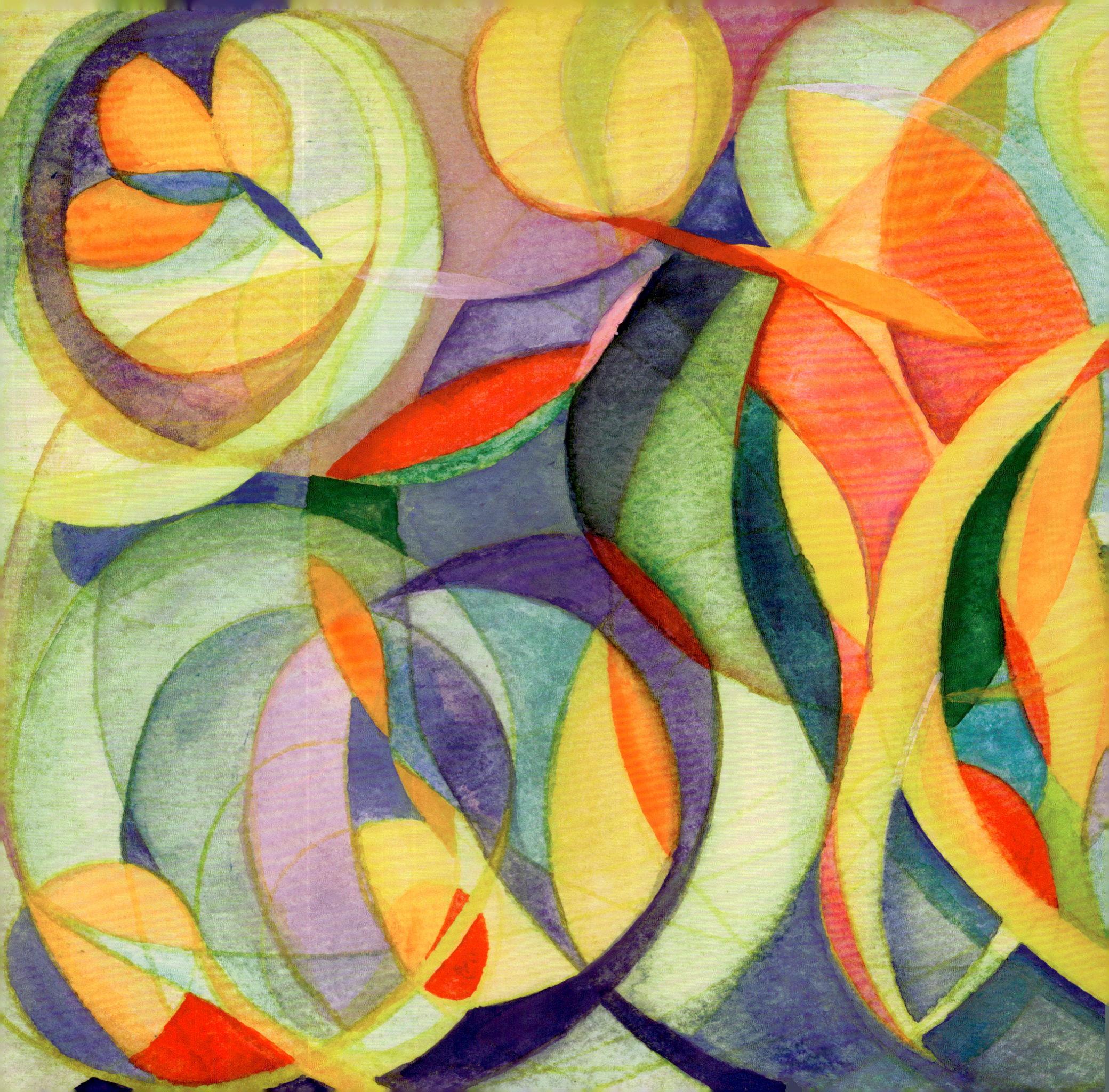

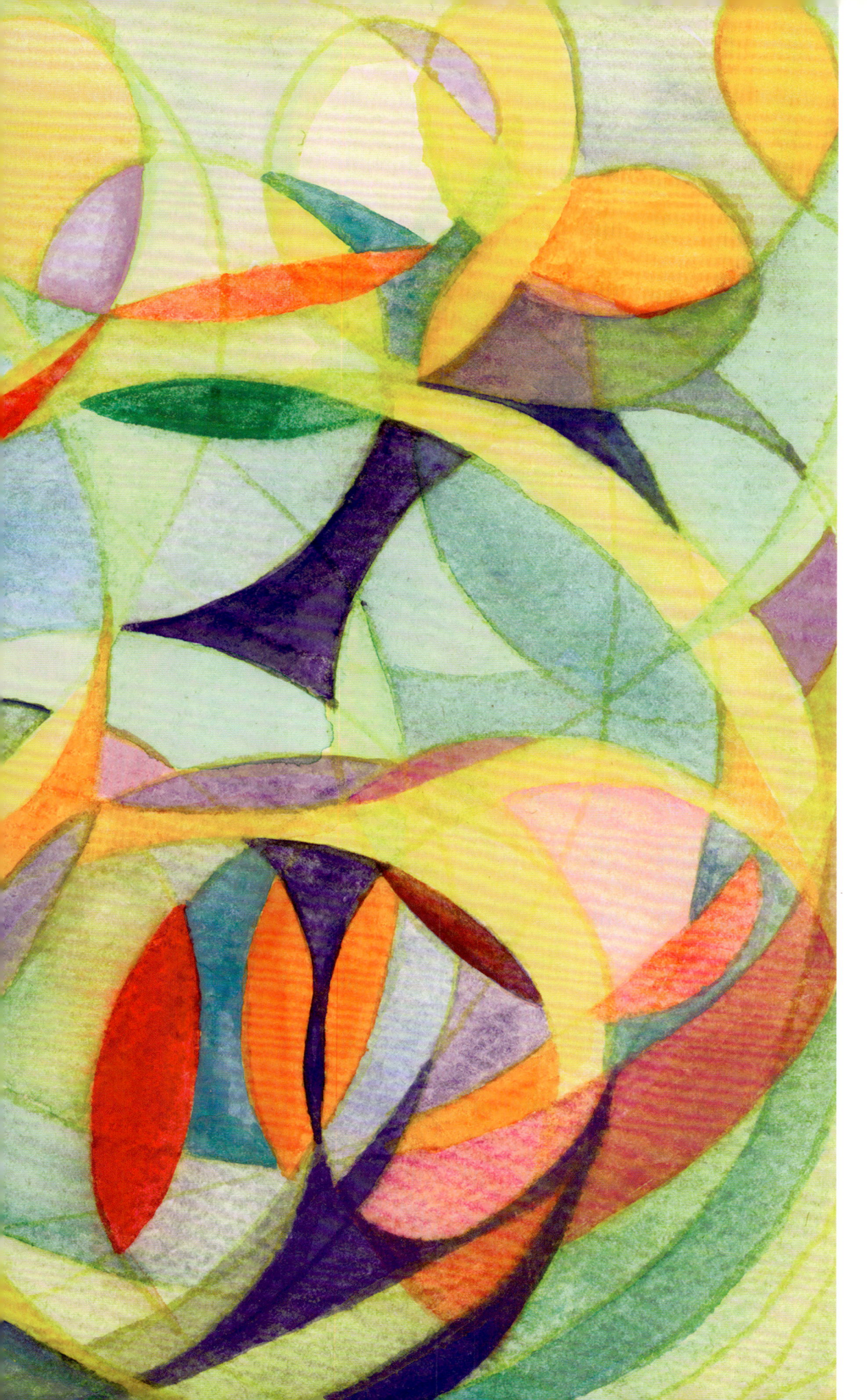

LIVING WATER
8 IN X 14 IN
WATERCOLOR/GOUACHE, 2003

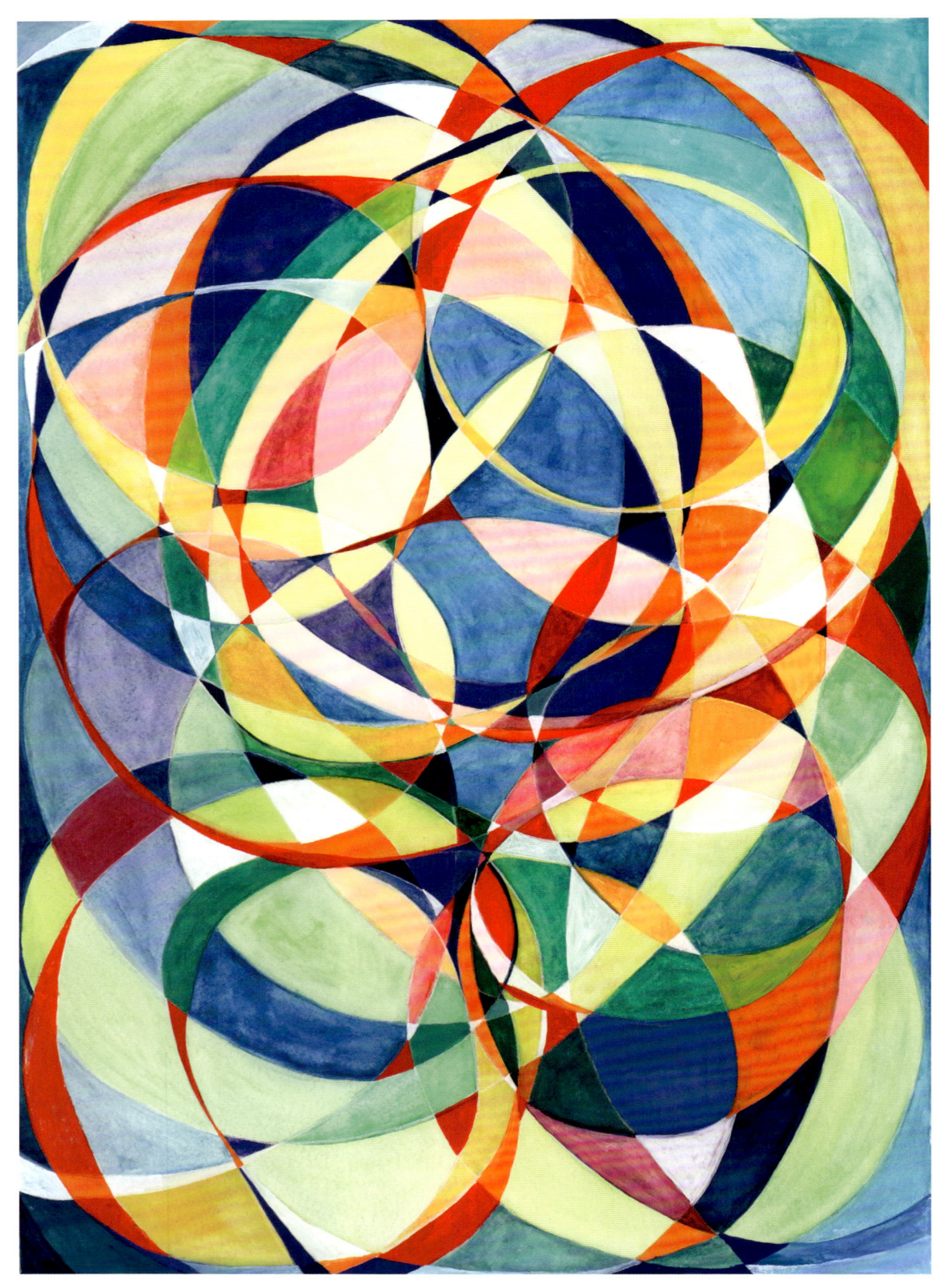

LIVING WATER 2

20 IN X 14 IN
WATERCOLOR/GOUACHE, 2003

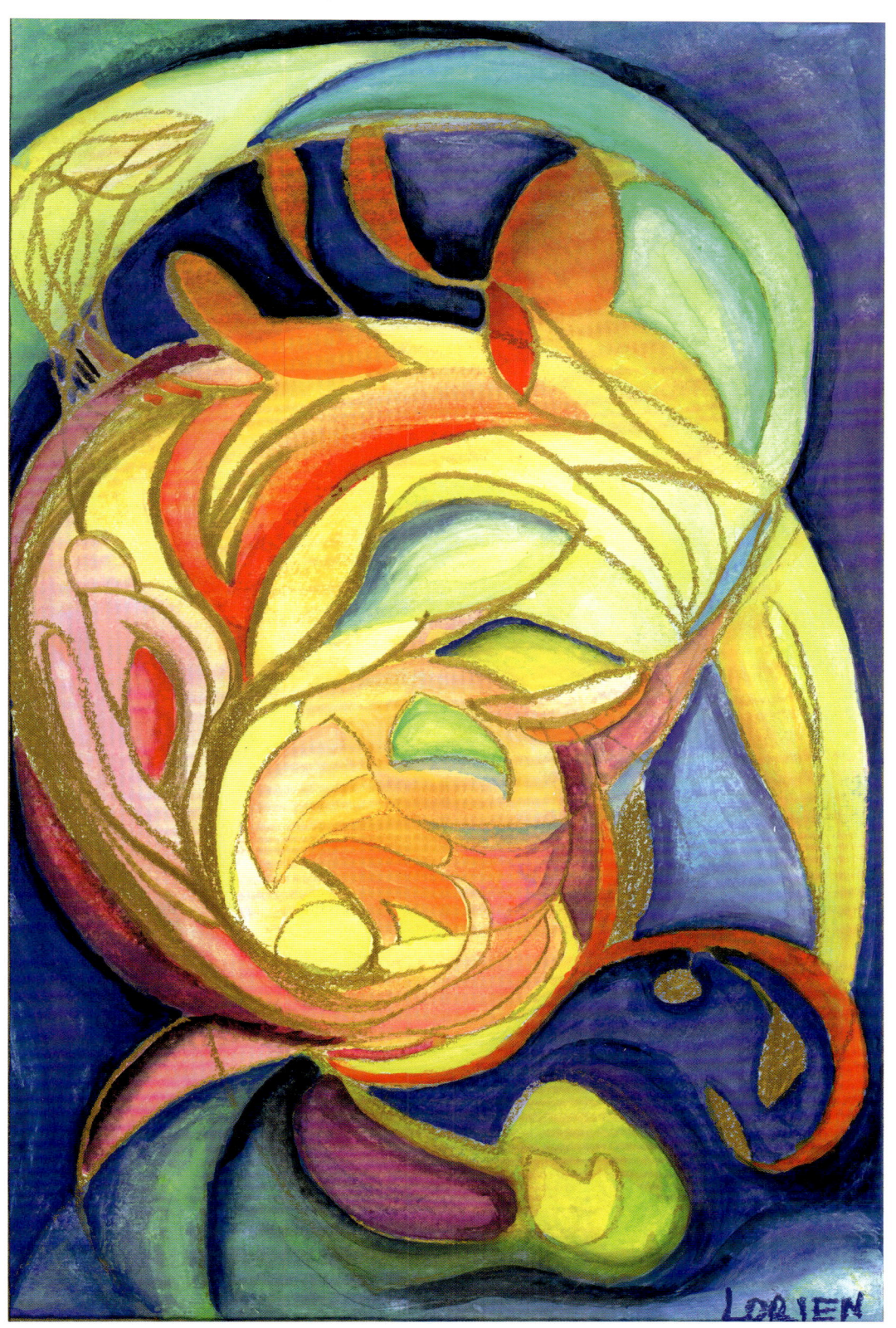

LIVING WATER 3
20 IN X 14 IN
WATERCOLOR/GOUACHE, 2003

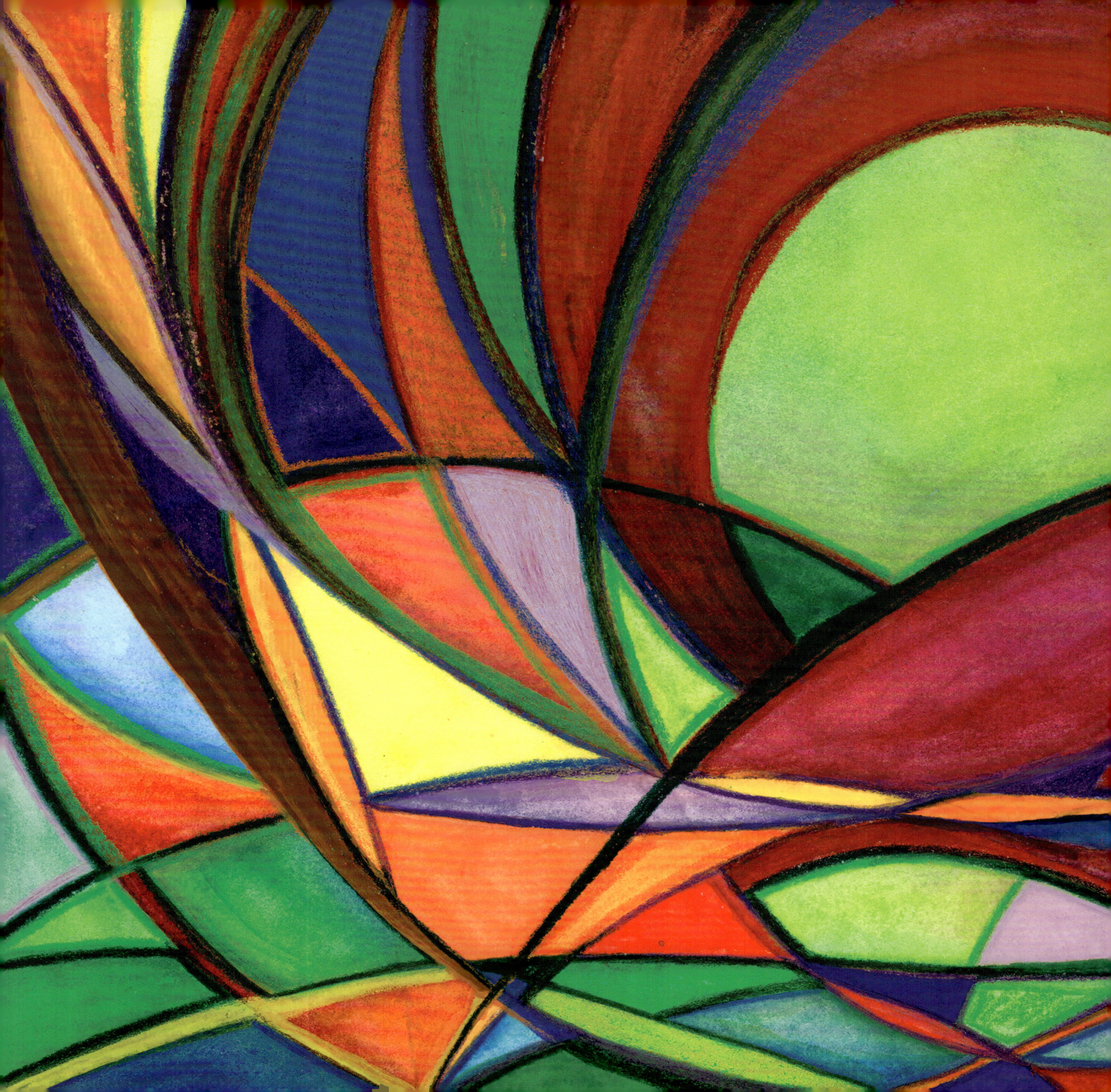

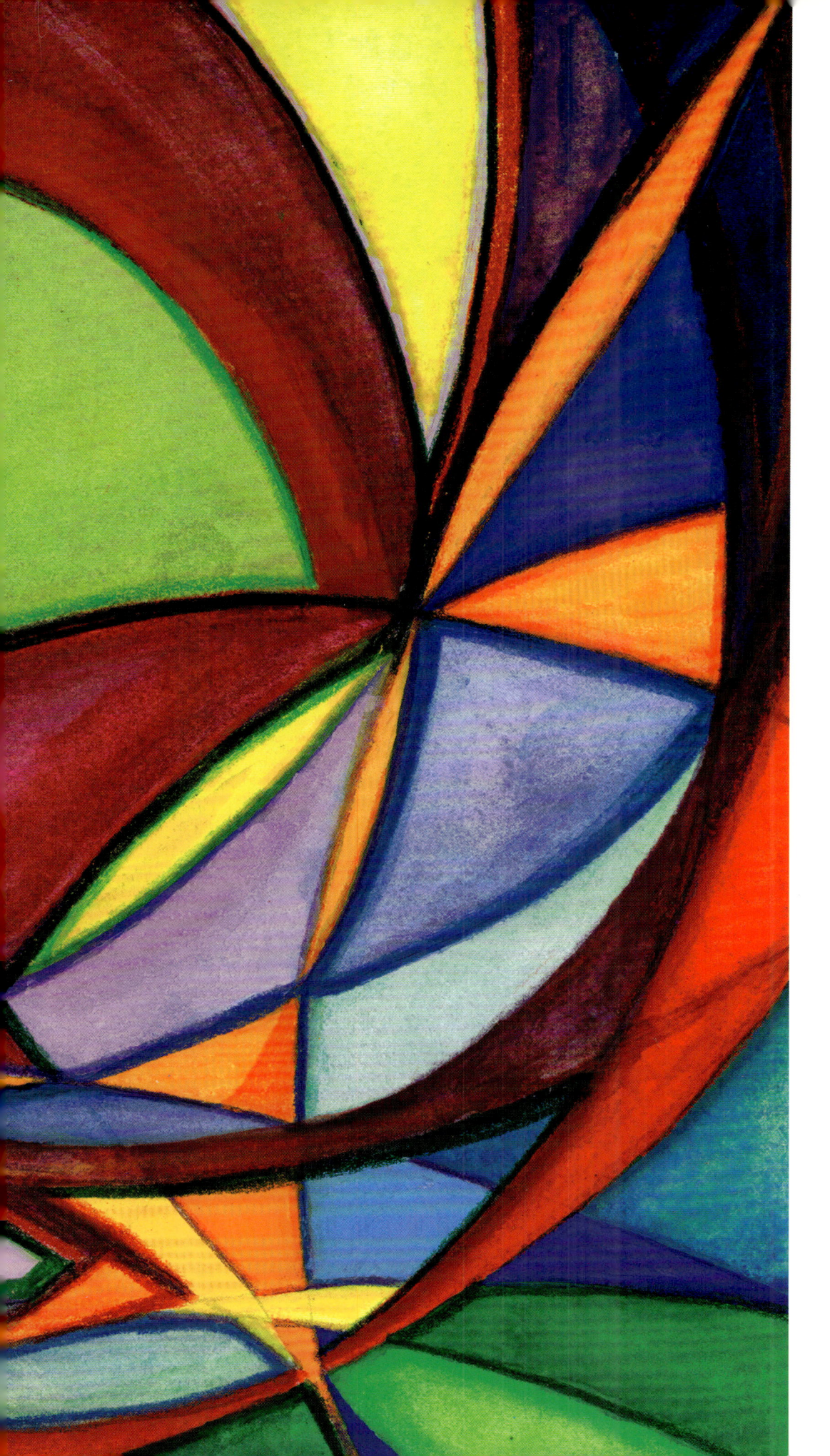

LIVING WATER 4
8 IN X 14 IN
WATERCOLOR/GOUACHE, 2003

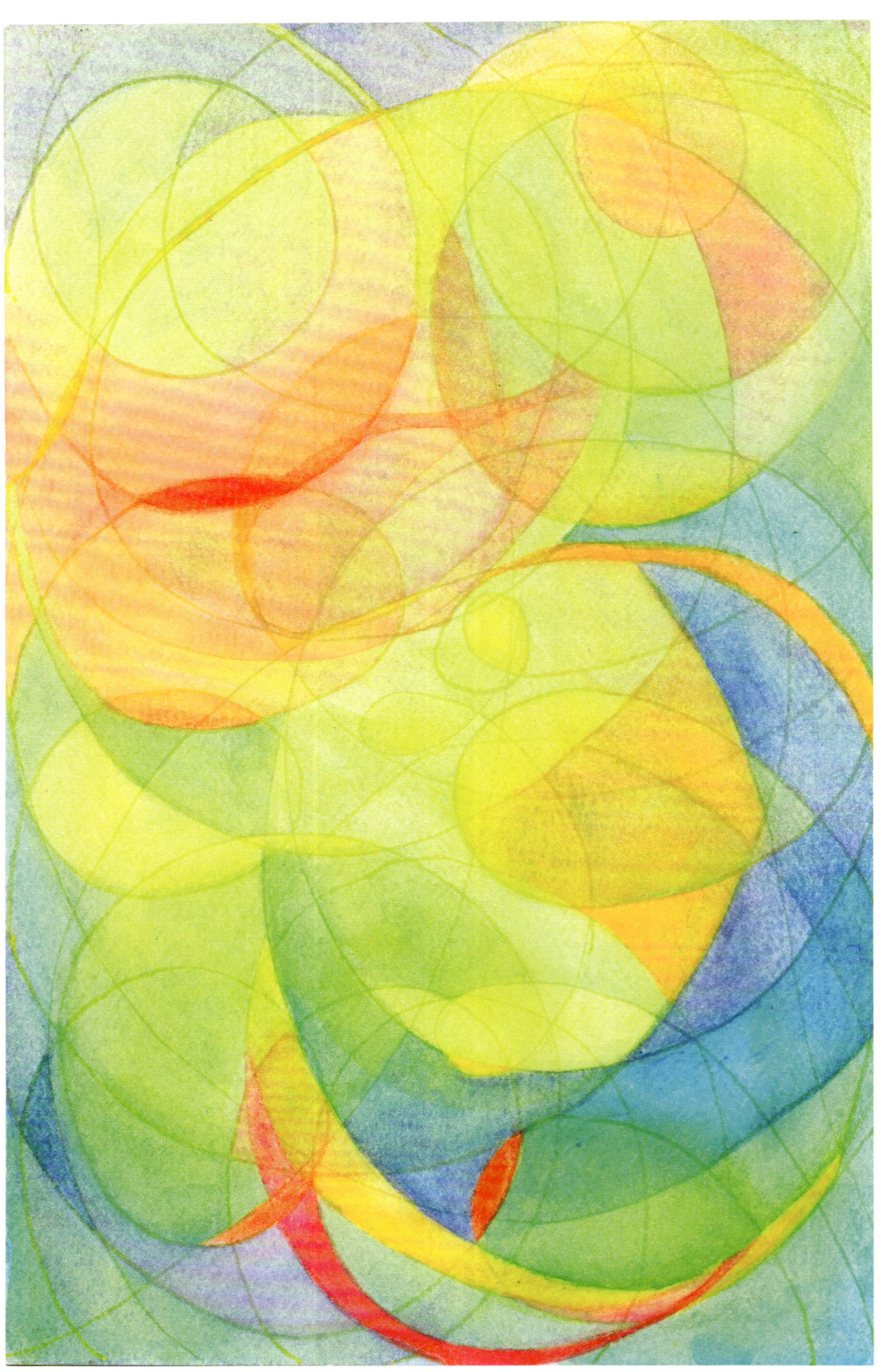

LIVING WATER 5

12 IN X 8 IN
WATERCOLOR/GOUACHE, 2003

GUITARRA ALEGRE *(RIGHT)*

40 IN X 30 IN
WATERCOLOR/GOUACHE, 2002

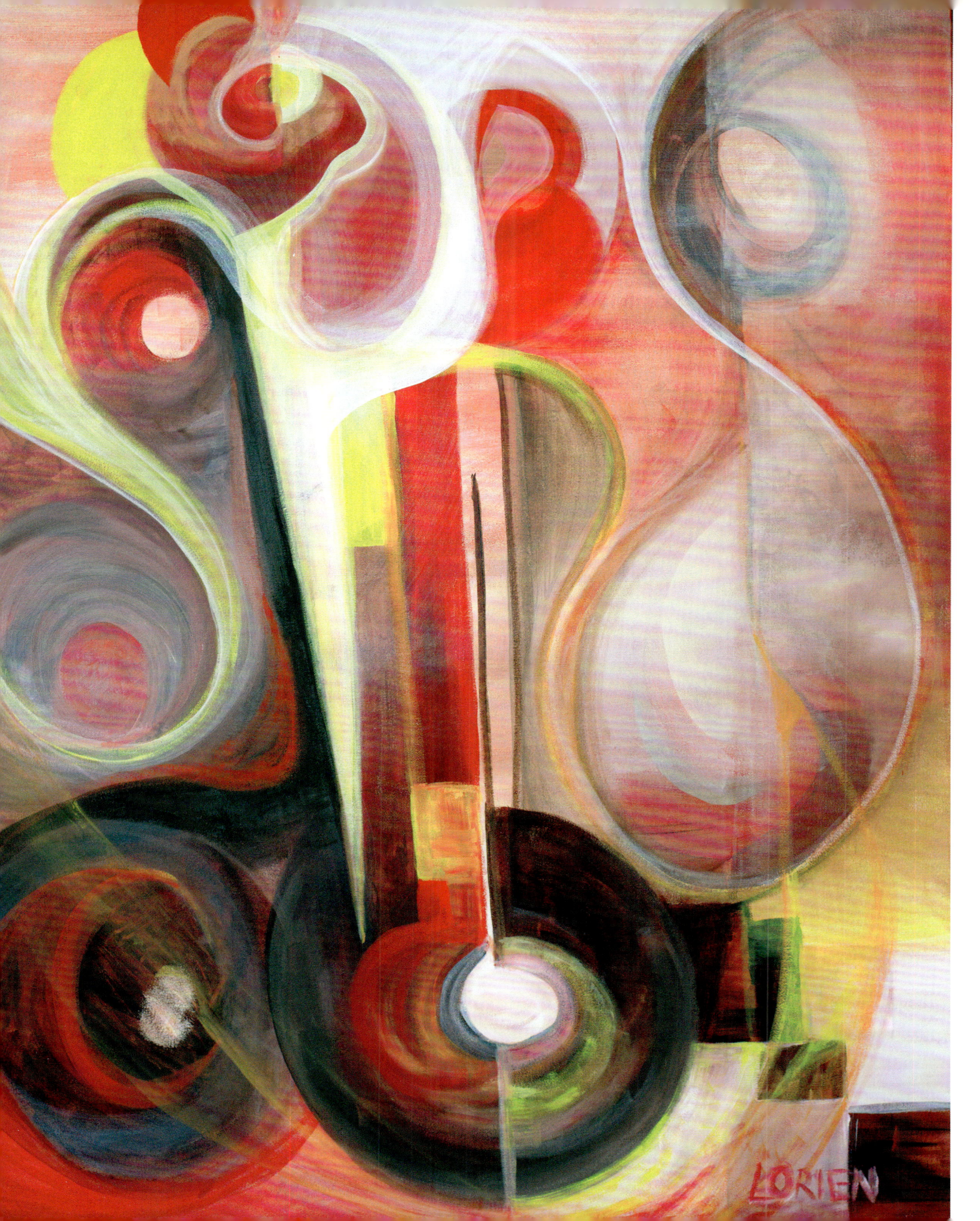

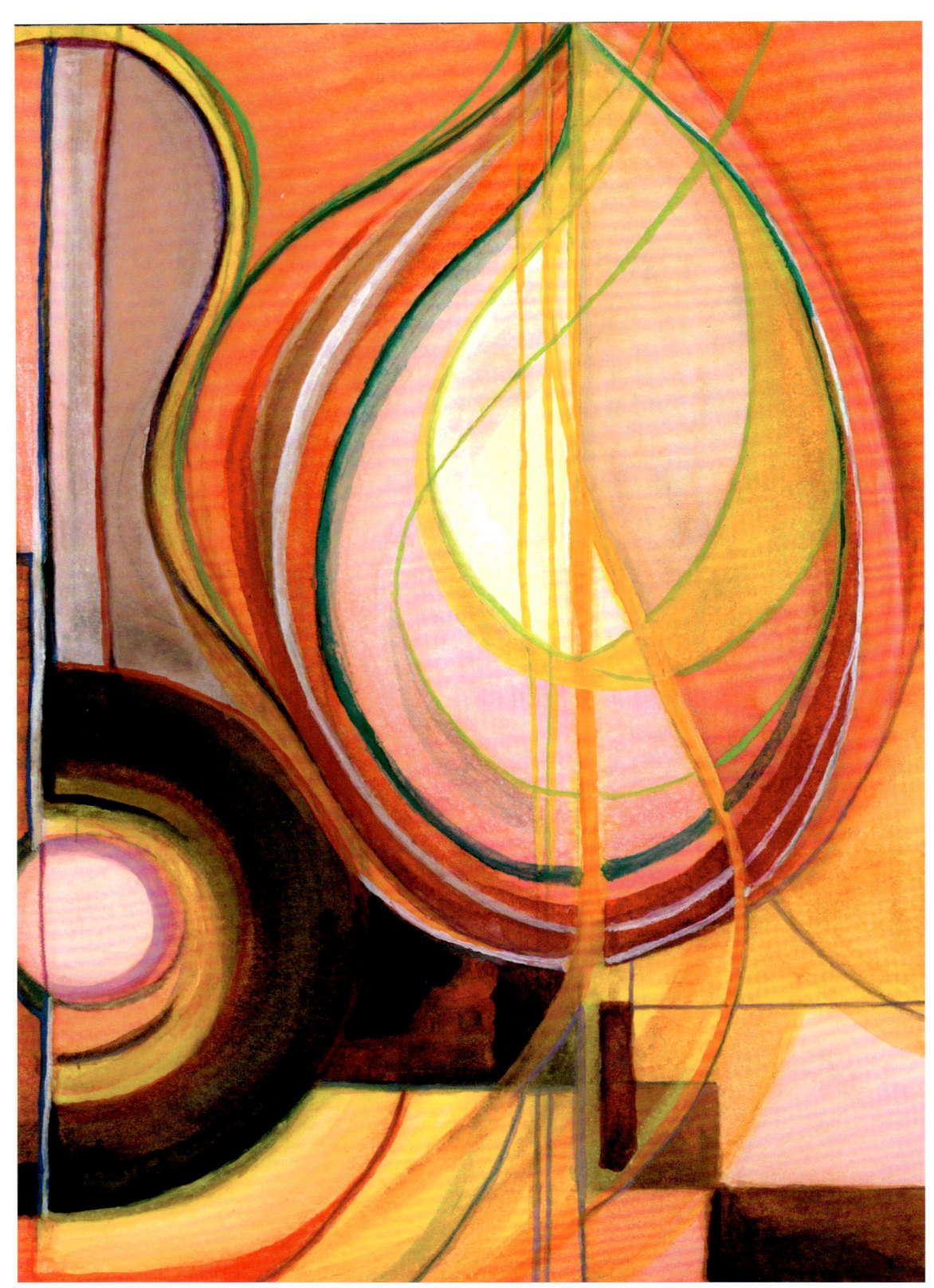

GUITARRA ALEGRE 3

10 IN X 8 IN
WATERCOLOR/GOUACHE, 2003

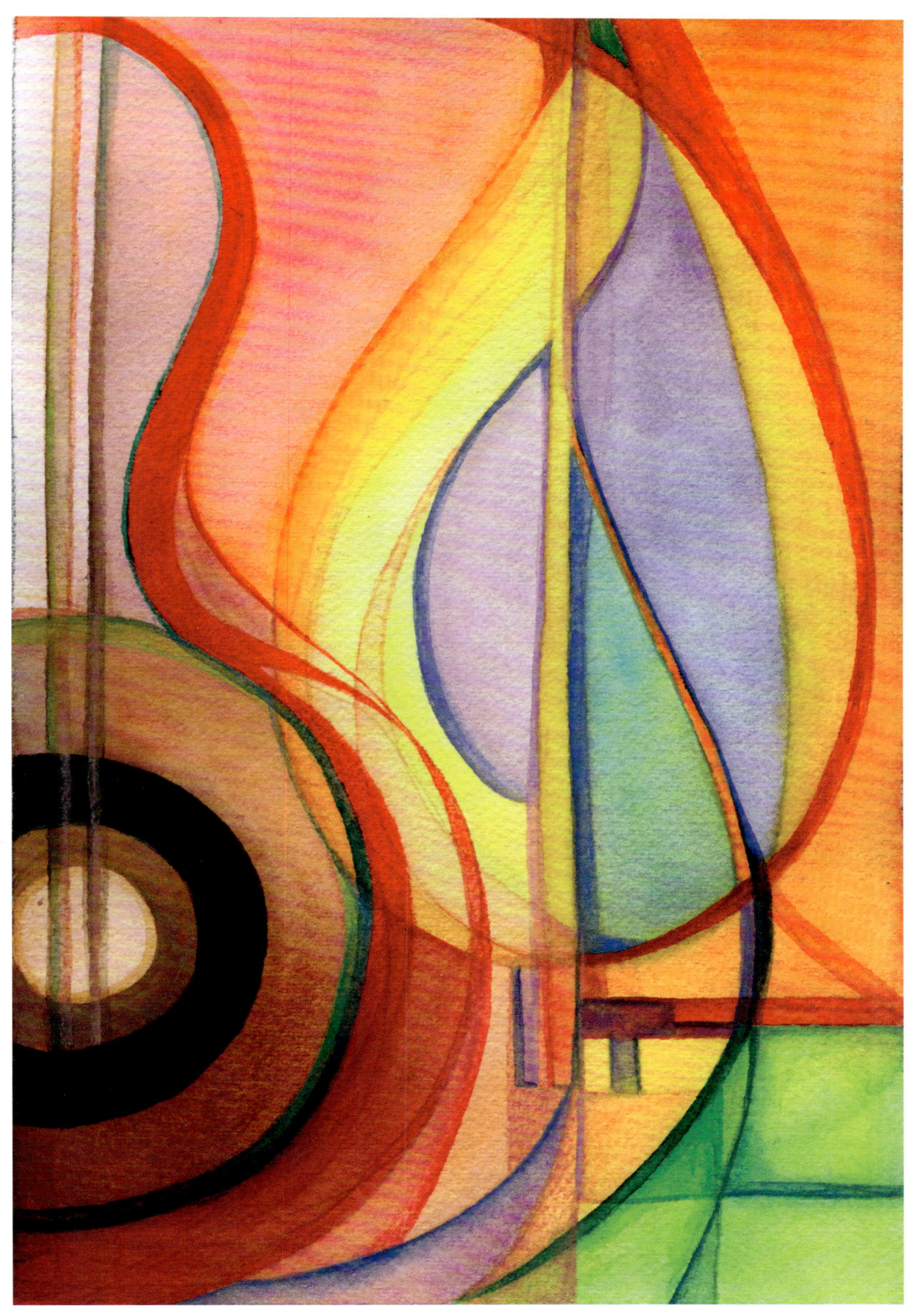

GUITARRA ALEGRE 4
8 IN X 5 IN
WATERCOLOR/GOUACHE, 2003

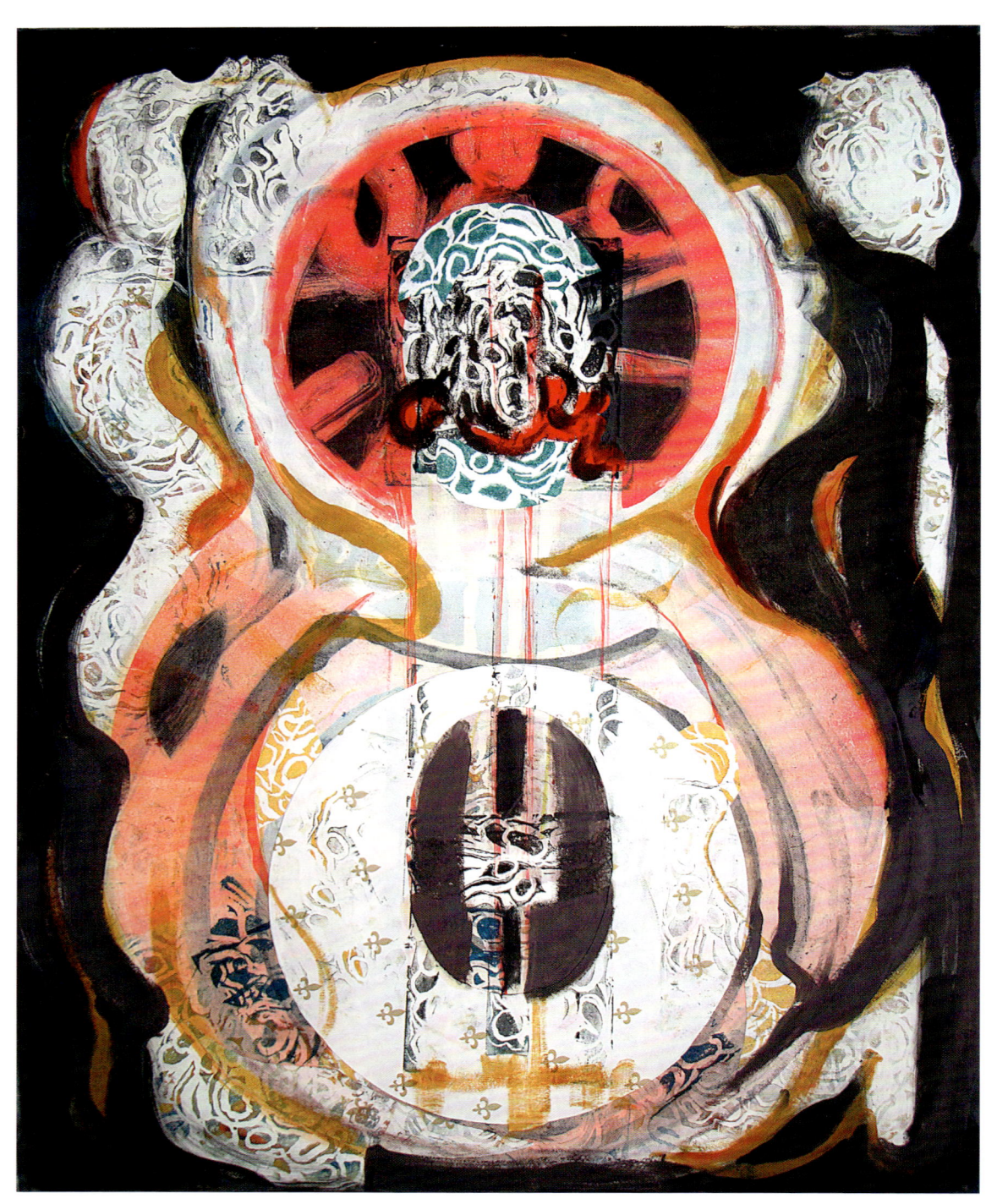

GUITARRA MONOTYPE 1

20 IN X 16 IN
MONOPRINT, 2008

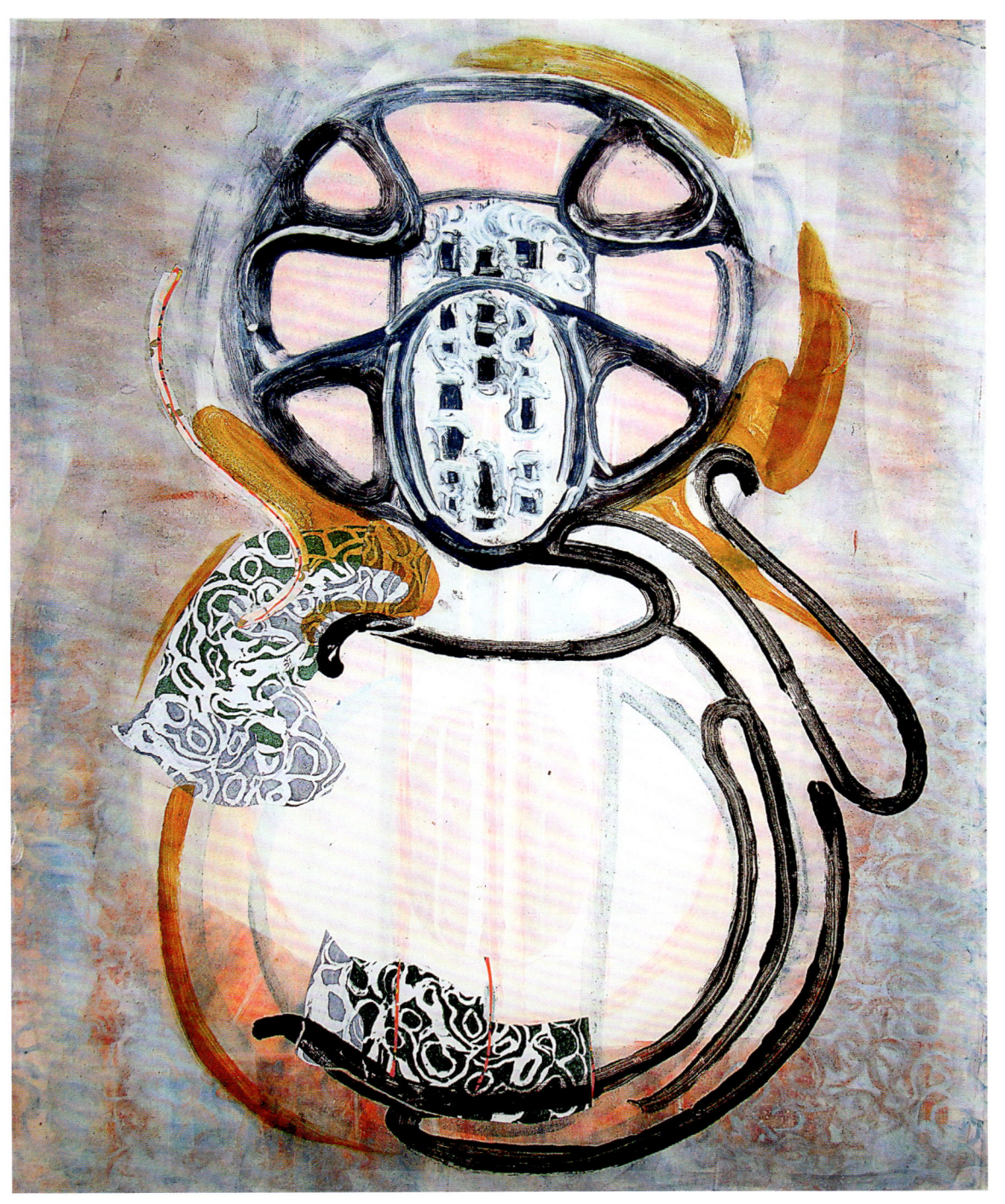

GUITARRA MONOTYPE 3
20 IN X 16 IN
MONCPRINT, 2008

RAYUELA 1
10 IN X 8 IN
PASTELS, 2009

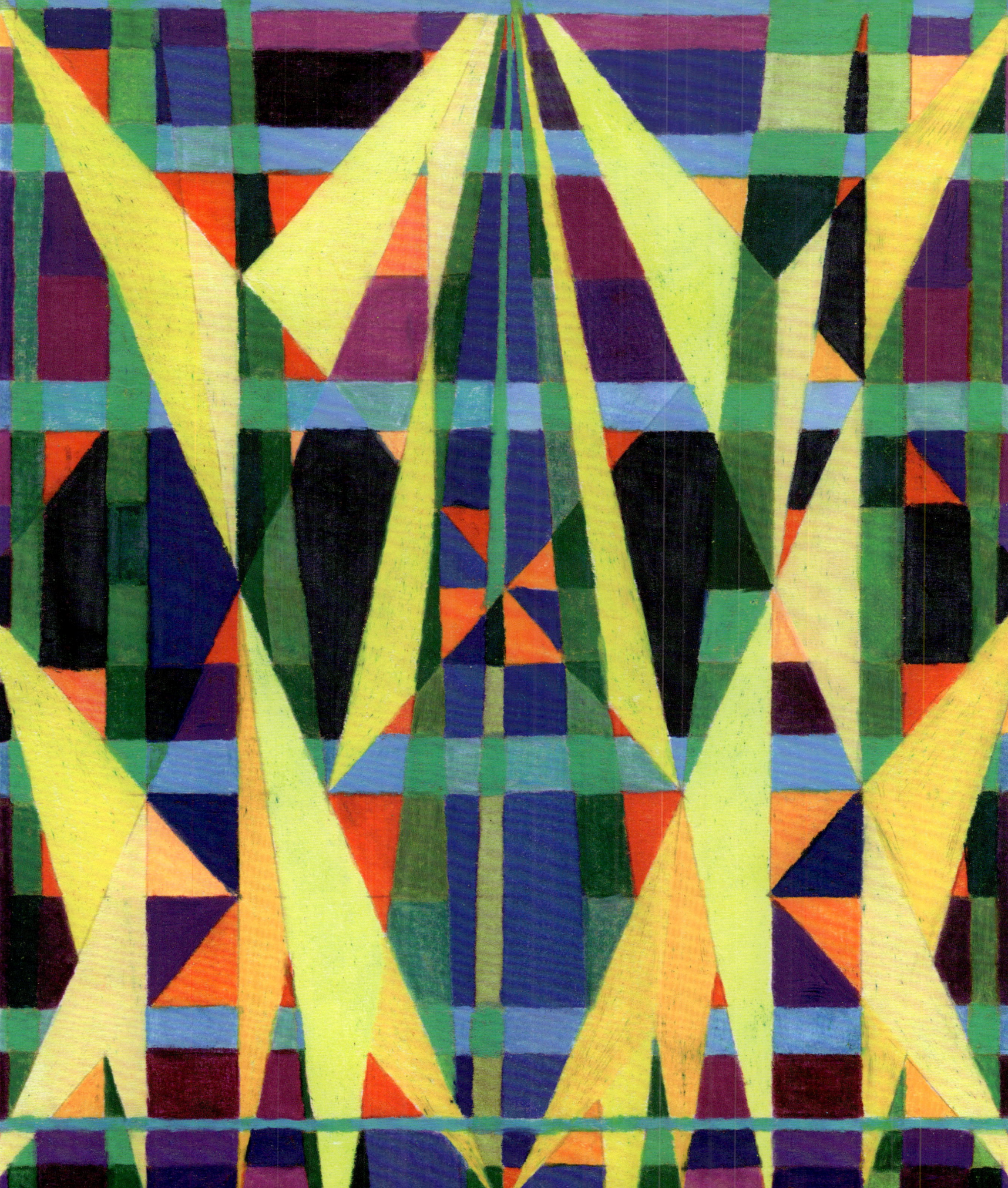

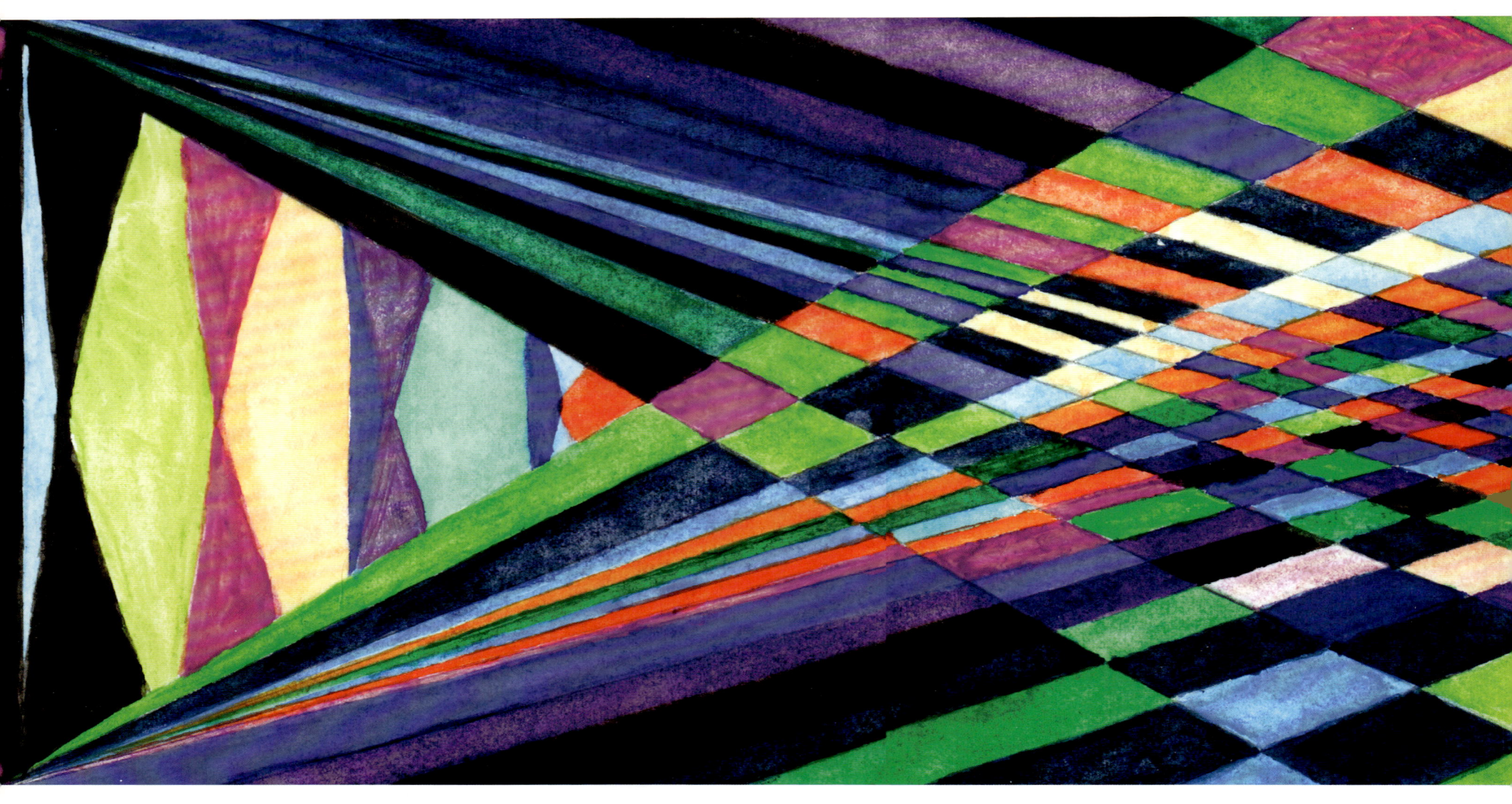

RAYUELA 5
4 IN X 20 IN
WATERCOLOR/GOUACHE, 2009

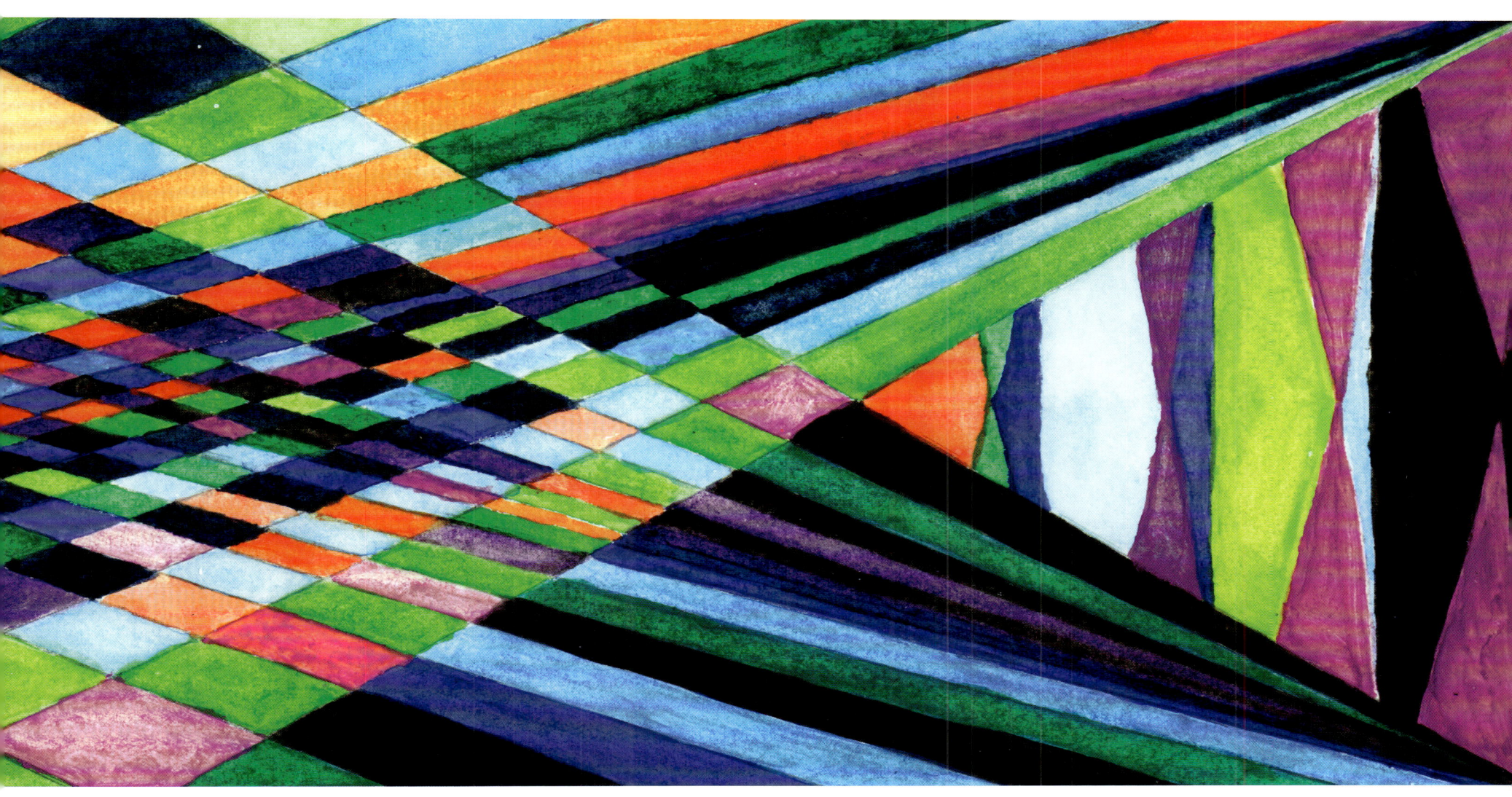

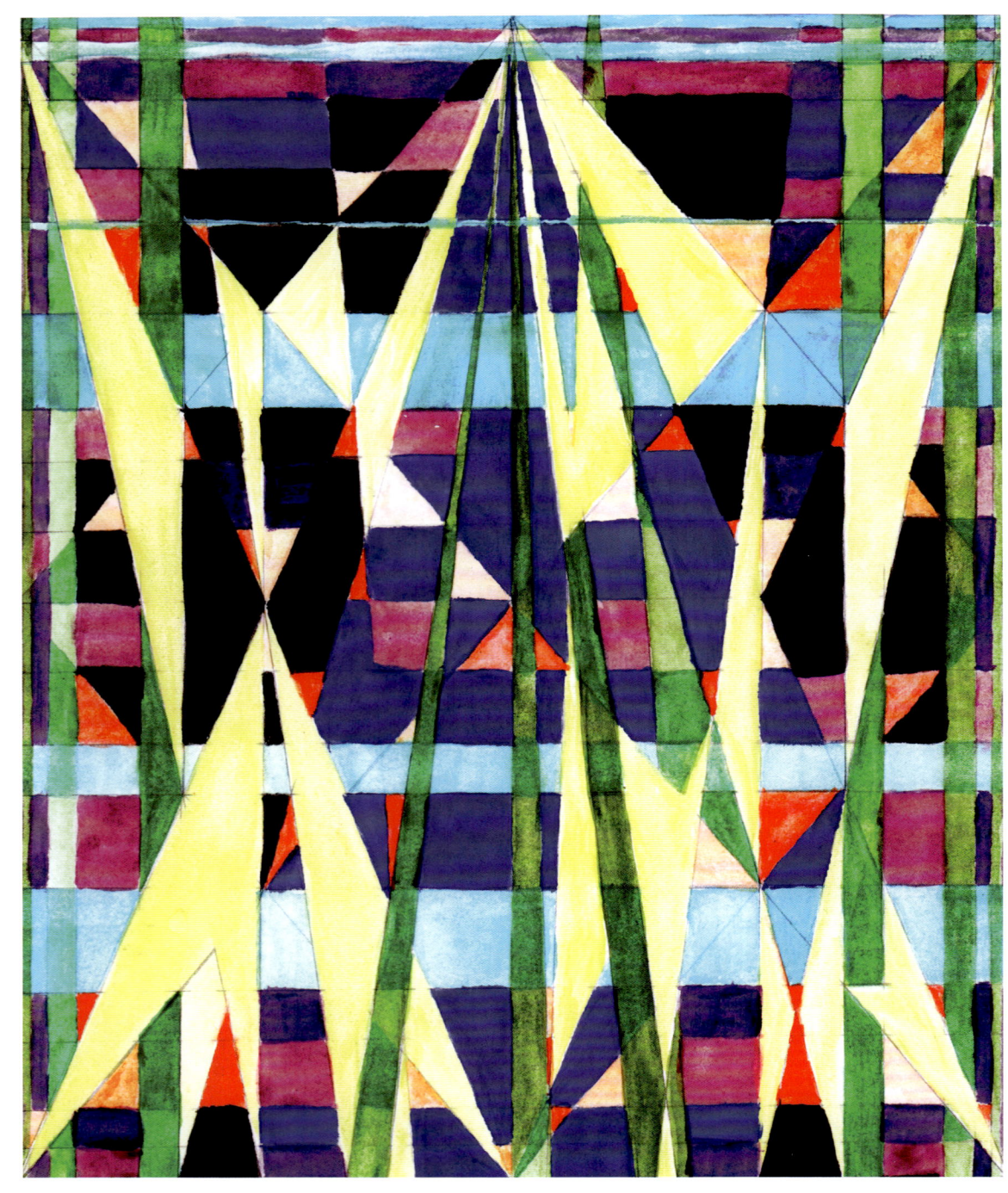

RAYUELA 2
10 IN X 8 IN
WATERCOLOR/GOUACHE, 2009

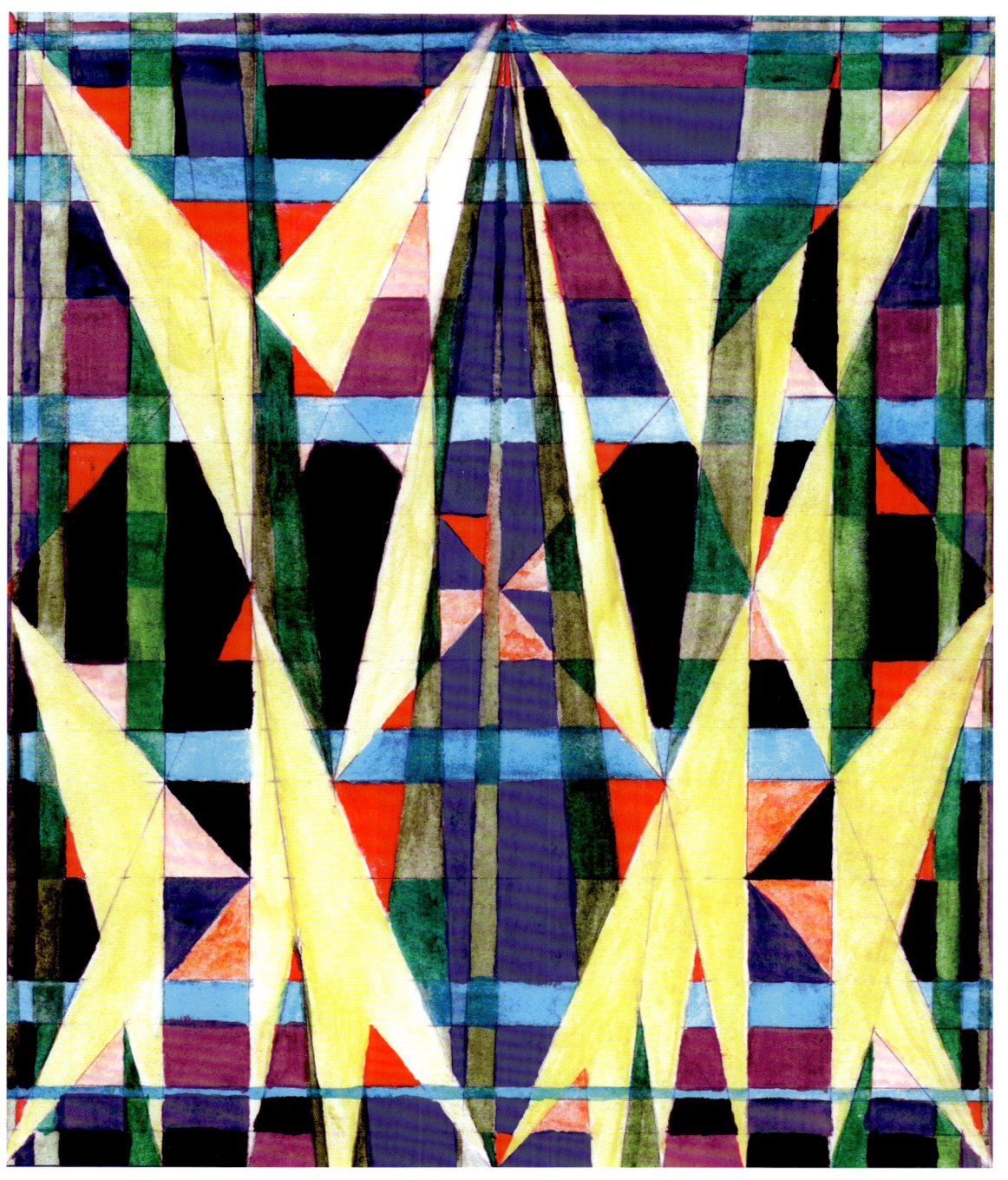

RAYUELA 3
10 IN X 8 IN
WATERCOLOR/GOUACHE, 2009

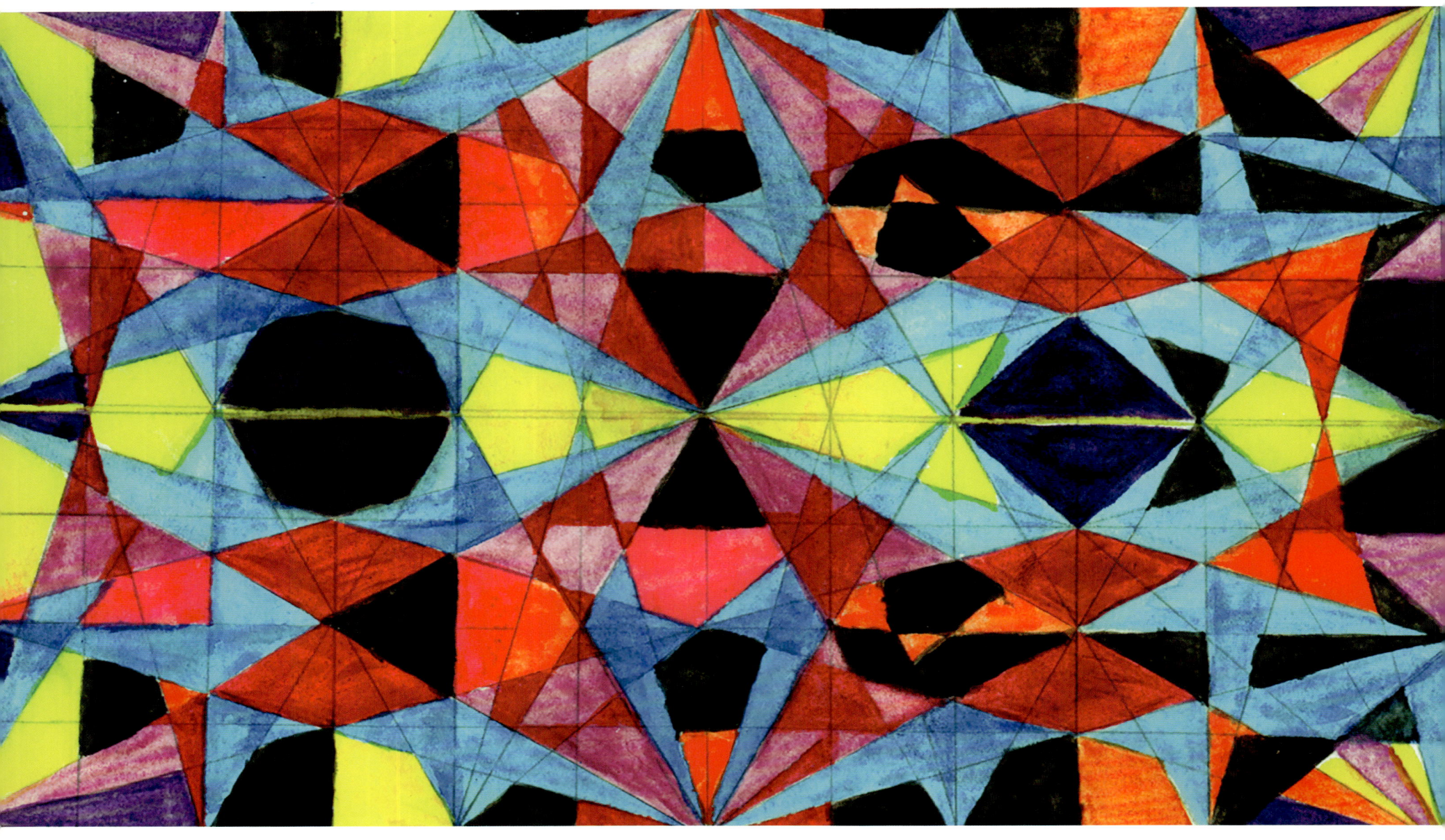

RAYUELA 4
4 IN X 20 IN
WATERCOLOR/GOUACHE, 2009

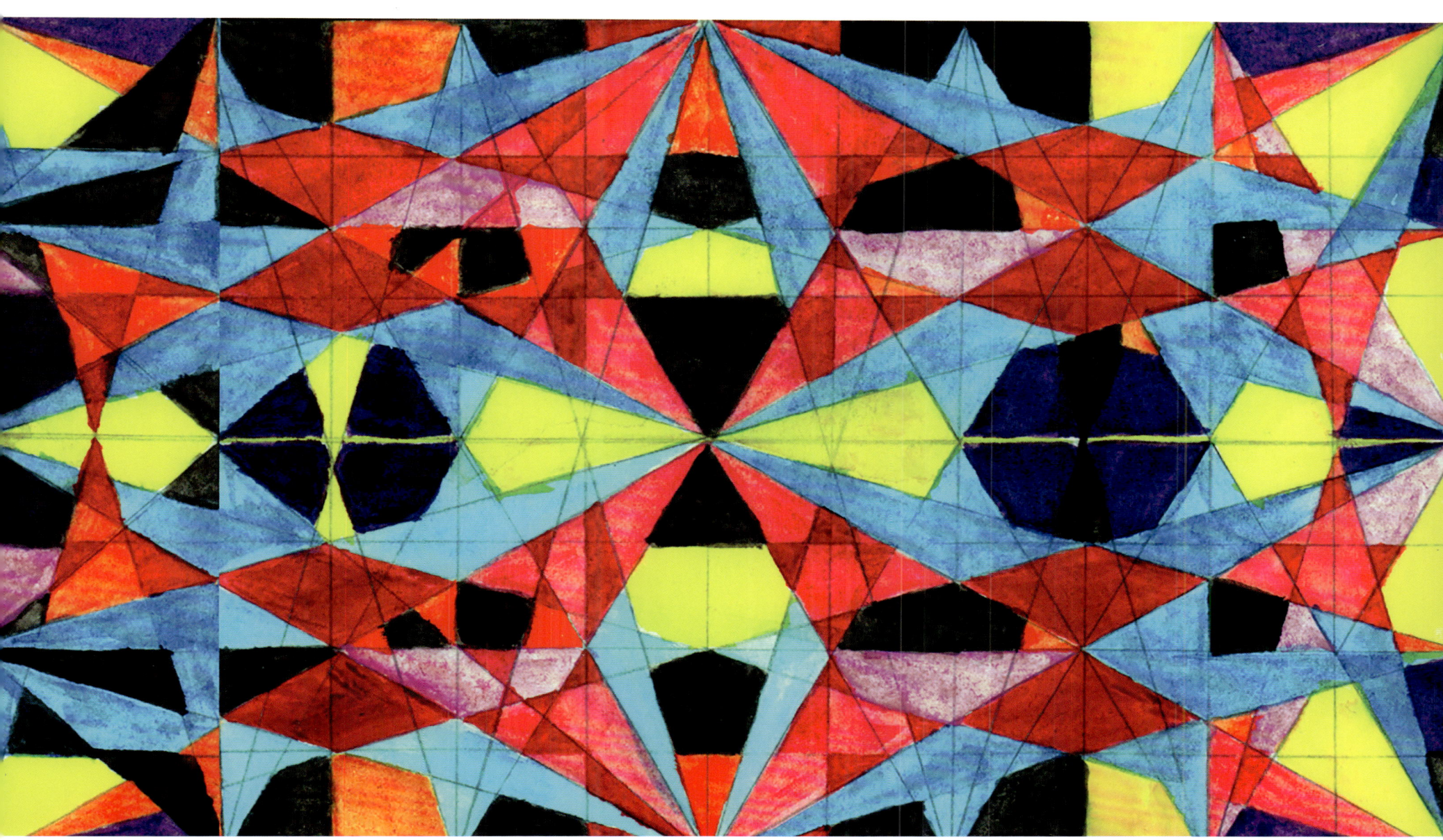

FIRST *WHEEL* WITHIN A *WHEEL* PAINTINGS

BY JOHN MENDELSOHN

THE CIRCLE IS AMONG THE GREAT SYMBOLS OF HUMAN EXISTENCE – IT IS OUR NATURAL LIFE, INTIMATE, CELLULAR, AND CYCLICAL; IT IS OUR TRANSCENDENTAL LIFE, EXPANSIVE, AND WITHOUT BEGINNING OR END.

The circle is similarly dual in its abstract possibilities, generating both a fecundity of geometric forms and a poetry of ordered energy.

In her series of watercolors, *Wheel within a Wheel*, Lorien Suárez allows circles to engender a world of curving forms, often dizzying in its complexity, yet open, light-filled, and lyrical. In that world, circles (and occasionally ellipses) overlap and converge creating a fugue of arcs and sections. Geometry has an unpredictable power here, bringing to life new, eccentric shapes and penetrating vectors. The allusion to patterns of natural growth abound in the spiral, pod, seed, and flower-like forms that emerge organically from the underlying matrix. At times we seem to be in aquatic or uterine depths, at others we are in a green-gold atmosphere shot through with sunlight.

Nature exists here, as well, in the dynamics of movements that ripple like water, float like liquid-borne life forms, refract like crystals, and expand like growth itself. Yet, the abstract clarity of the shapes and the precision of their relationships make clear that we are in a place that is as cosmic as it is terrestrial. There are intimations of the constellations and the galaxies, and of the invisible forces that bind the universe together. Suárez's circles recall the heavenly spheres which, according to esoteric belief, produced a musical, celestial harmony.

Wheel within a Wheel, the series title, is taken from the prophet Ezekiel's vision of fiery concentric wheels, with rims "full of eyes", that bore four winged creatures. Moving through the sky, this startling phenomenon was a powerful, multi-directional revelation of God's glory, the divine essence present in every aspect of reality.

Suárez's reference to this image sensitizes us to the ecstatic feeling in her work, and to its spiritual dimension. The appeal here is neither to doctrine nor to an elevated state, rather it is to the awareness that spirit is embodied in the visible and in our inspired acts of vision. At the same time, her work suggests that in the visible world there is a creative energy that works in mysterious ways. Inventive, playful, and abundant, it animates living things and the microcosmic structures of the realm they inhabit. That energy enlivens forms, and colors, and the endless intoxicated pleasure we take in them.

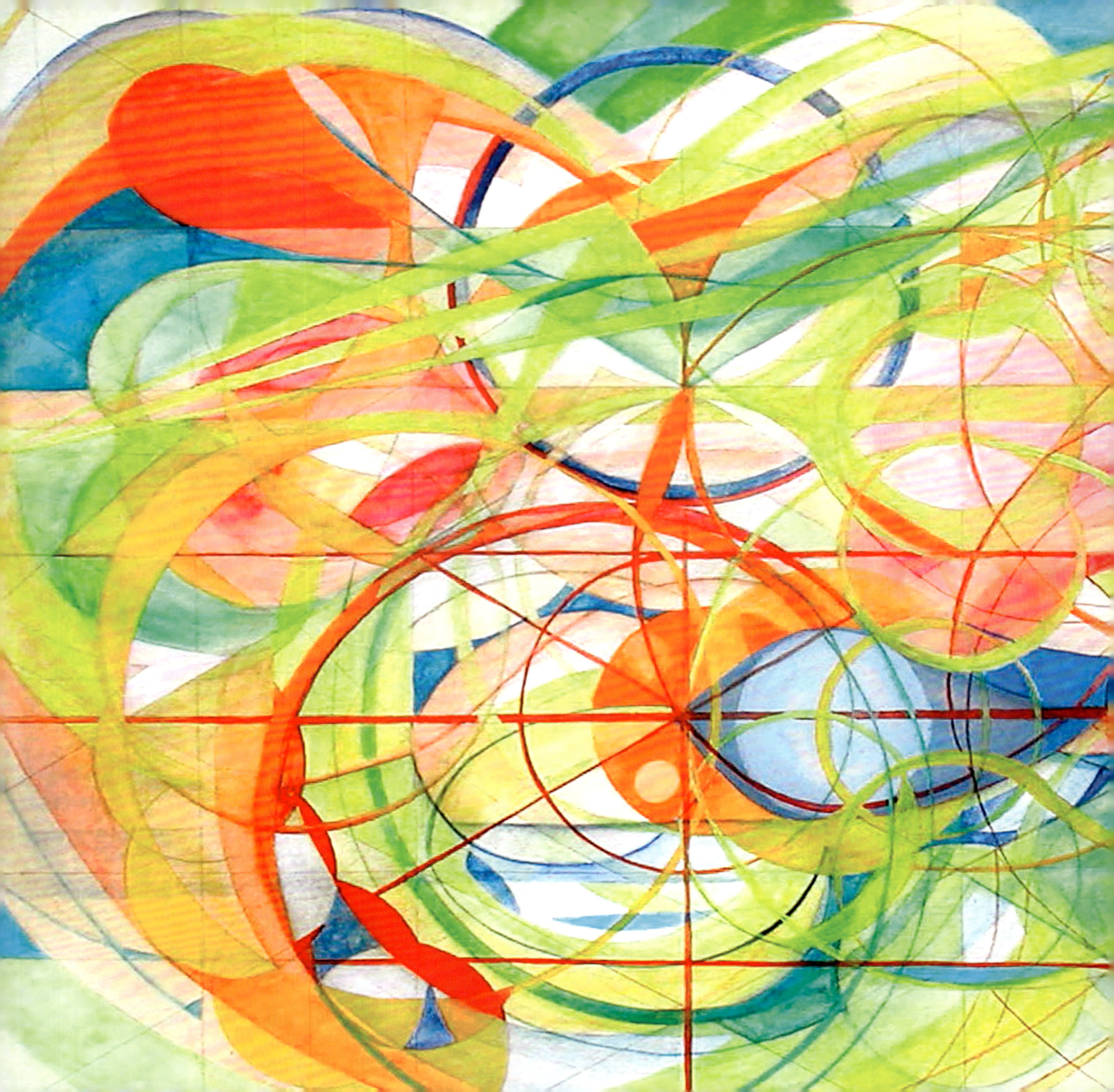

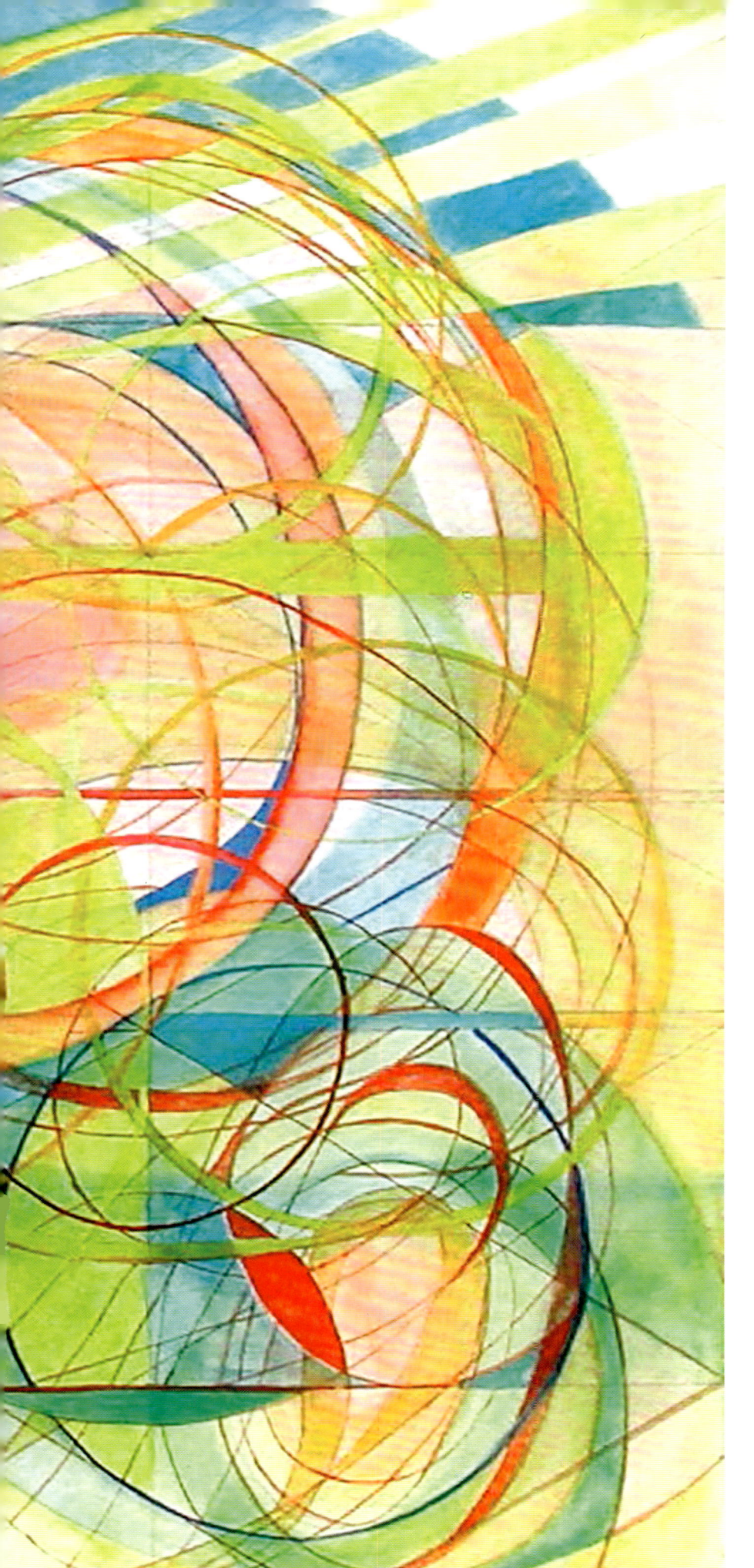

WHEEL WITHIN A WHEEL 1
14 IN X 20 IN
WATERCOLOR, 2003

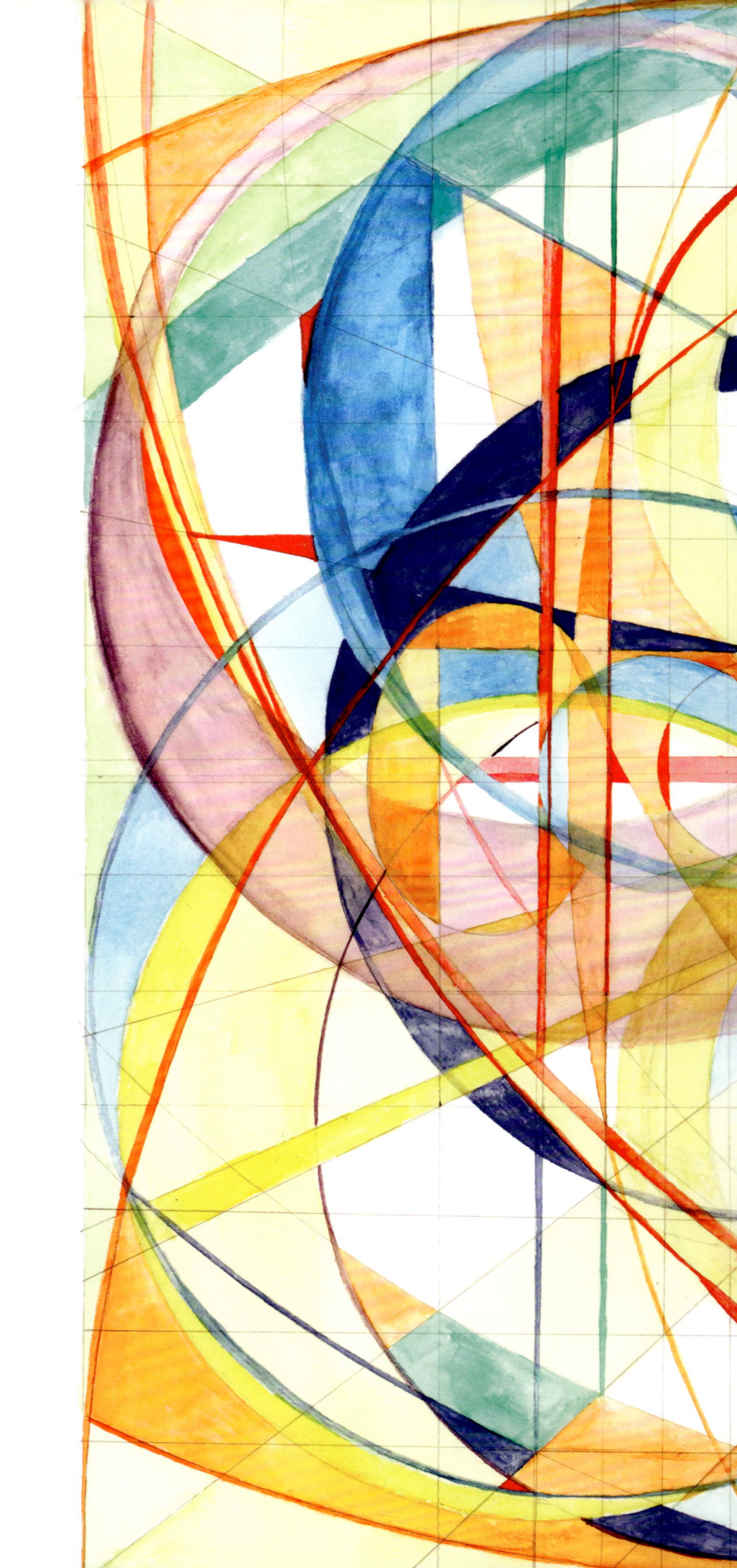

WHEEL WITHIN A WHEEL 2

14 IN X 20 IN
WATERCOLOR, 2003

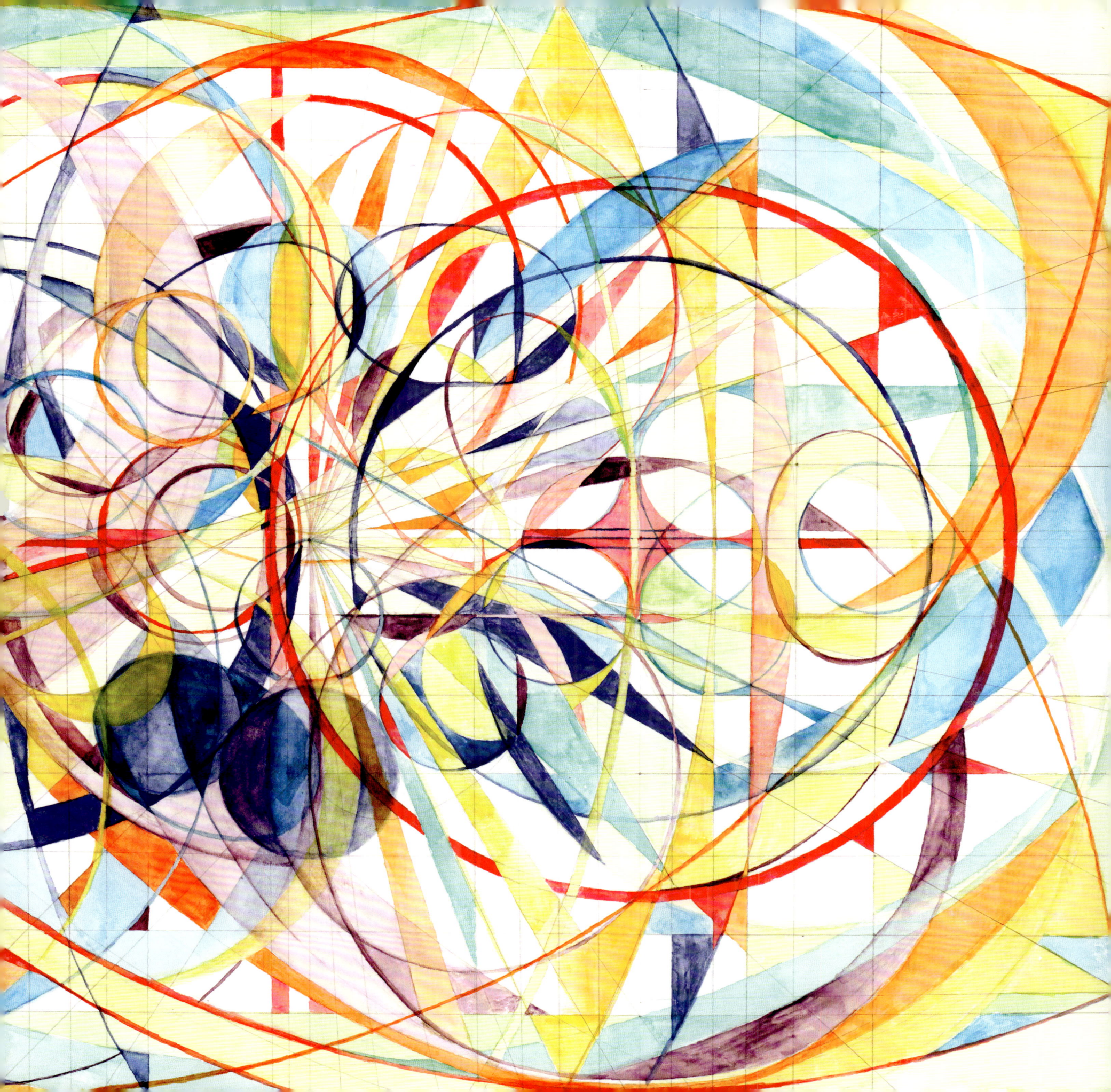

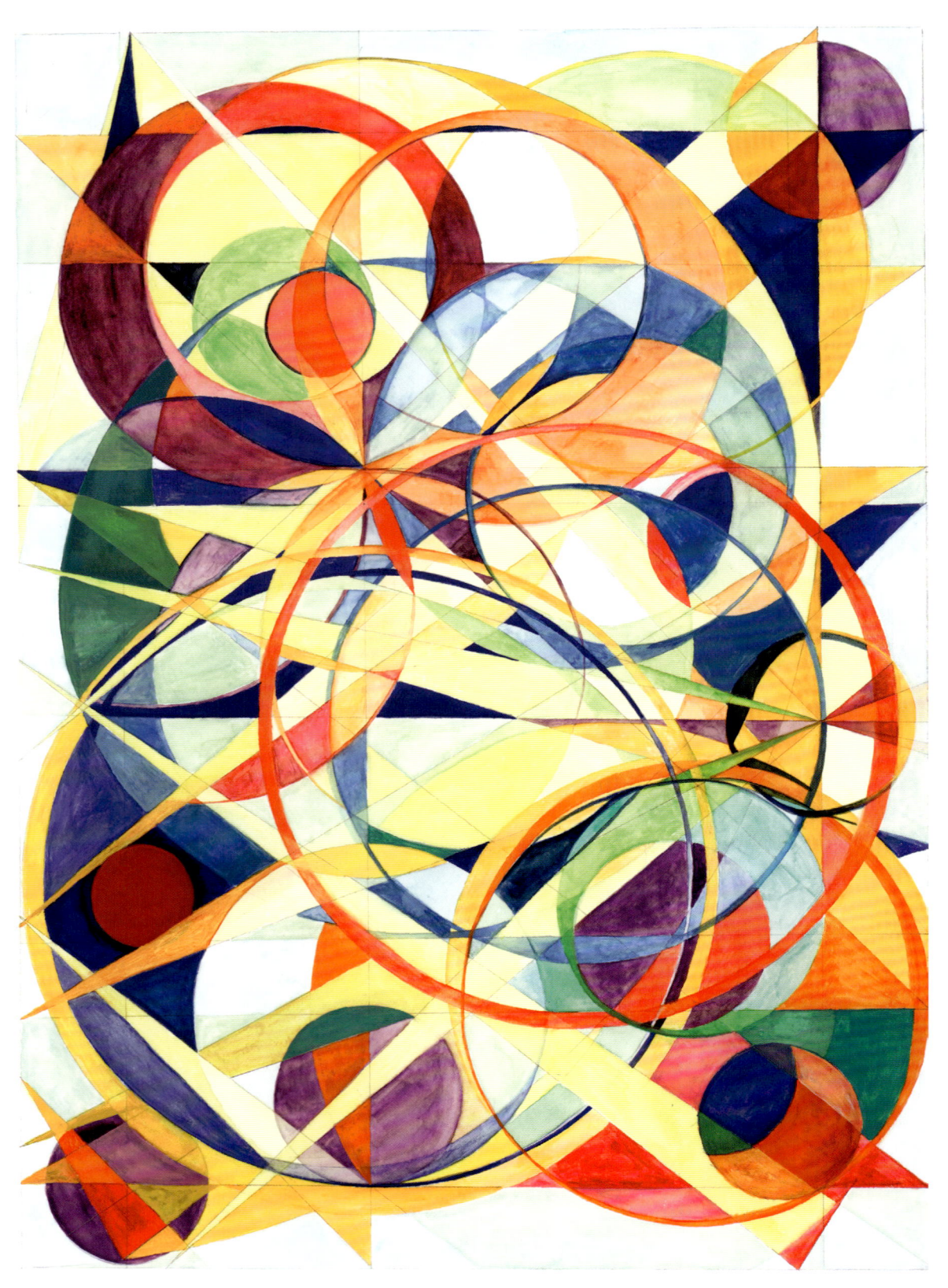

WHEEL WITHIN A WHEEL 3
20 IN X 14 IN
WATERCOLOR, 2003

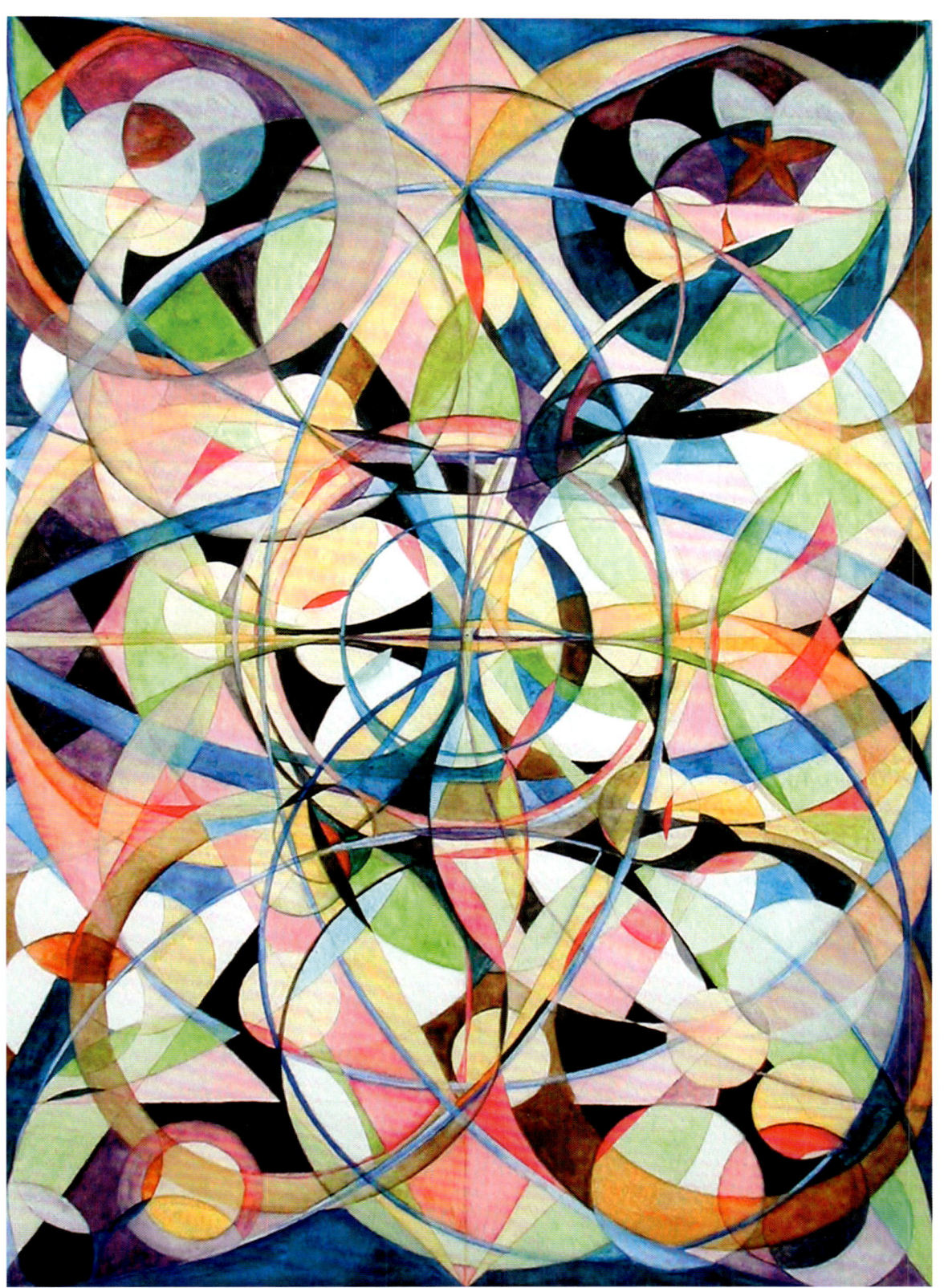

WHEEL WITHIN A WHEEL 4
20 IN X 14 IN
WATERCOLOR, 2003

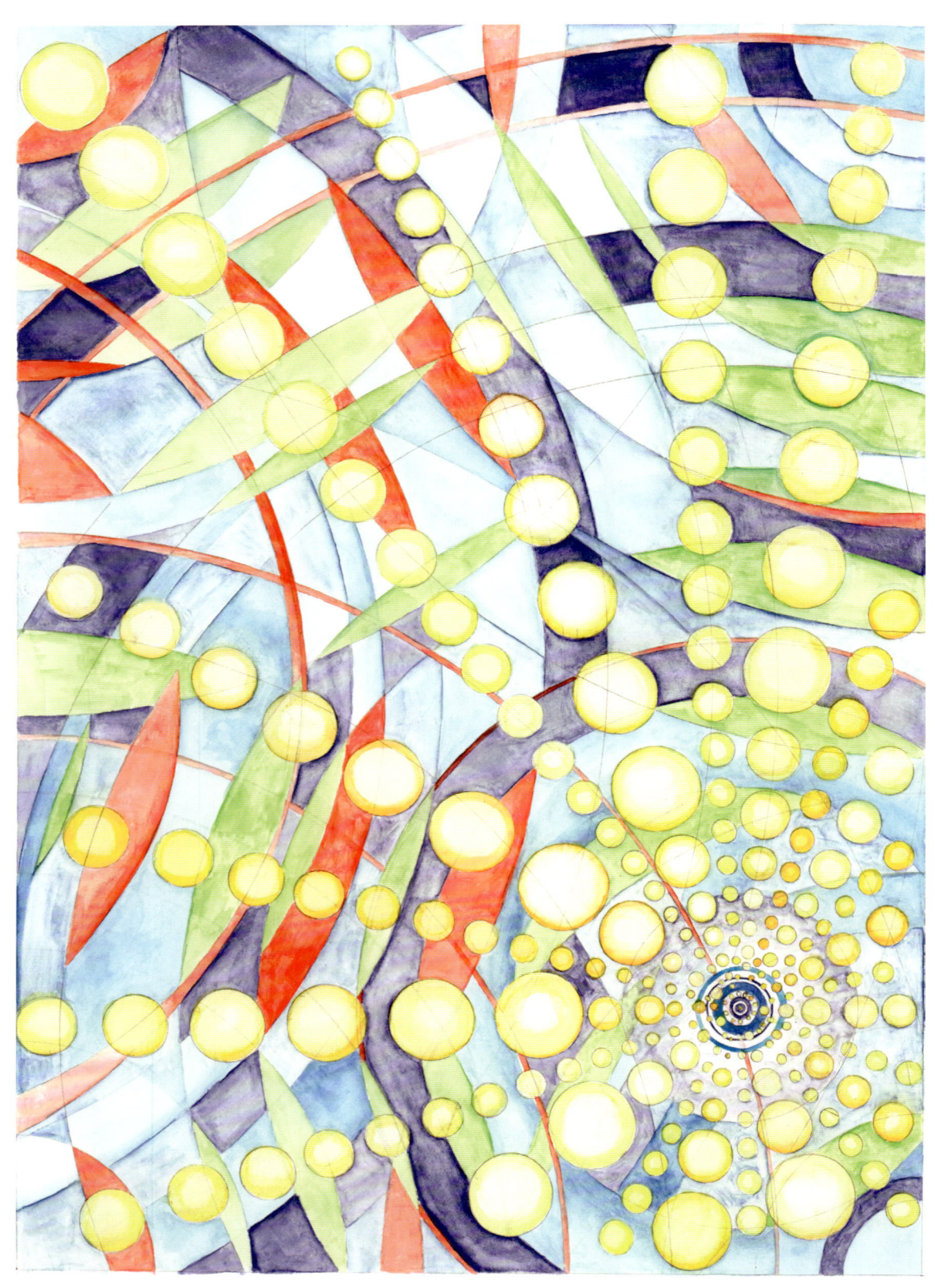

WHEEL WITHIN A WHEEL 9

20 IN X 14 IN
WATERCOLOR, 2003

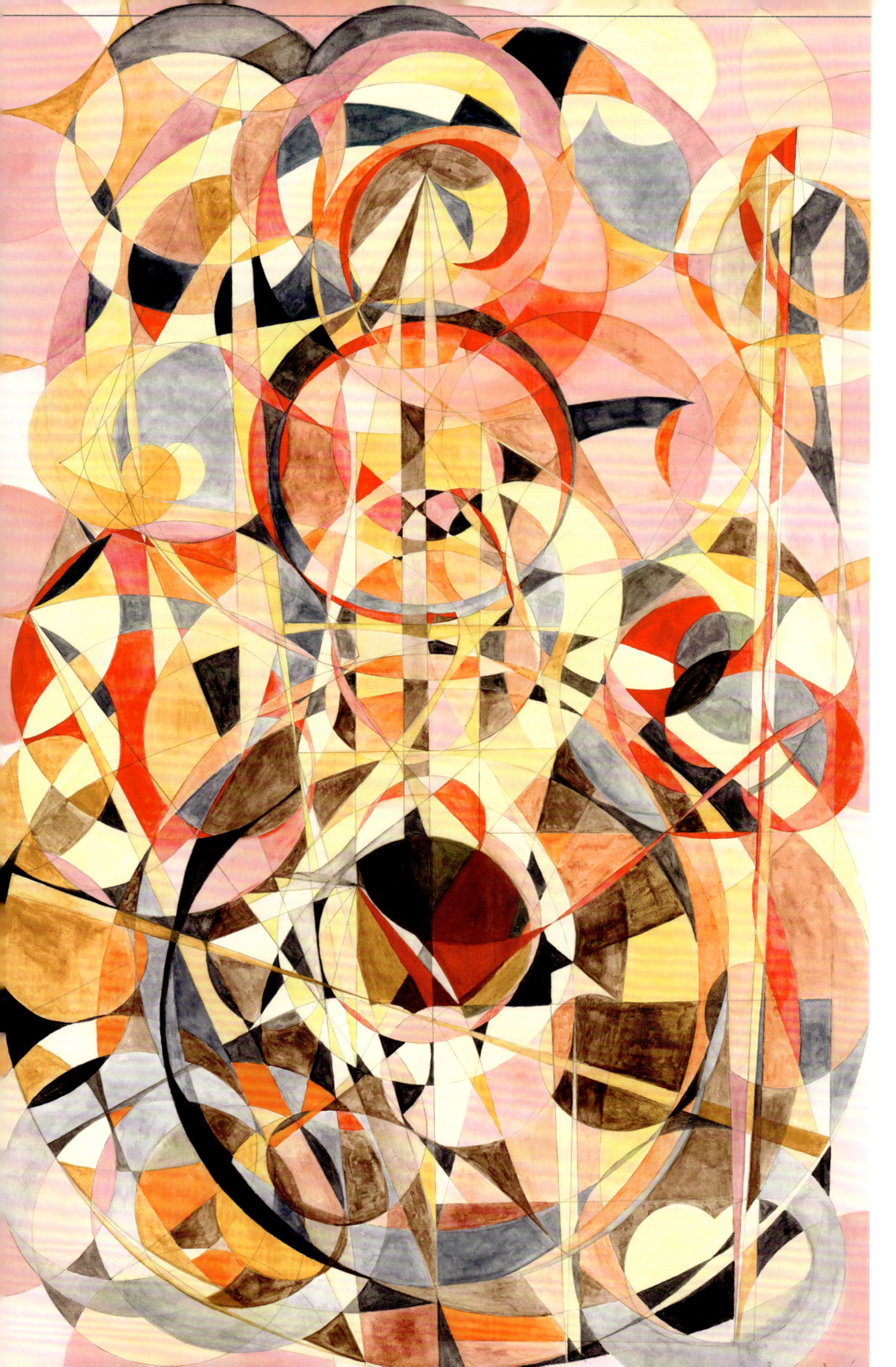

WHEEL WITHIN A WHEEL 15

29 IN X 18 IN
WATERCOLOR, 2003

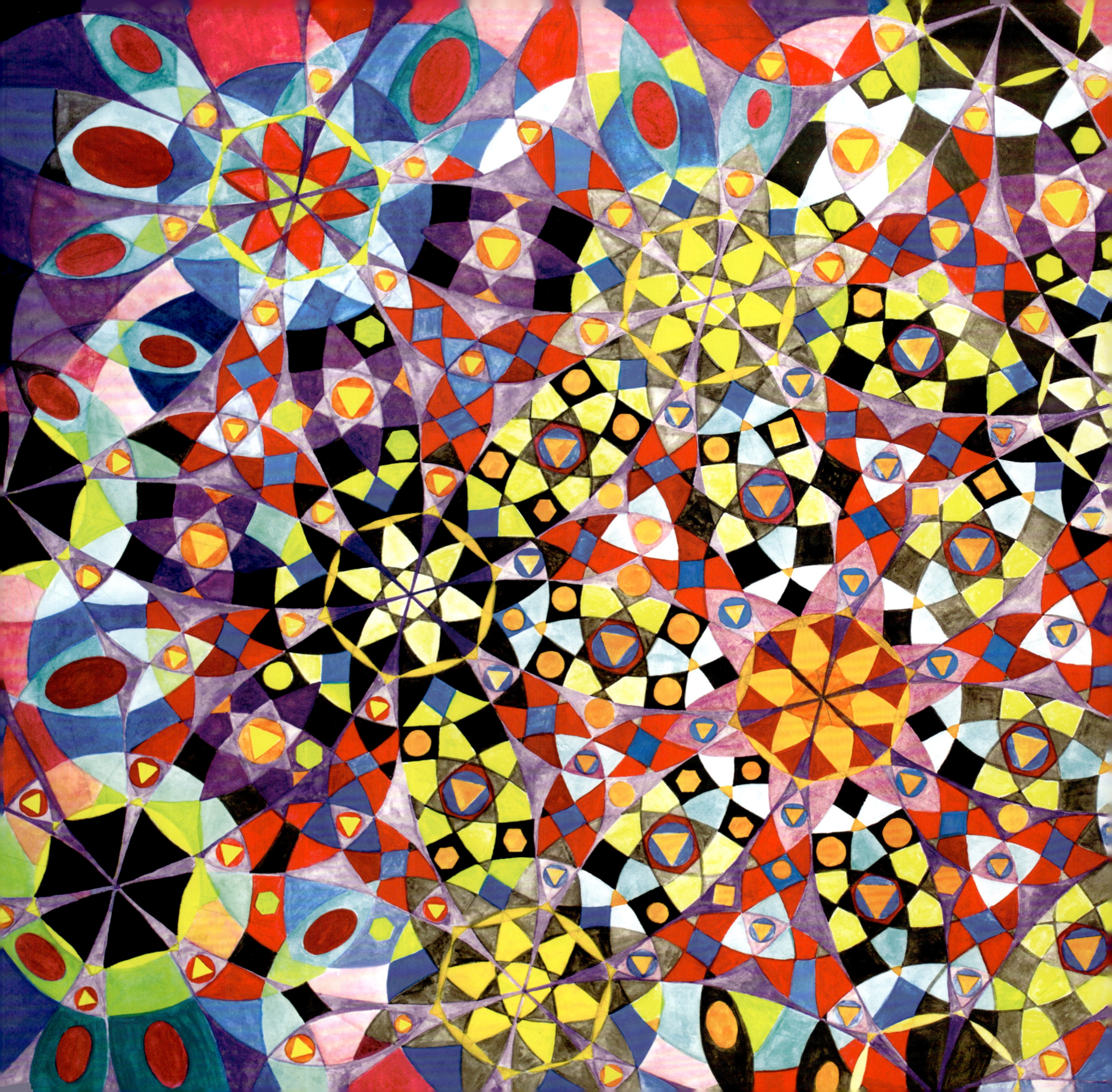

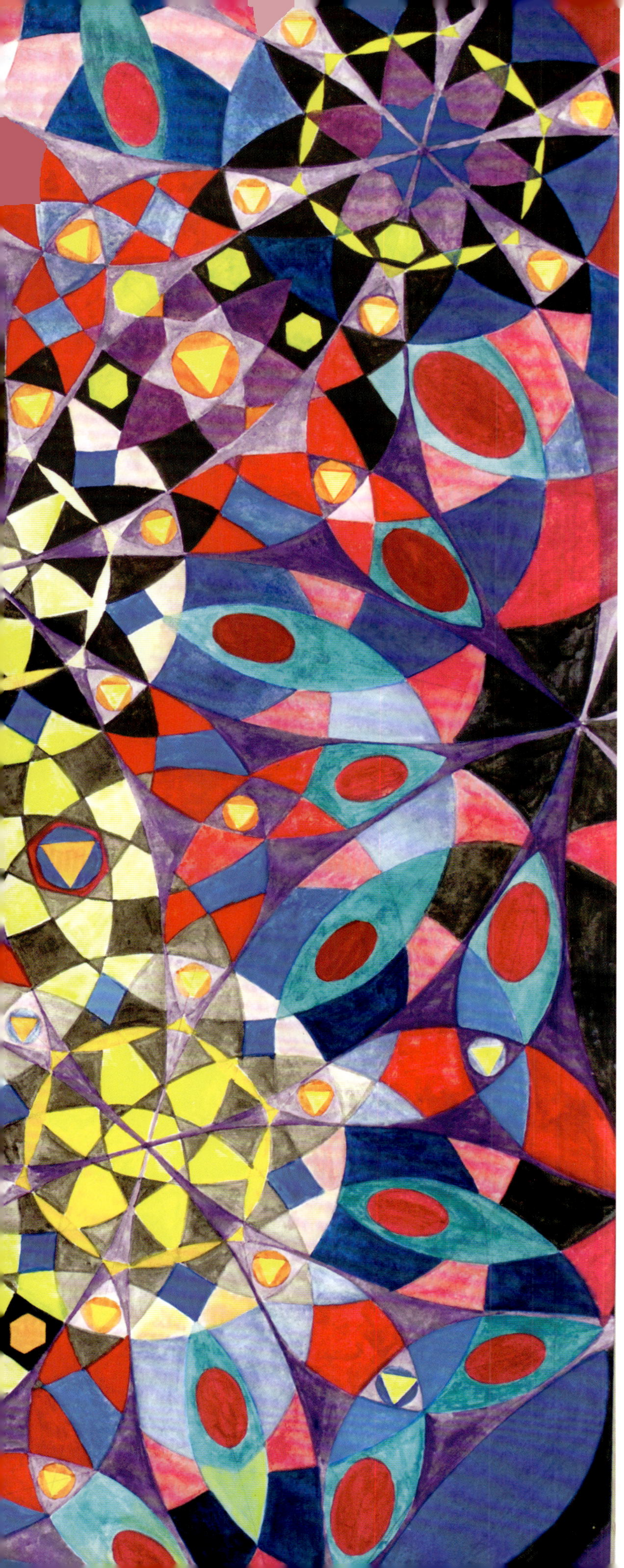

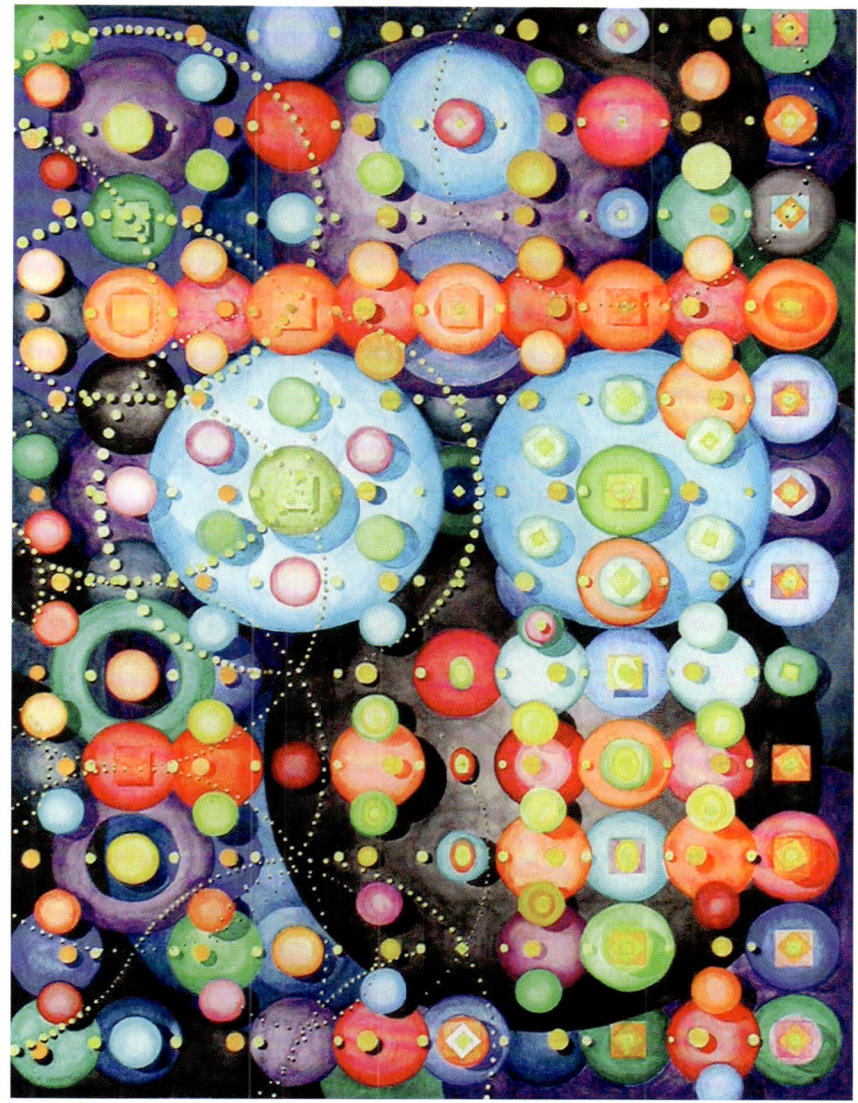

WHEEL WITHIN A WHEEL 16 *(LEFT)*

22 IN X 30 IN
WATERCOLOR, 2003

WHEEL WITHIN A WHEEL 17

30 IN X 22 IN
WATERCOLOR, 2003

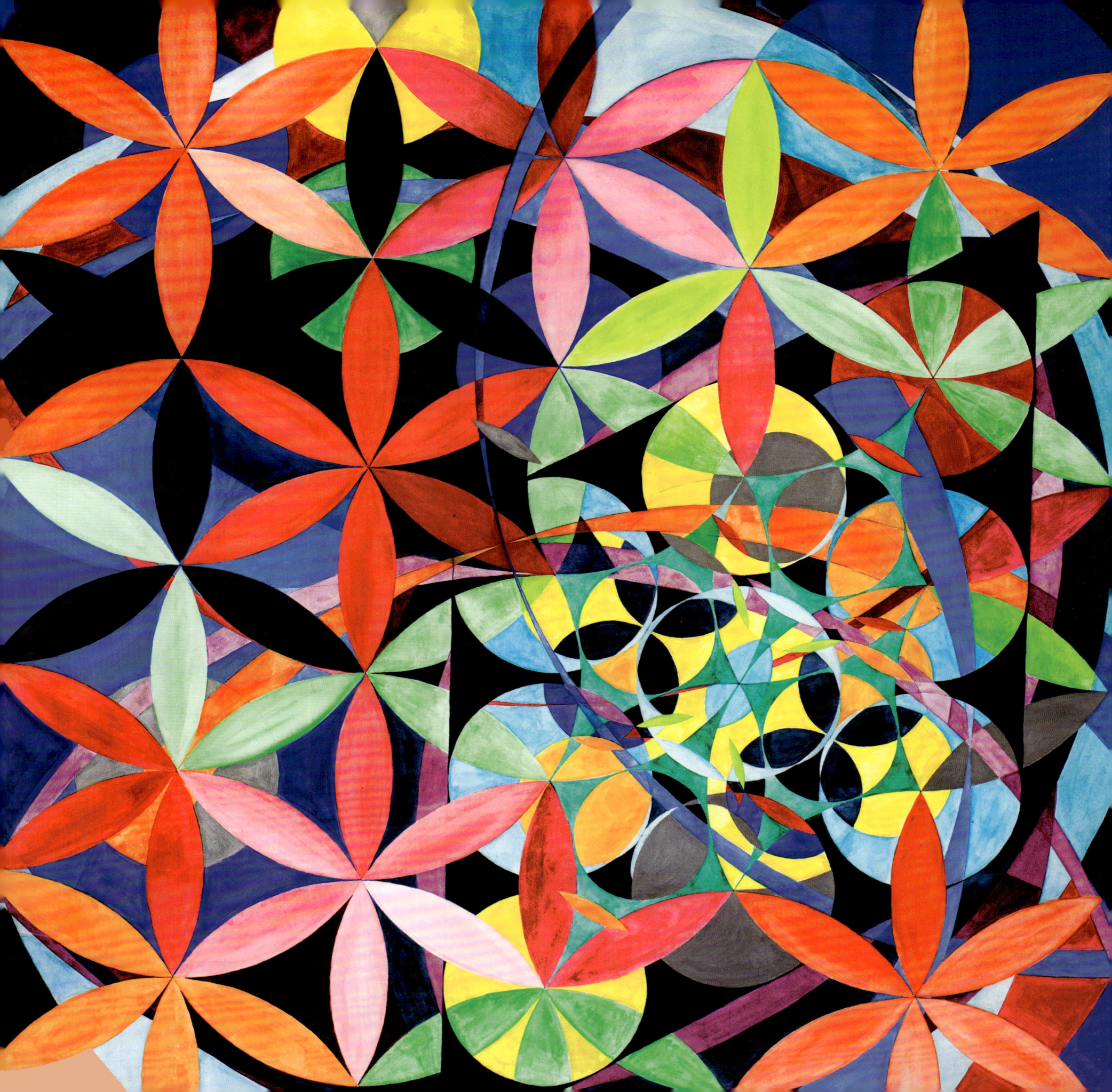

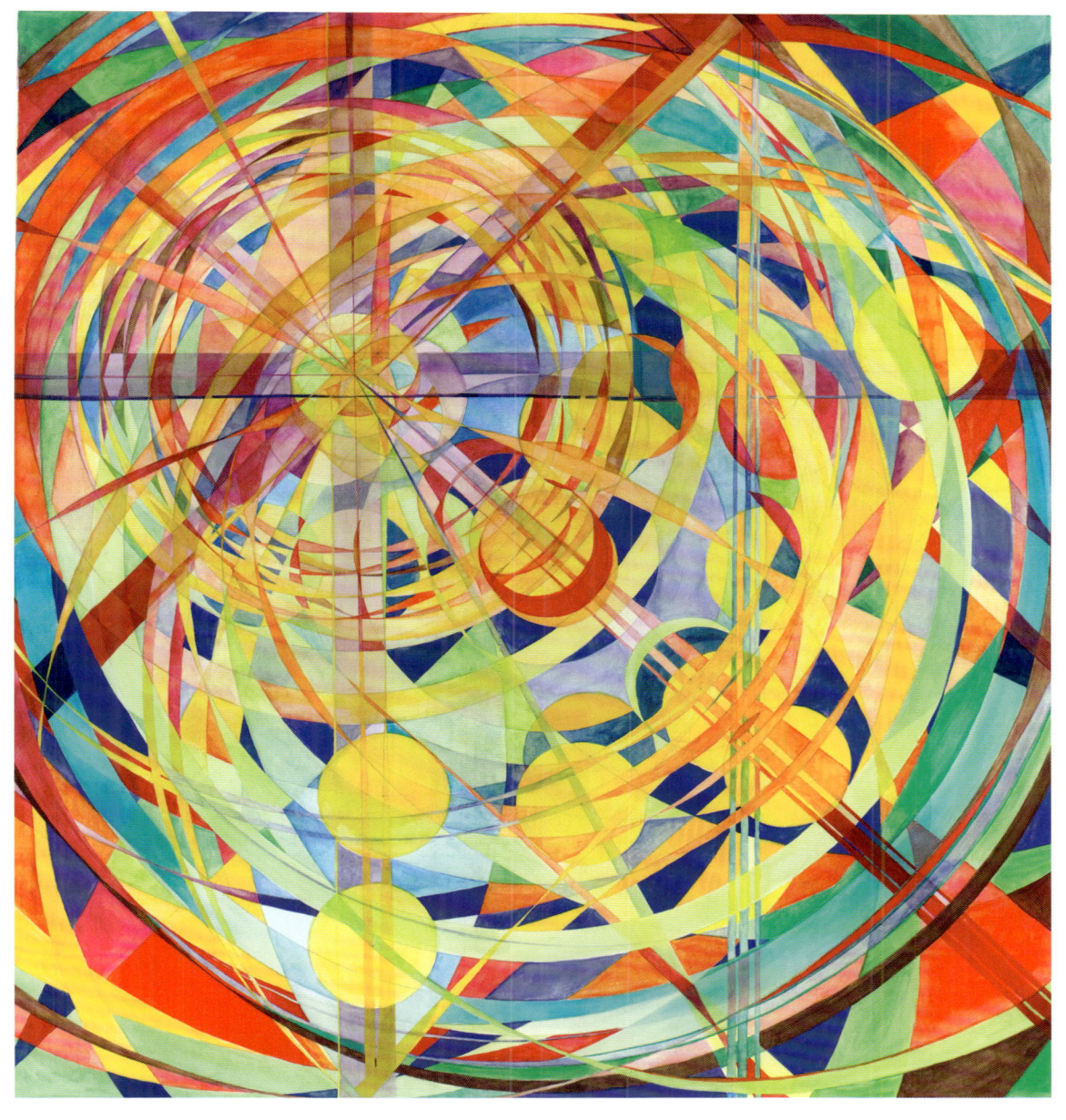

WHEEL WITHIN A WHEEL 18 *(LEFT)*

51 IN X 48 IN
WATERCOLOR, 2004

WHEEL WITHIN A WHEEL 22

51 IN X 48 IN
WATERCOLOR, 2004

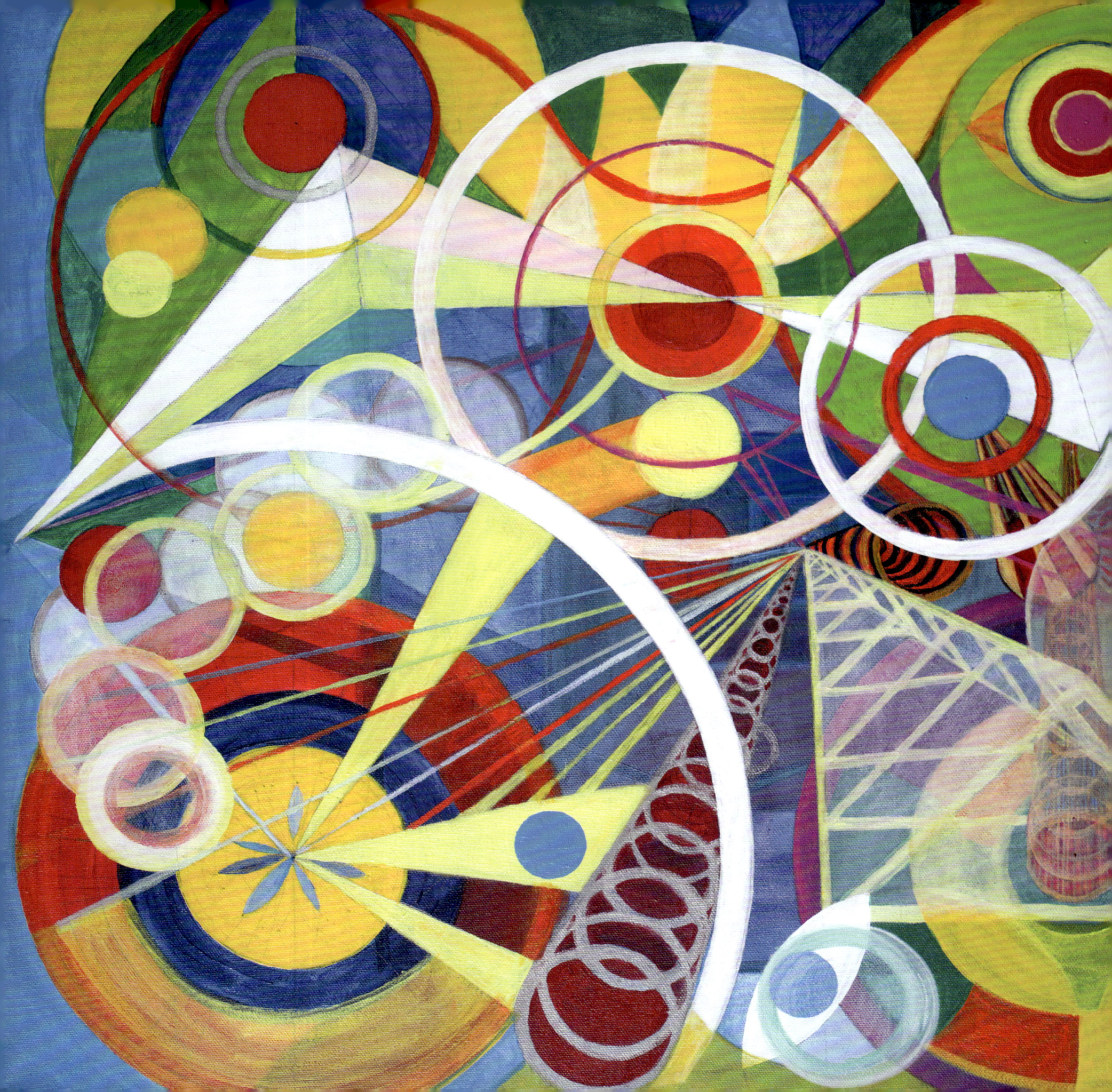

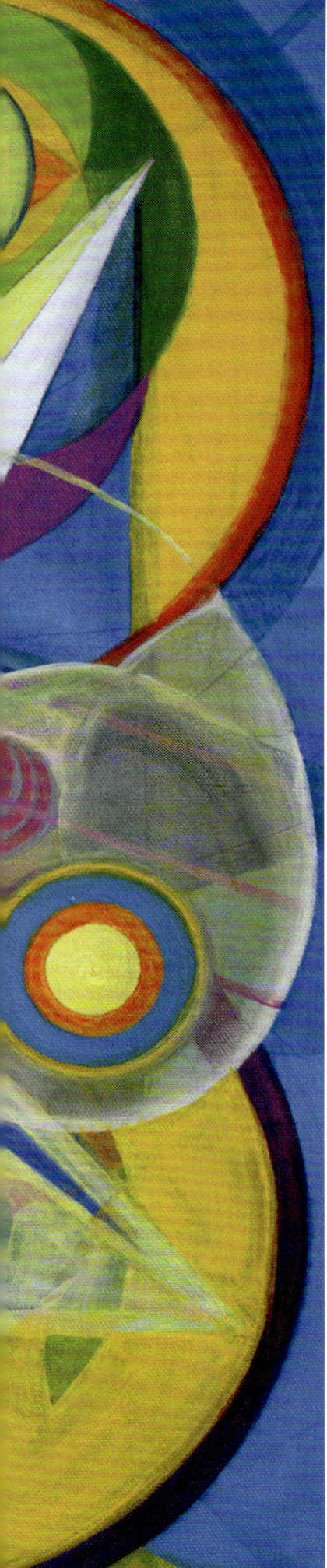

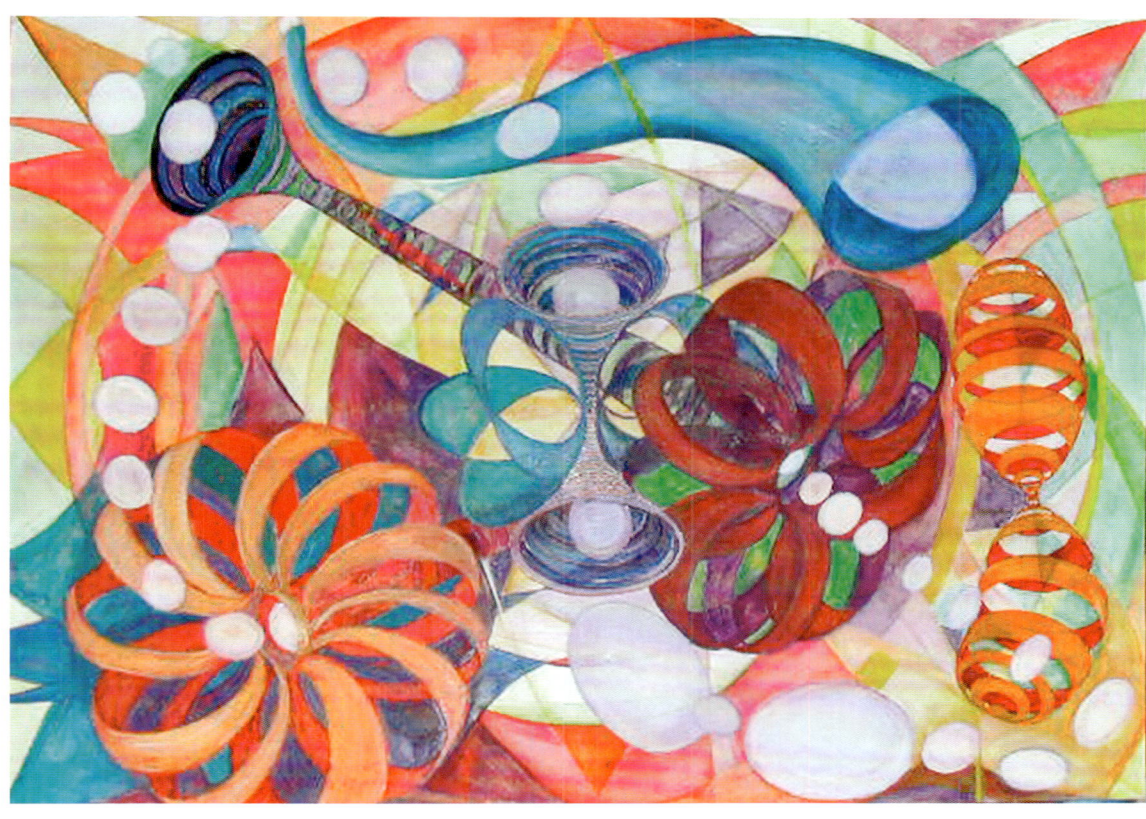

WHEEL WITHIN A WHEEL 23 *(LEFT)*

24 IN X 18 IN
ACRYLIC, 2004

WHEEL WITHIN A WHEEL 24

14 IN X 20 IN
WATERCOLOR, 2004

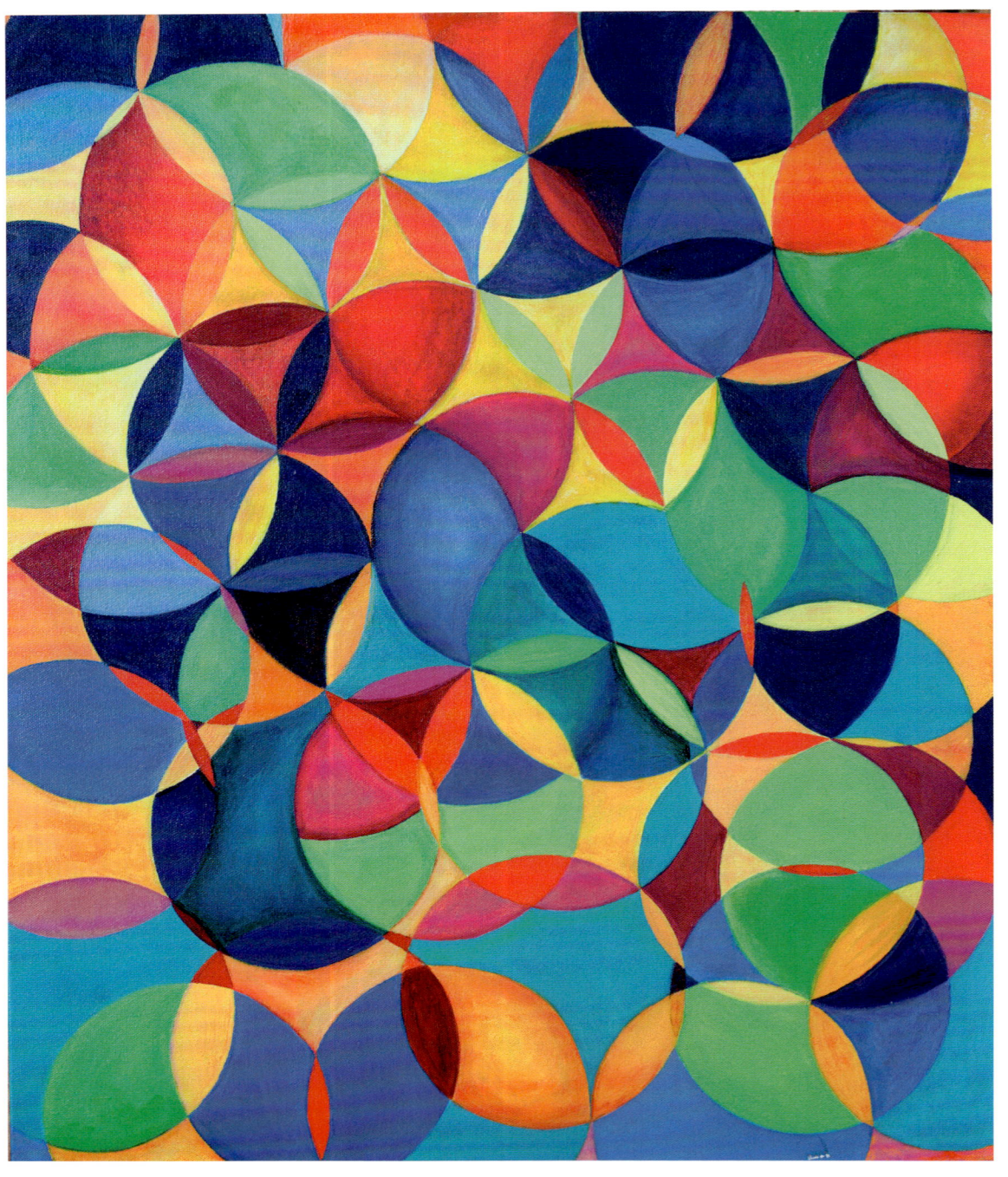

WHEEL WITHIN A WHEEL 28

24 IN X 18 IN
ACRYLIC, 2004

WHEEL WITHIN A WHEEL 33 *(RIGHT)*

36 IN X 36 IN
ACRYLIC, 2005

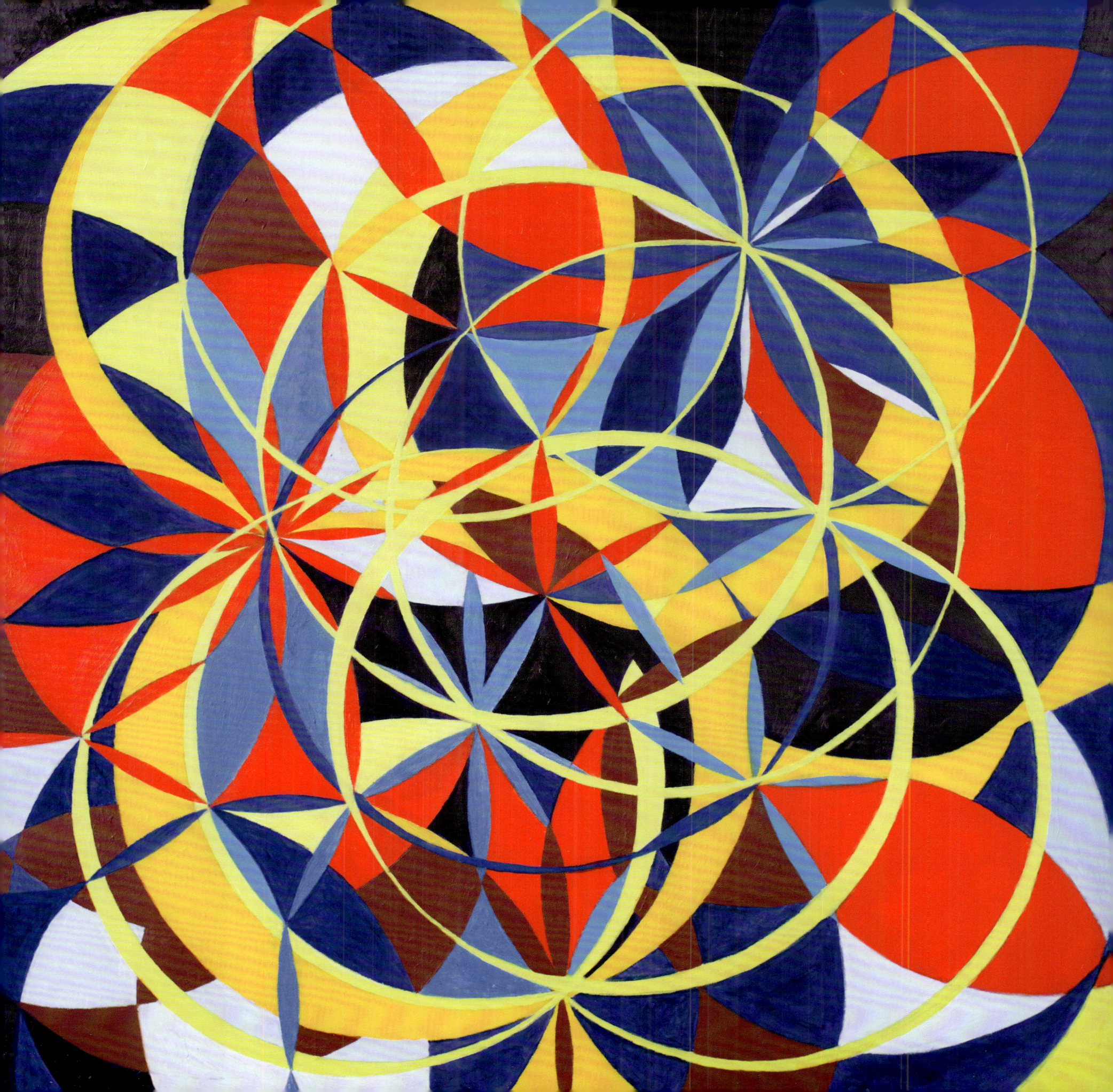

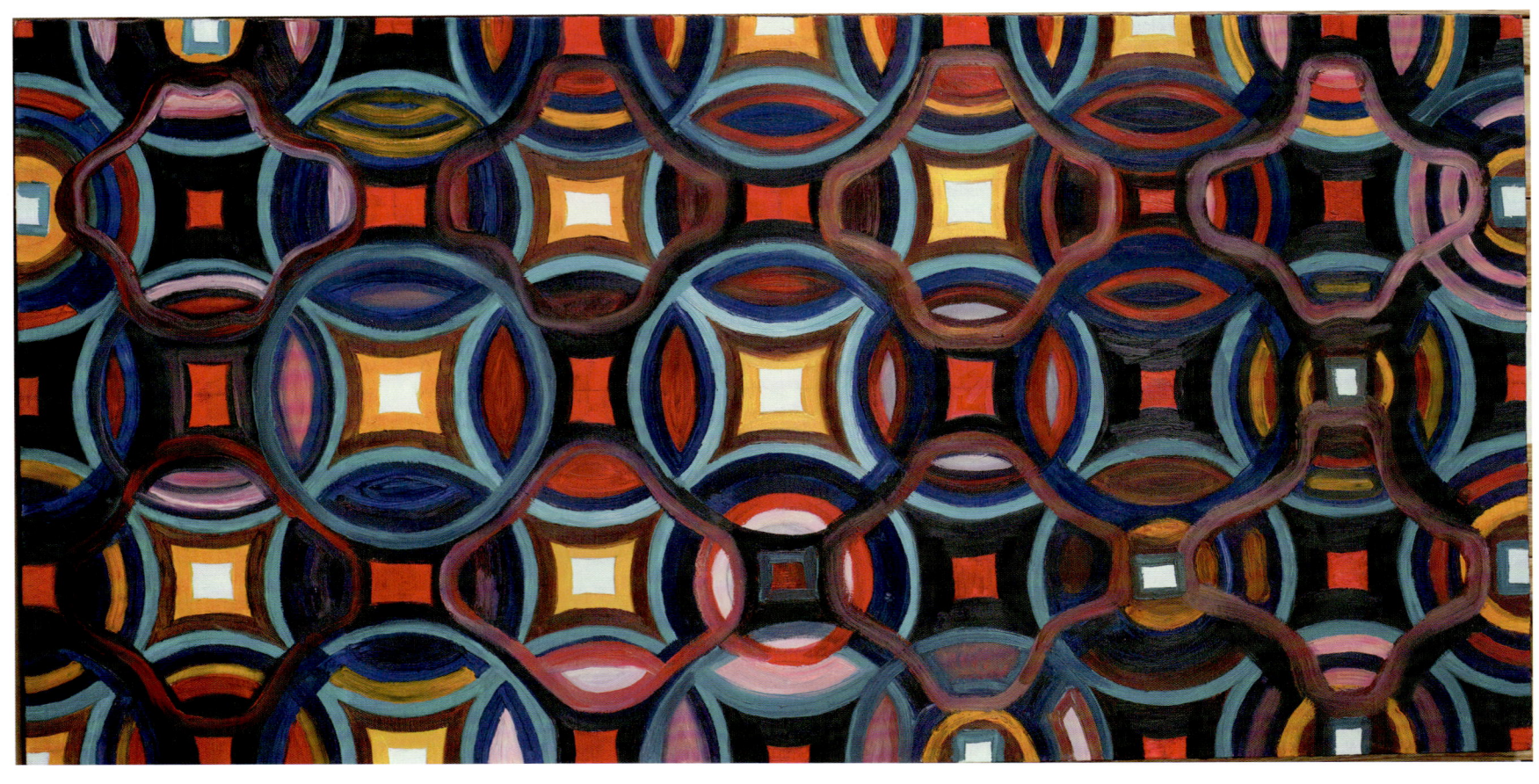

WHEEL WITHIN A WHEEL 36
24 IN X 48 IN
OIL, 2005

WHEEL WITHIN A WHEEL 34 *(RIGHT)*
12 IN X 9 IN
WATERCOLOR, 2005

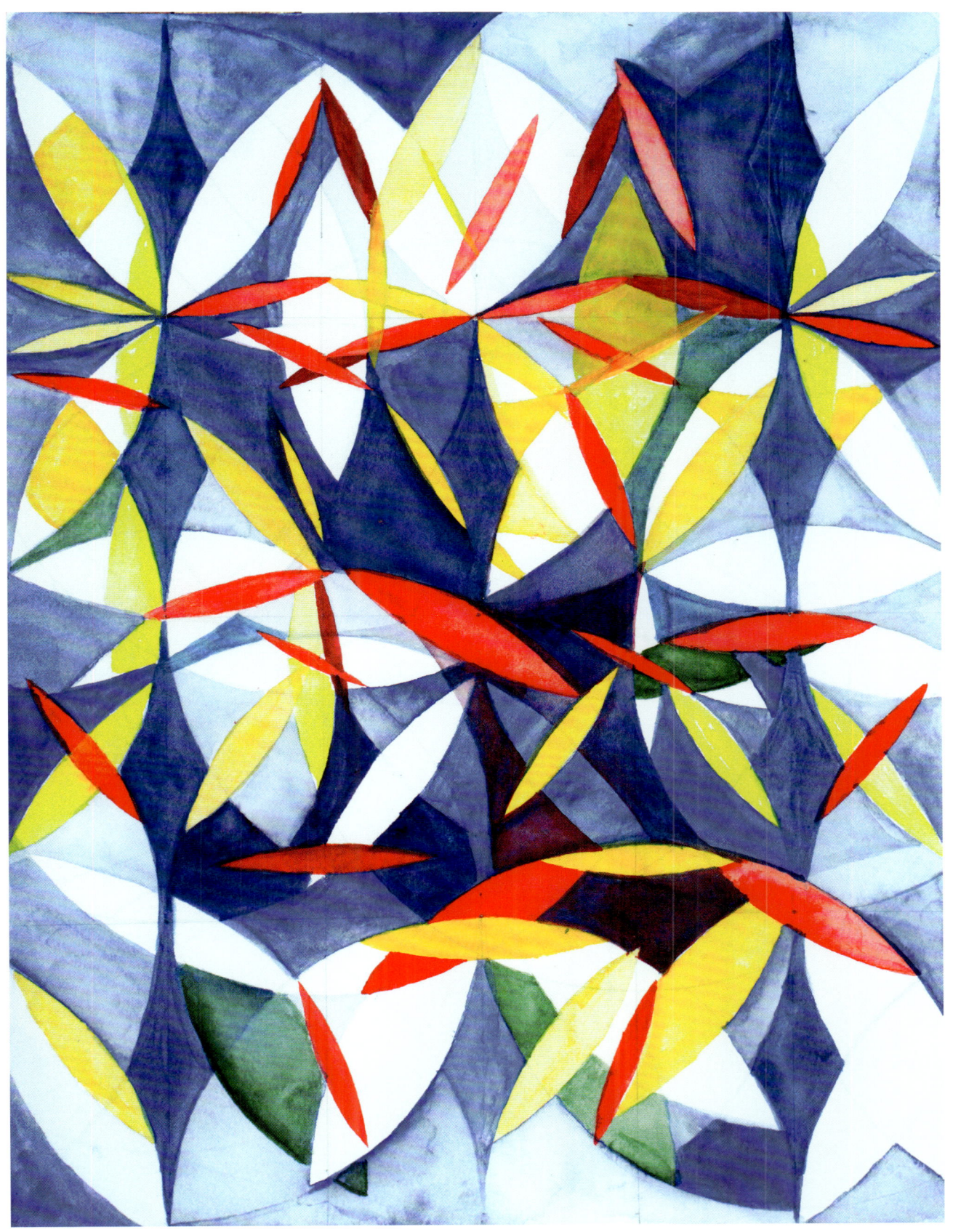

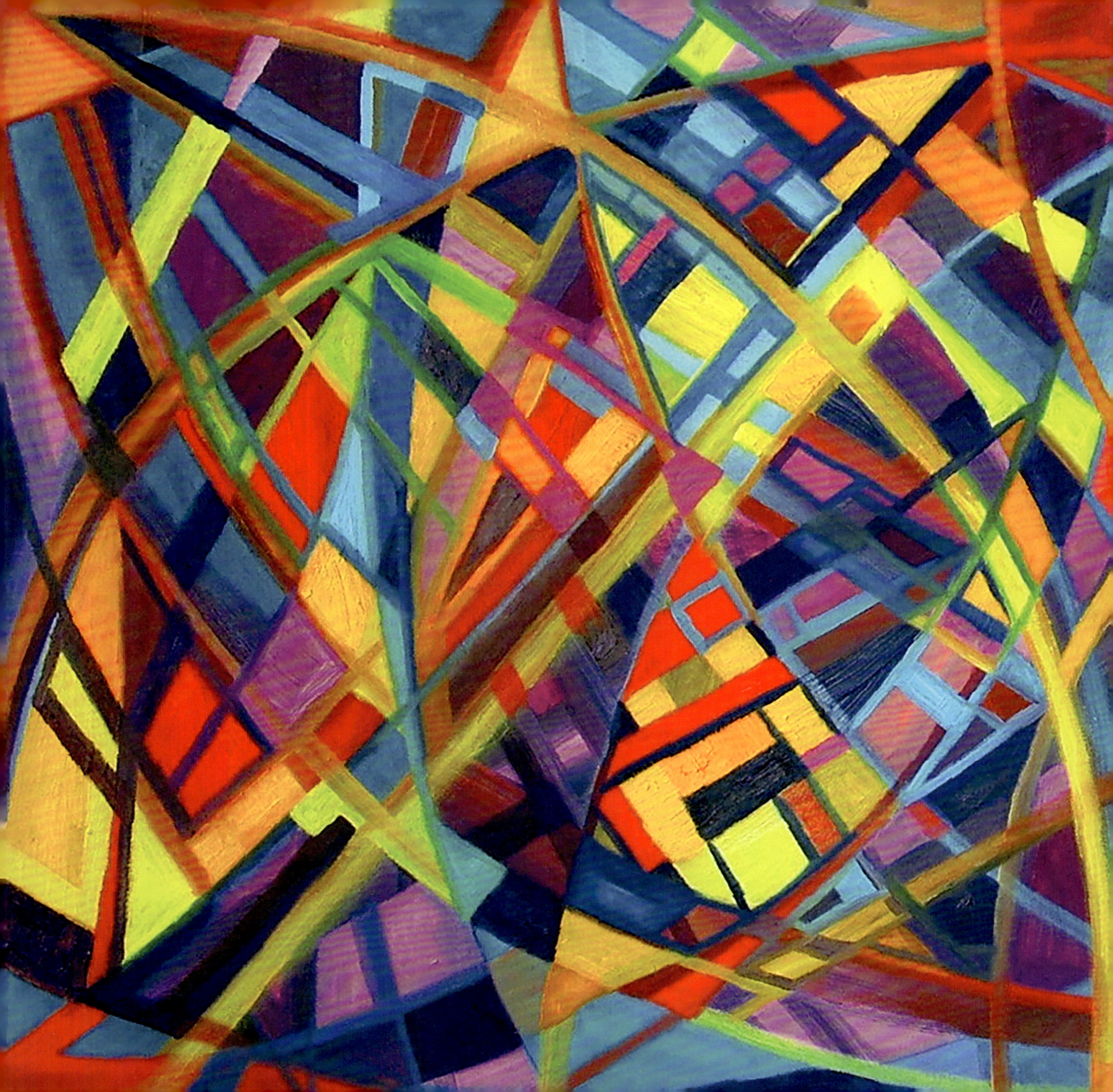

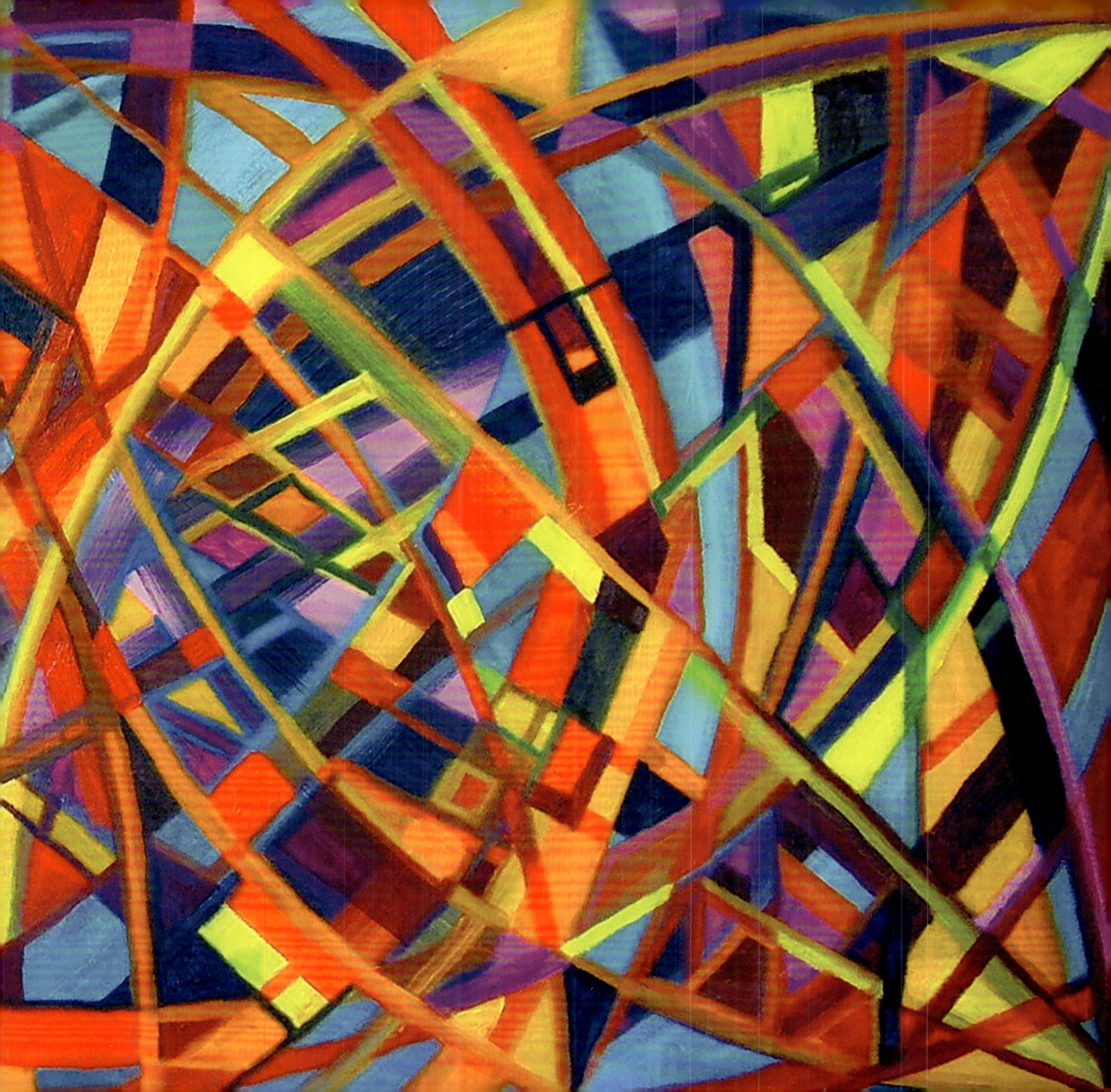

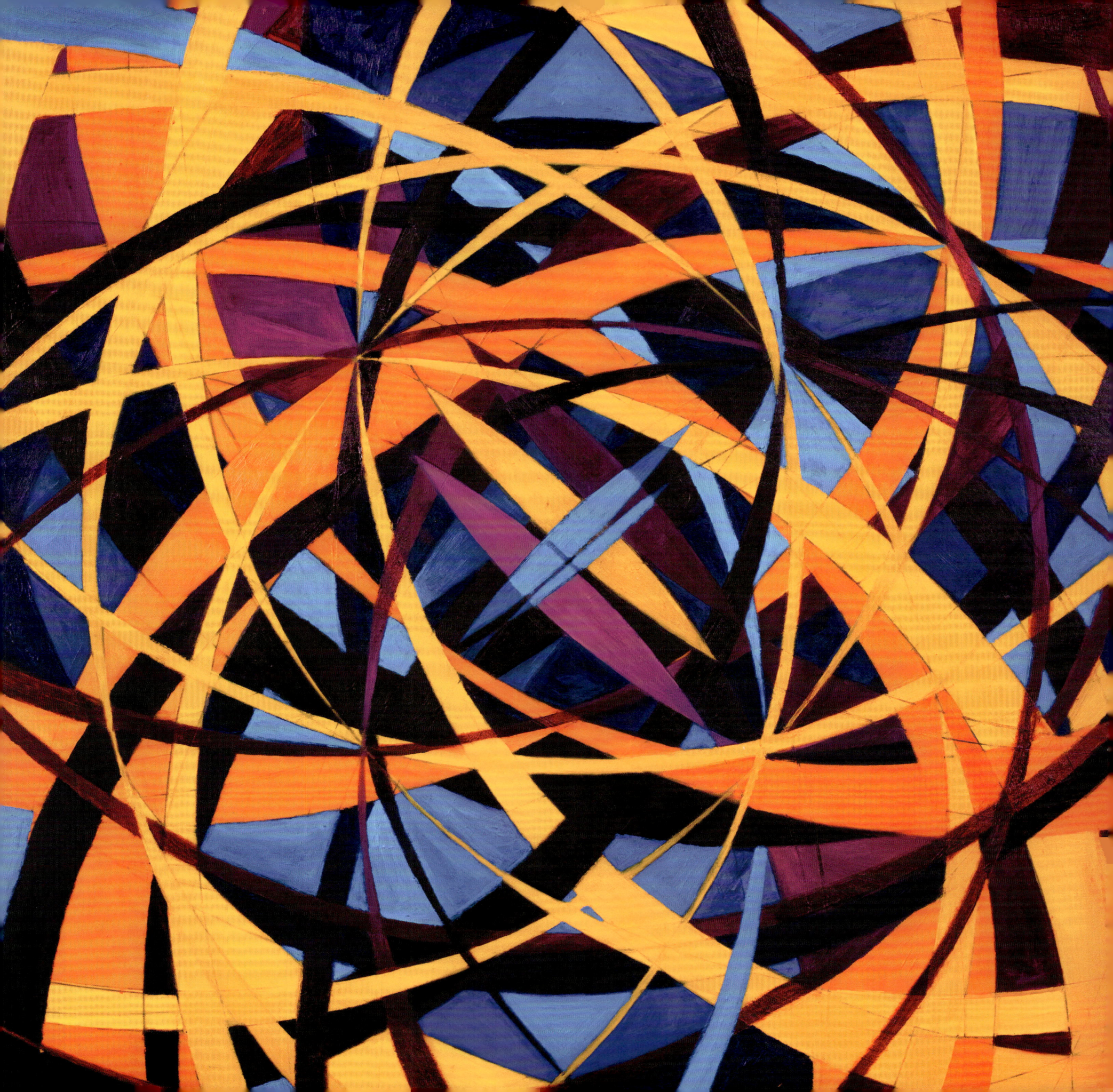

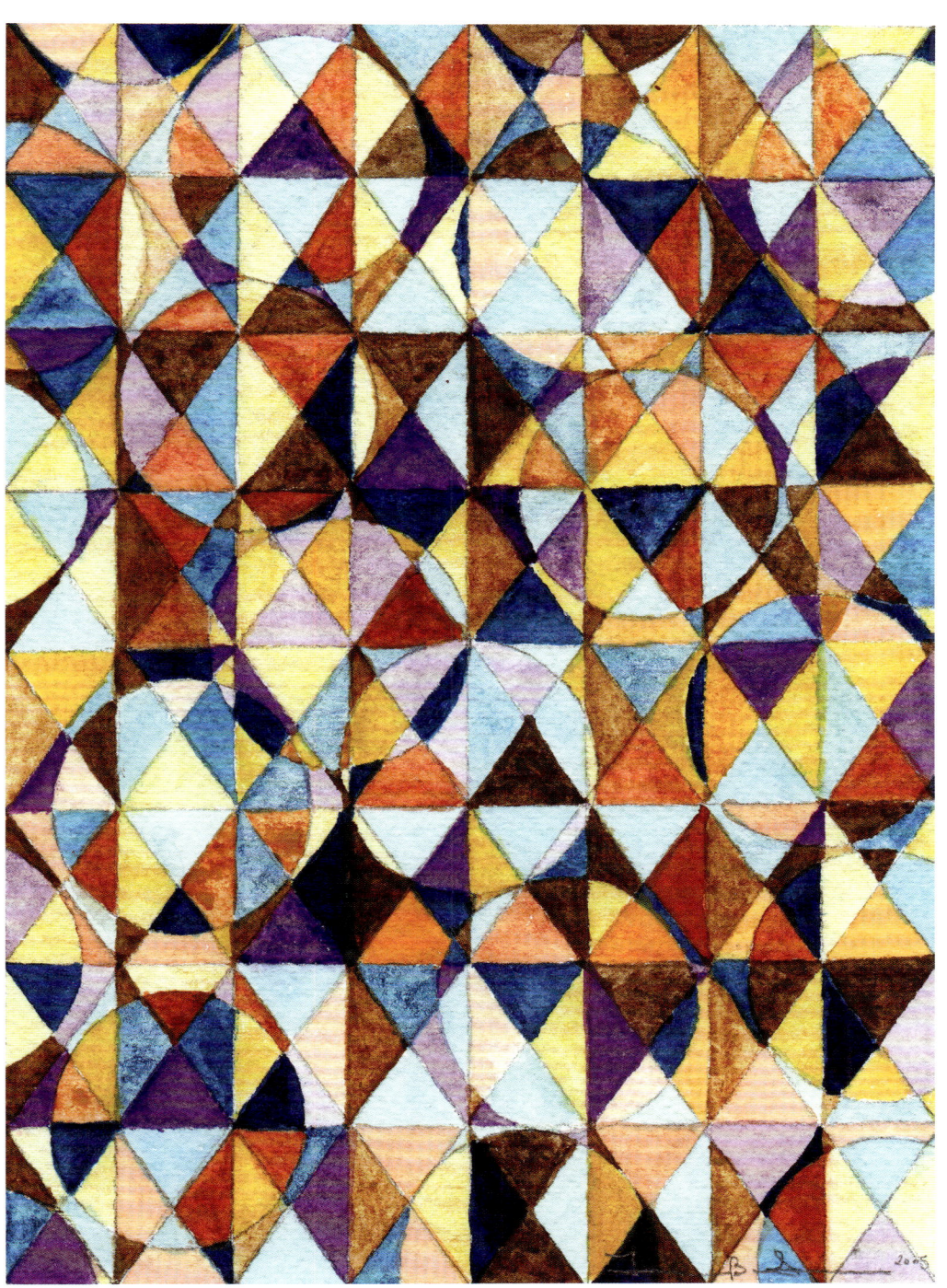

WHEEL WITHIN A WHEEL 37 *(PREVIOUS)*
48 IN X 24 IN
OIL, 2005

WHEEL WITHIN A WHEEL 38 *(LEFT)*
48 IN X 48 IN
OIL, 2005

WHEEL WITHIN A WHEEL 39
6 IN X 4 IN
WATERCOLOR, 2006

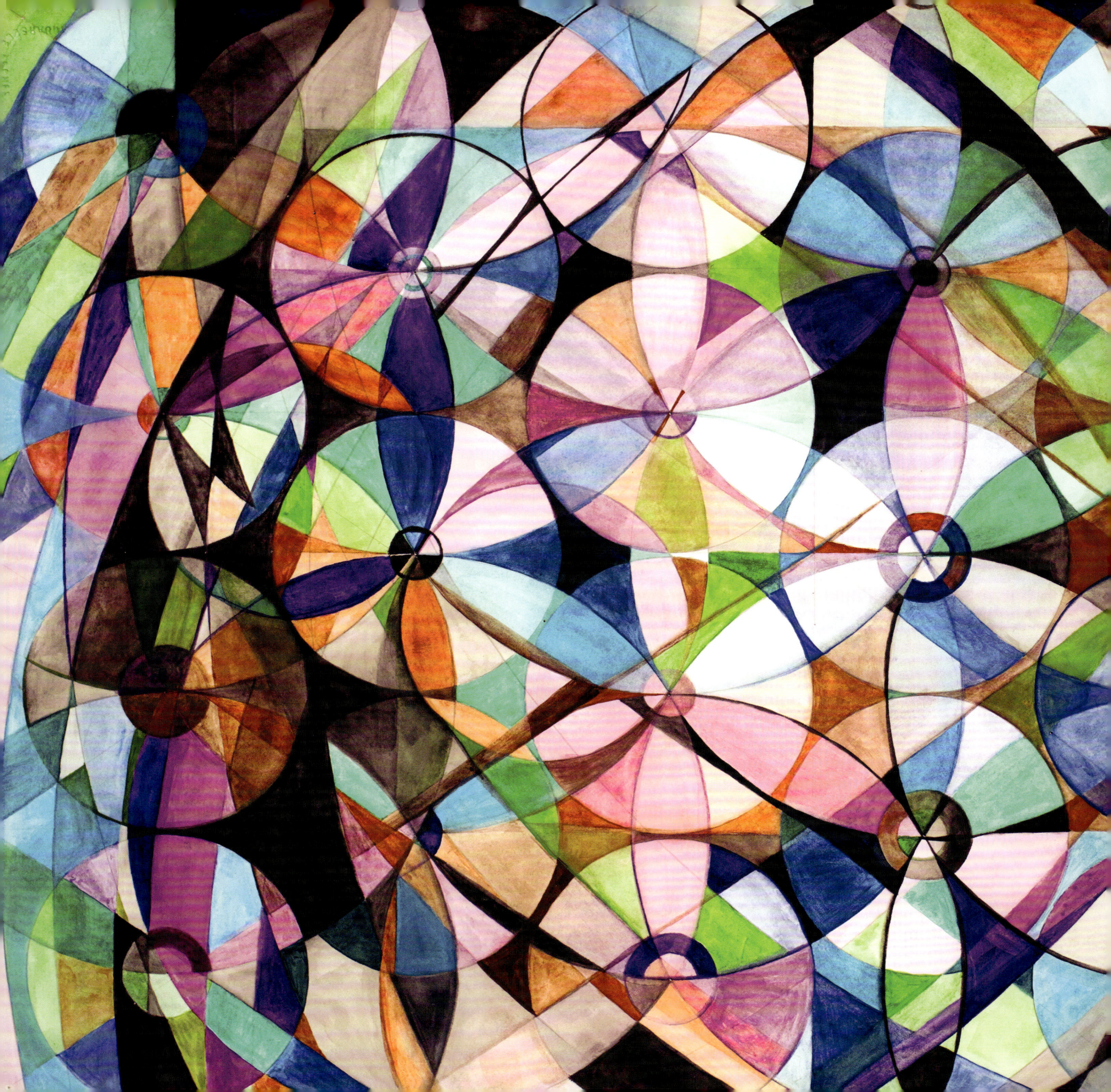

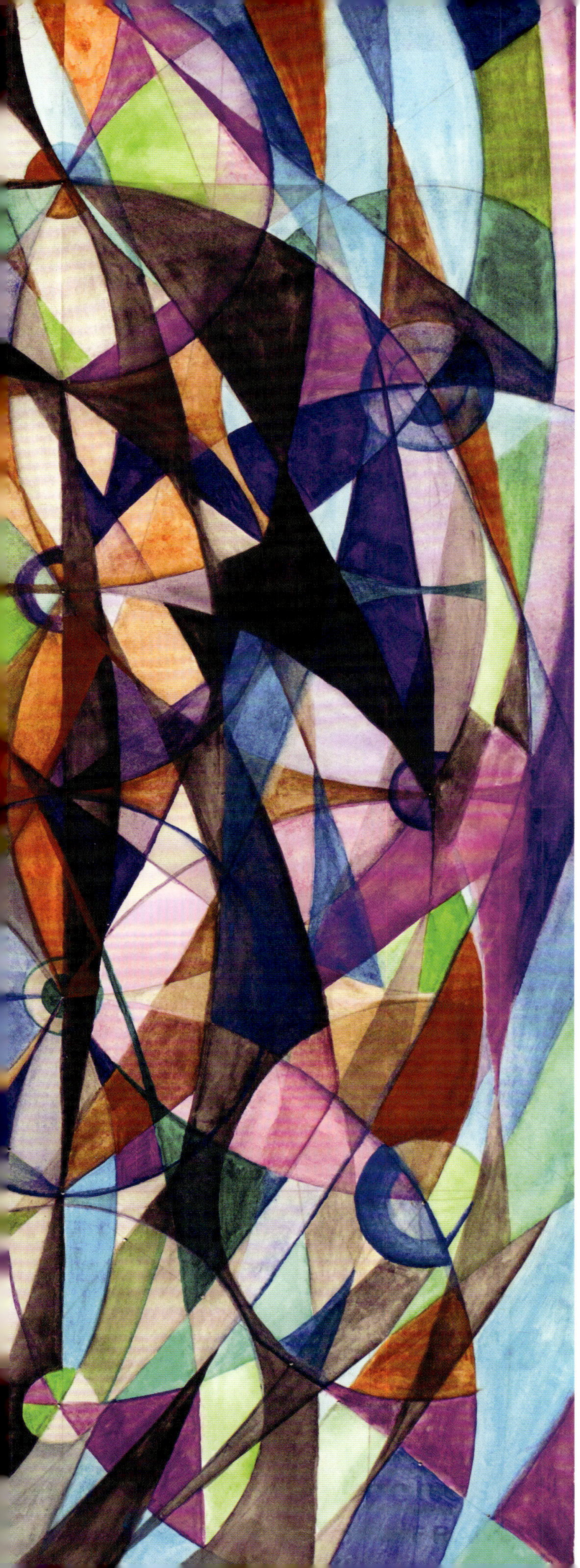

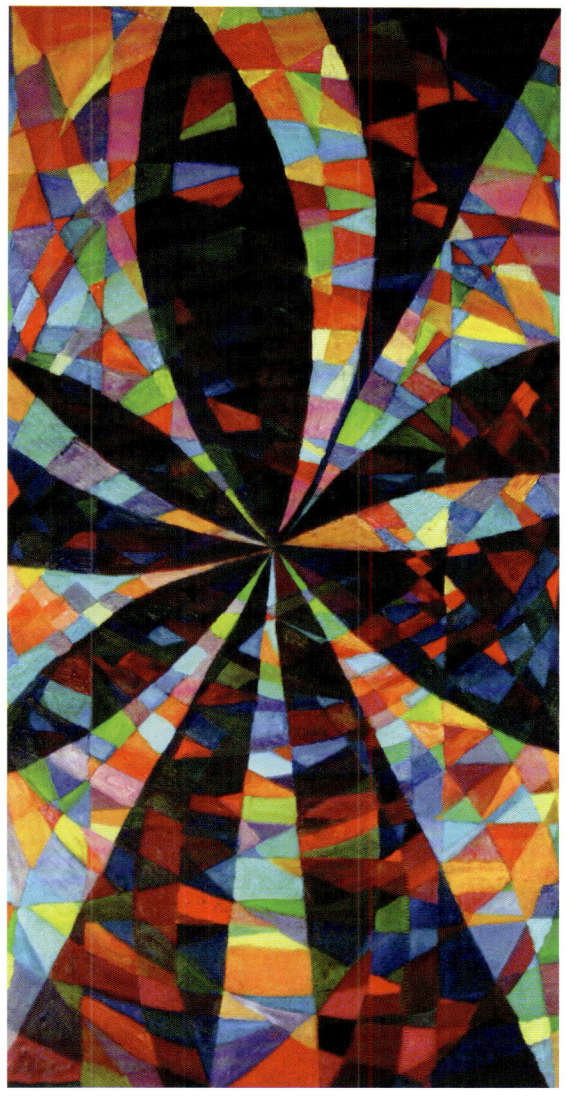

WHEEL WITHIN A WHEEL 43

48 IN X 24 IN
OIL, 2006

WHEEL WITHIN A WHEEL 41

30 IN X 22 IN
WATERCOLOR, 2005

WHEEL WITHIN A WHEEL SERIES

5 YEARS LATER

SIMPLY COMPLEX

BY EVAN SENN

A KALEIDOSCOPIC EXPLORATION IN THE INTERACTION BETWEEN COLOR, SHAPE AND LINE, VENEZUELAN-RAISED AND PALM DESERT, CALIFORNIA-BASED ARTIST LORIEN SUÁREZ FINDS THE INNATE BEAUTY IN OUR NATURAL WORLD INSPIRING AND MOTIVATING, AND CREATES COMPELLING WORKS OF ART THAT EXPRESS THAT FASCINATION.

Her colorful and detailed works of art are meditative yet expressive. The complex intricacies of biological forms ignite Suárez's creative mind and inspire a visual response to the experience of knowing truths about our world and our existence.

Suárez was raised in Venezuela and came to the U.S. as a teenager with her family. Well-educated, having earned degrees in California, Spain and Belgium, Suárez has used her passion for knowledge to help her art practice become and remain engaged with her surroundings. She is enamored with the Latin American minimalists, Teilhard de Chardin, metaphysics, mystical readings, meditation, natural geometry, fashion, botany, color theory, and the concepts of perfection and imperfection, among many others.

A theorist at heart, her artwork reflects the internal yearning for truth and understanding. She is constantly creating worlds within worlds in her art. The subtleties present in her visual artworks feel as though they divulge the colorful secrets of the universe with the simple language all beings understand—color, shape and line.

"When sophistication is thought of as an appreciation and sense of taste, based on an extended gamut of experience, then these concepts start to lose their discrepancies," Suárez says. "The concepts almost feed off each other. These sort of paradoxes–non-dual patterns–begin to show up more as I do the research and practical process design work, thinking alongside my art-making work."

Her current body of work transforms all materials and all boundaries into her personal expression of life and vitality. Her signature style of geometric abstraction feels rooted

in the Latin American minimalists, the American Hard Edge Abstraction and the work in the Salon des Réalités Nouvelles. Pushed toward a visual expression at an early age, Suárez was able to hone her craft to express herself through color and line alongside her studies in school. Her dedication to her studies later on in life helped craft outstanding academic skills in research, furthering her fascination with theory and artistic expression.

Suárez finds inspiration in observing plant life and finding the creative tensions in biological foundations, nature's designs and the imperfection or abnormalities of the natural world. Having spent much of her life in the tropics, the bold color and palpable atmosphere inherent in that area of the world have permeated her expressive work to infuse bits and pieces of each world she feels connected to. "The living, growing geometries have their own life-giving magnetism," according to Suárez. "I am continually in a discovery space; there's just an endless quality to what can be discovered in these living geometries and their arrangements and patterns alongside color."

Alongside the botanical geometry in her work, there are aspects of urban city life, sprawling metropolis', the busy chaos of evolution and expansion; there are also elements of her childhood home of Venezuela, with the bright colors, thick and heavy energy and constant movement. These pieces of the puzzle have come together so naturally to build the unique body of work that is Suárez's signature style, and her own personal perspective on the world.

Writers like Philip Ball helped push Suárez into scientific qualities of color and patterns in nature, with books like *The Self-Made Tapestry: Pattern formation in Nature*. Studying other experts, like Johanness Itten and Josef Albers also fueled Suárez's interest in color theory and play. When she was a child, she admits, she spent much time looking at and loving the art of Carlos Cruz-Diez and Jesus Soto at the Museum in Caracas. Their use of color, kinetic energy and geometric abstraction were very influential on Suárez's growing interests in energy, color, line and expression.

She has exhibited all over the world, most recently at the Venice Biennale, where she received great praise for her work in "New Voices in Latin America," curated by Dr.

Milagros Bello from Miami, Florida. Suárez's geometric botanicals have been collected as fine art pieces, home décor and even as clothing pieces. The abstract patterns Suárez utilizes translate easily onto the body.

Suárez has always been captivated by the art of fashion, beautifying everyday items, and using her abstract designs to enhance the human form, as well as the art itself. To bridge the gap between fine art and fashion is not an easy task, but Suárez is one of those keen artists who creates work that feels specifically made for movement, life and touch.

Her paintings, predominantly made in watercolor and gouache, feel as though they are already moving, so it is no wonder that so many find her textile designs and clothing items so hypnotic.

Suárez's practice and output as an artist sits alongside the great abstractionists in art history. Meditative and bold like Carmen Herrera, intuitive and full of truth like Sol LeWitt, emotive minimal like Eva Hesse or John McLaughlin, Suárez is unafraid to tackle the complexities in this world with

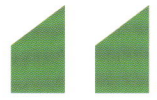

I need to make art to be alive... Over time, as a meditative practice, art has even become a form of life in itself.

simplicity, simultaneously finding intricacies in the real world austerities. Unable to stop creating since she was a small child, Suárez's eye for visual expression rivals the poets and writers of a bygone era, rich and full of multiple entendre and interactions.

"I need to make art to be alive," Suárez says. "I'm not at my best when I haven't been making art. Art has basically taken hold of me as the pivotal axis that has defined my life. Over time, as a meditative practice, art has even become a form of life in itself. It's basically how I communicate. I'm moved to create in response to what I experience and discover through contemplation of my natural environment."

She hopes that her own methodologies and discovery processes may ignite a similar curiosity in her viewers as well, potentially helping viewers become more appreciative of the contemplative aspects and the seeming magical connections found in science and in nature. Viewers can feel the energy that fuels her practice—the dynamic, creative life force that permeates everything in the natural world, everything that connects living beings to one another.

**Evan Senn is the Editor-In-Chief of Culture Magazine, Assistant Editor for YAY! LA Mag, and founder of Rogue Arts. She has an M.A. in Art History and is a Curator, Editor and Writer. She has contributed as an arts writer for more than twenty publications, and teaches Art History at Laguna College of Art & Design.

EVOLUTIONARY ABSTRACTION

BY BRITTNI WINKLER

UPON FIRST GLIMPSE AT ONE OF LORIEN SUÁREZ'S LARGE-SCALE ABSTRACT WATERCOLORS (5'-7' PAINTINGS), THERE IS A STRONG TENDENCY TOWARDS TRANSPARENCY AND FLUIDITY THAT MAKES EACH OF HER PIECES POSSESS AN ETHEREAL QUALITY THAT IS LIGHT AND BUOYANT.

Through a process of "combining watercolor with gouache and acrylic paint on paper, Suárez creates a surface that can be manipulated with a layering process of color washes, brush strokes, and overlapping design elements". The first words that come to mind when viewing Suárez's works are kinetic, organic, transparent, fluid, and structured. All of these terms somewhat contradict the other and the creation of this discrepancy through watercolor abstract pieces is an interesting route to explore. In an interview with Suárez we discussed the creation of her artworks as being, "The time when I am most alive and aware of the creative dynamism of life. I would describe this artwork-awareness as joy".

As an abstract artist, Suárez is creating the perception of movement and growth of living forms. Through her particular use of geometry there is what she describes as a "sensorial experience of nature in our immediate environment"—where the shapes and symmetries that Suárez creates symbolize plant growth, flowers, waves, spirals in shells, pinecones, and also mineral structures such as crystals. In Suárez's painting series *Wheel within a Wheel* 47, 49, 50 (each painting 62 in x 45 in) each piece is symbolic of an "aspect of the dynamic symmetries of growth". Each piece has a wide color spectrum with geometric patterns that repeat and overlap one another. Some have black backgrounds and others have more transparent qualities with white backgrounds. Each piece of the paper is divided intricately into an immersive, multi-layered atmosphere. She relates these paintings to the manner in which leaves and petals interconnect and form, how each has a particular placement and how this comes back to concepts like the axial symmetry of the circle. The effect is to stimulate a visual sense of expansion, movement and vibrancy through strict and controlled use of the perceptions of movement, form, and color through the use

of watercolor and paper. *Wheel within a Wheel* is titled after Ezekiel's vision of the "Wheel within a Wheel amidst the glory of God."

Some of Suárez's more recent artworks such as, *Chromatic Crystals* and *Prismatic Crystals* focus on the geometric nature of the twining laws that define the structural growth of seed crystals. Instead of focusing on plants and movement, her new study and focus of crystals adds another element of structure to her watercolors. There is an interesting layering of opposition that develops with the crystals between the use of watercolor and its creation of paintings of ethereal structures of the crystals that are quite strong. In *Prismatic Crystals*, Suárez explores geometric patterns using rectilinear forms as opposed to circles and more linear works such as in *Wheel Within a Wheel*. What is intriguing is that each crystal structure is repeated and builds upon itself, but is not uniform. Suárez combines the forms of the crystals into a geometric layout and then builds her own layers upon one another through an organic process that allows room for "the artistic response to grow within". Even though Suárez is working with a different subject matter in her new works she says, "I discover time and time again the infinite quality inherent to geometric patterns."

In this manner of creating artwork, Suárez is not attaching to any previous notions of the artwork—she allows it to come to life in the process with a standard idea of what should be accomplished by the end. "I usually start with an overall drawing on paper and then begin to paint, though the drawing will be altered as I paint, and the painting will be altered by the changes I make to the geometric patterns I explore", explained Suárez, "A natural bond emerges for me with the materials and instruments I use in my work process. These tools facilitate the crafting of a design onto a blank surface – as an open space."

The scale at which Suárez is working with watercolor and the amount of time it takes her to finish large piece is anywhere from a couple of months to an entire year. She describes each artwork as "an ongoing building process", where she sets aside the readymade notions

and keeps the process entirely organic and evolving. This type of process of creating an artwork can be seen as a transformative journey of welcoming the immediate moment and letting the imagination unfold. Suárez says that, "Over time, I also realized that art-making is a form of meditation. Through the process of discovery, creativity engenders the energy as passion from which the artwork emerges. When I am at work on art, I am completely engaged." This sense of engagement and concentration is expressed through Suárez's understanding of structure and fluidity in her artworks while also meshing them with high attention to detail and color schemes playing off of one another.

Lorien Suárez's love for art began as a child when she was living and attending school in Venezuela. Two particular Venezuelan artists strongly influence her career today, Jesus Soto and Carlos Cruz Diez. "I came to appreciate what they discovered and created –artworks that were revealing a fragment, an instance, from an endless pattern of an infinite

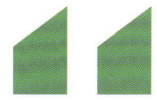

I discover time and time again the infinite quality inherent to geometric patterns.

reality (Soto) and that color as an element isn't static but has an ephemeral dynamism that's displayed as an endless variation of hues (Cruz-Diez.). She moved to the US for her Undergraduate career and studied History with high honors at UC Berkeley. She then pursued a graduate degree in Europe where she studied Business and History at Leuven, Belgium at the Katholieke Universiteit, the Universidad de Salamanca Spain, and at ESADE in Barcelona. Her artwork has been exhibited in curated shows in museums, galleries, cultural and educational center/institutions: SDAI, Riverside Art Museum, and Palm Springs Art Museum.

** Brittni S. Winkler is a curator and artist working out of Miami, FL. She is currently completing her MFA in curatorial practice and working as a Fellows research assistant at Florida International University. Her graduation show in 2015 will deal with the visual connection between art and yoga.

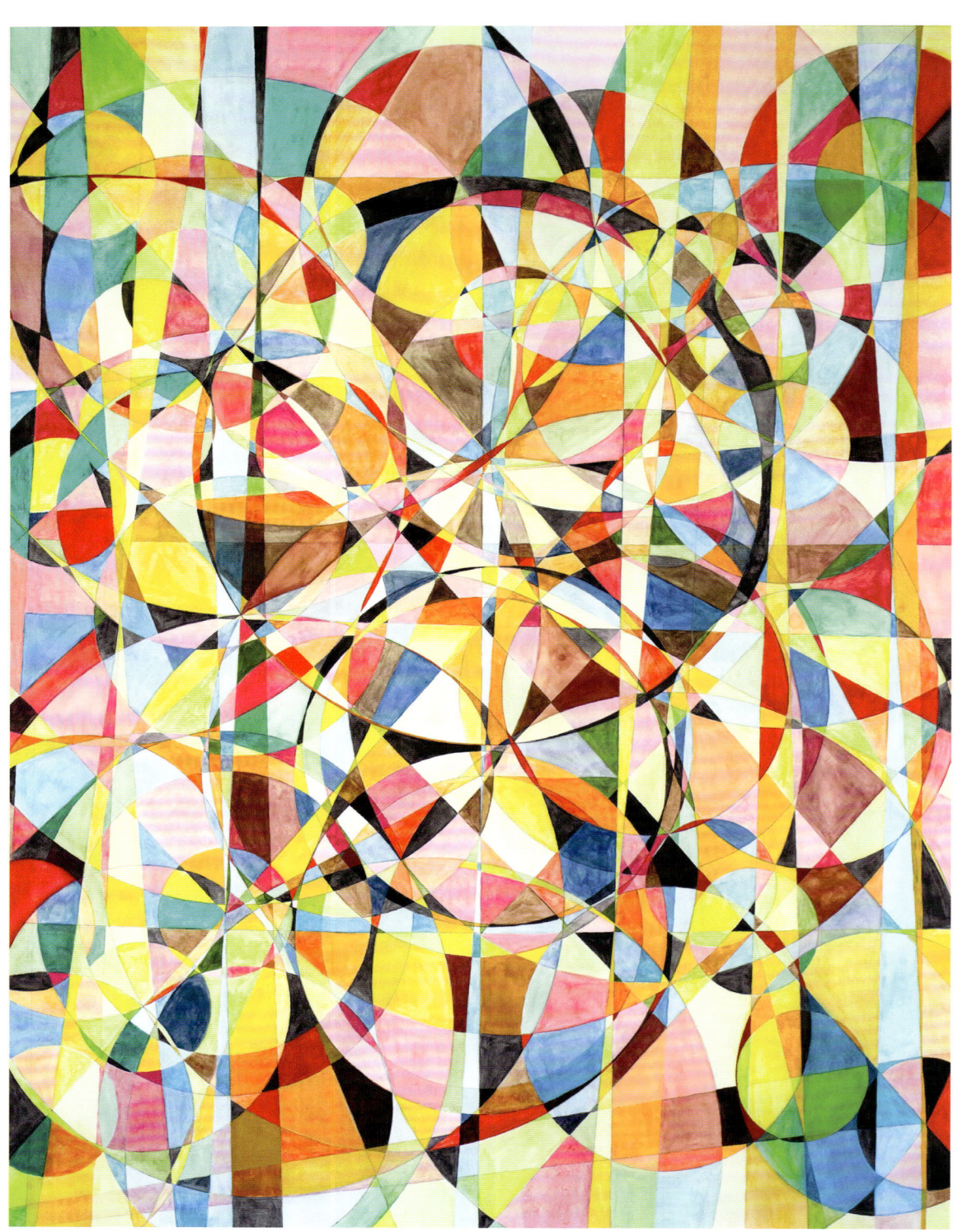

WHEEL WITHIN A WHEEL 44

68 IN X 48 IN
WATERCOLOR/GOUACHE, 2006

WHEEL WITHIN A WHEEL 45 *(RIGHT)*

51 IN X 51 IN
WATERCOLOR/GOUACHE, 2006

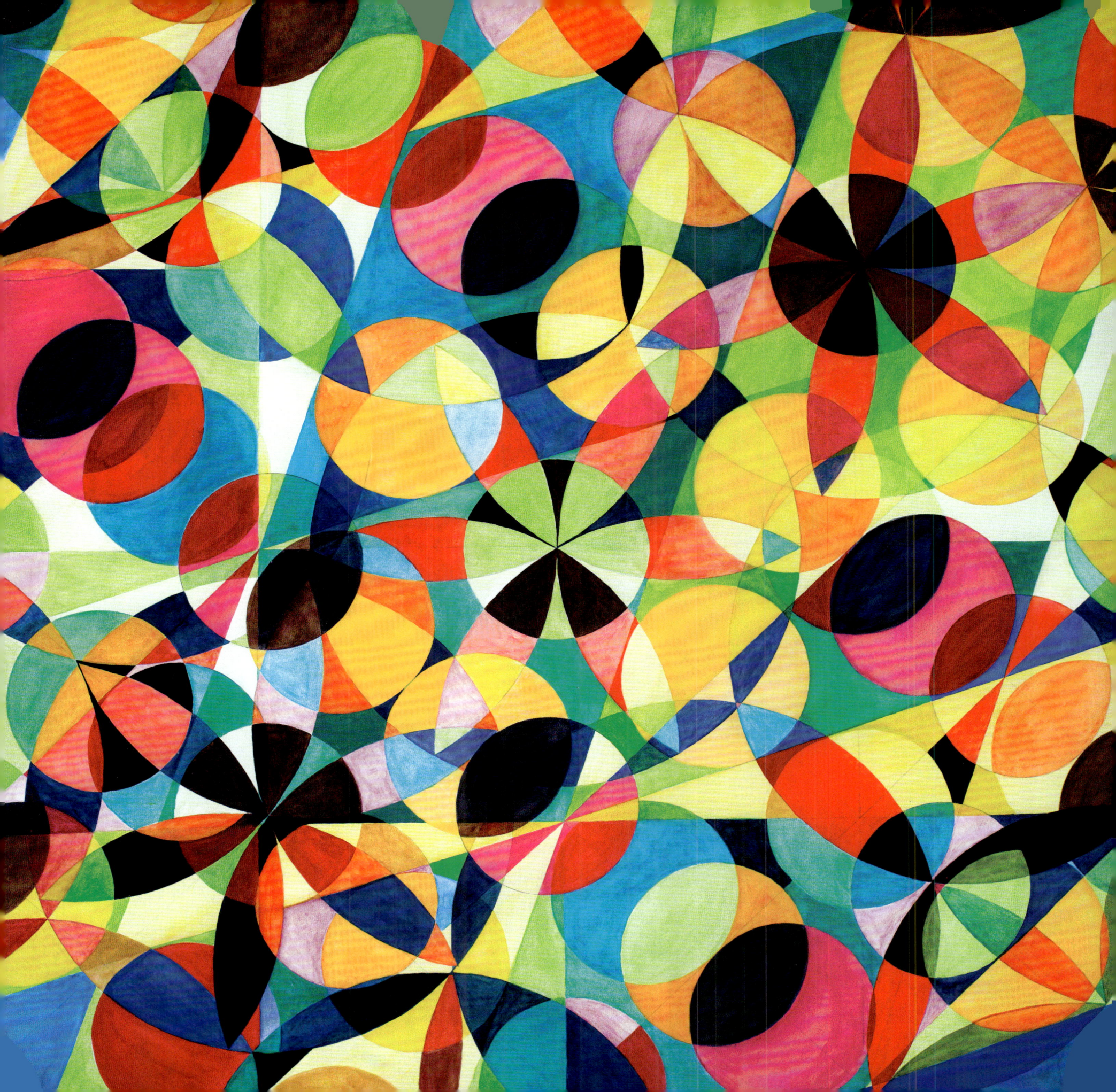

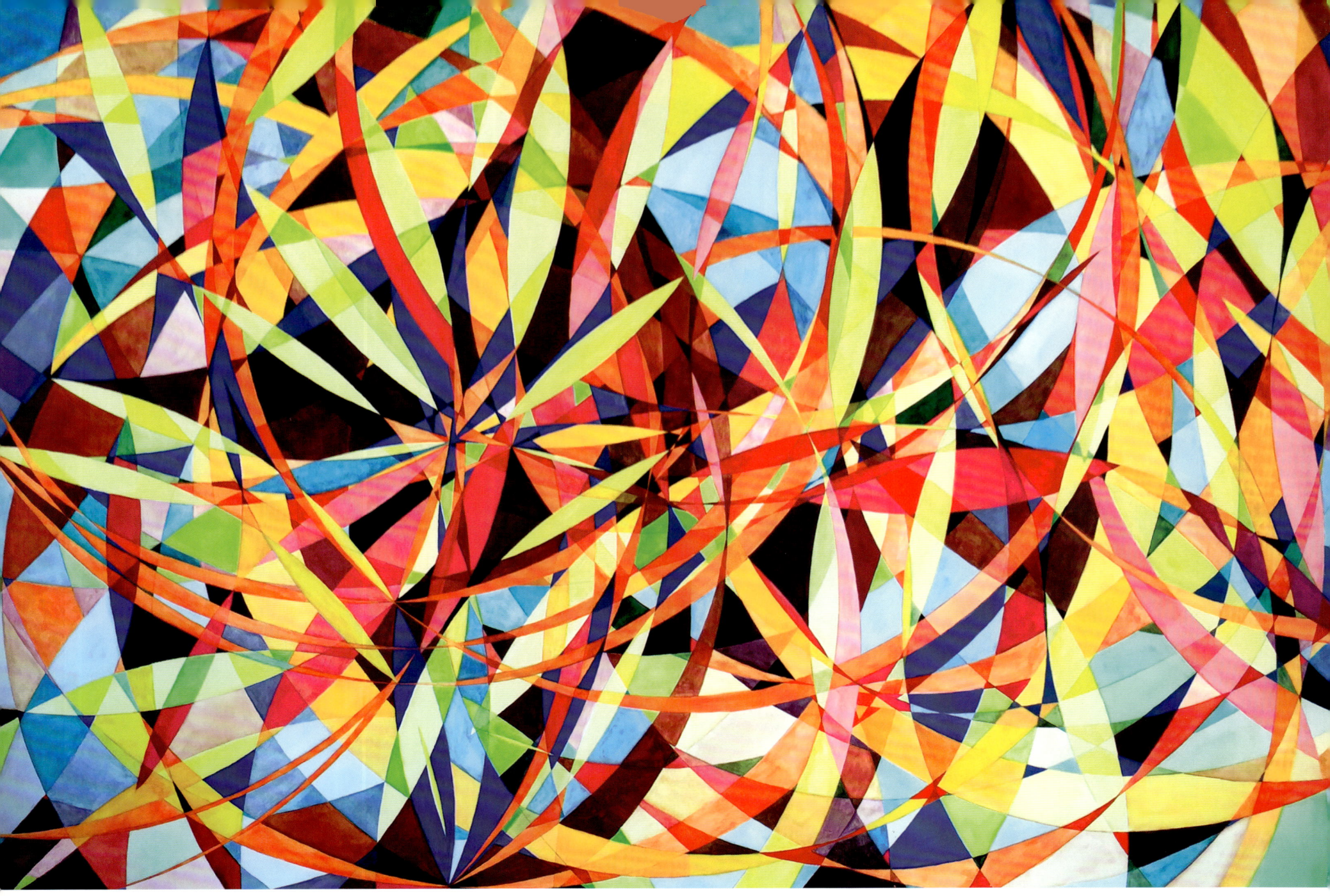

WHEEL WITHIN A WHEEL 46

51 IN X 72 IN
WATERCOLOR/GOUACHE, 2007

WHEEL WITHIN A WHEEL 47 *(RIGHT)*

62 IN X 45 IN
WATERCOLOR/GOUACHE, 2007

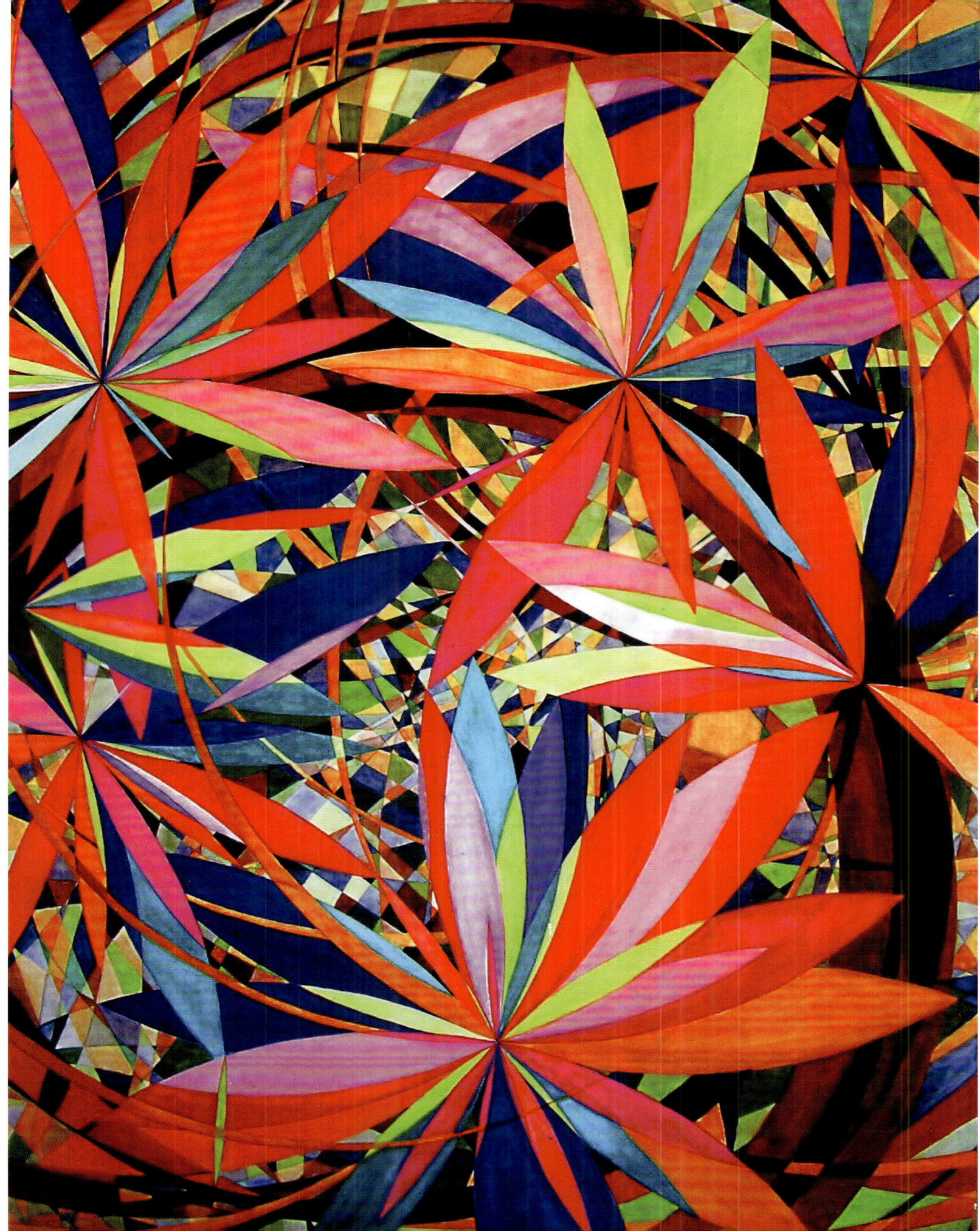

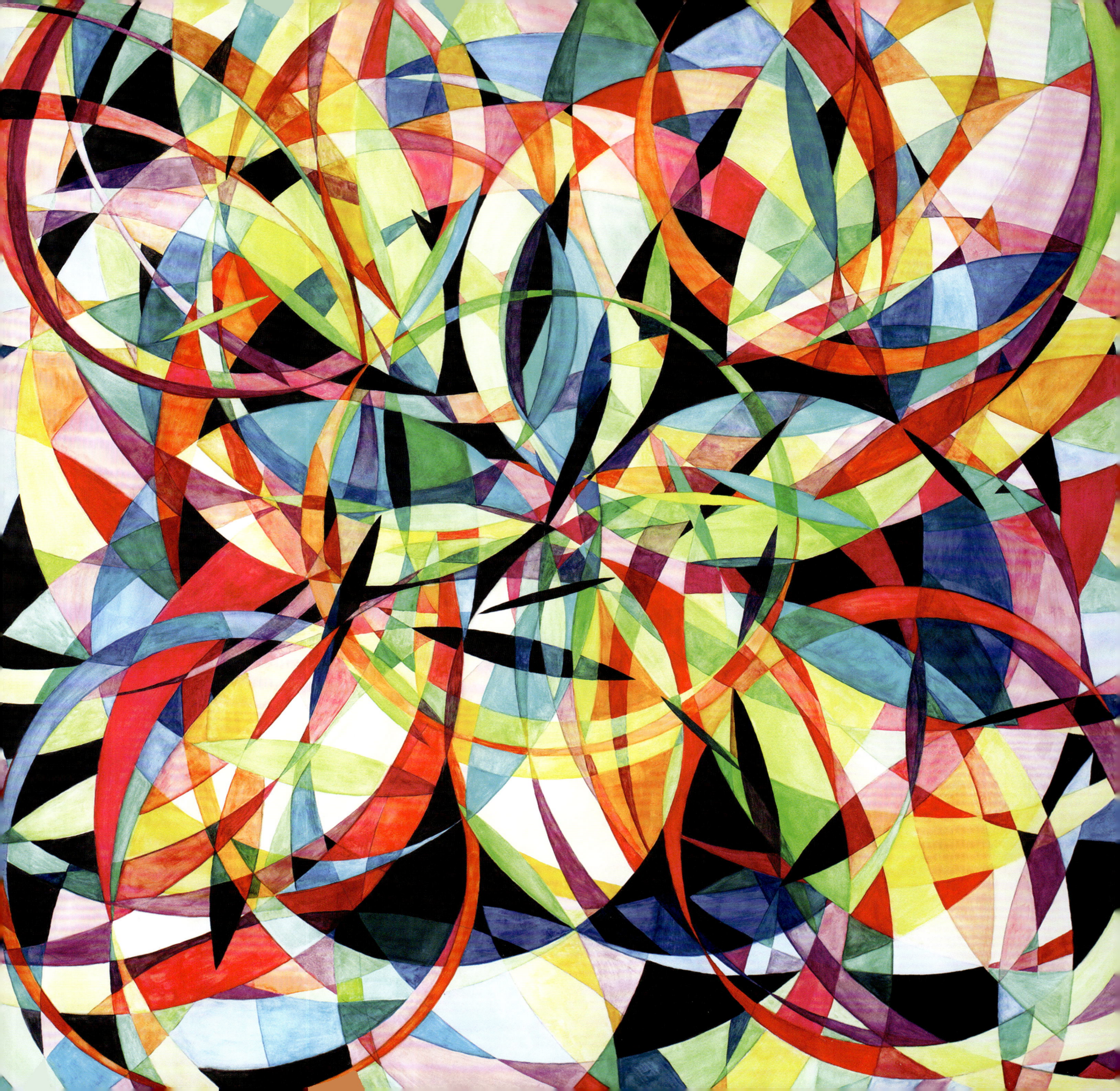

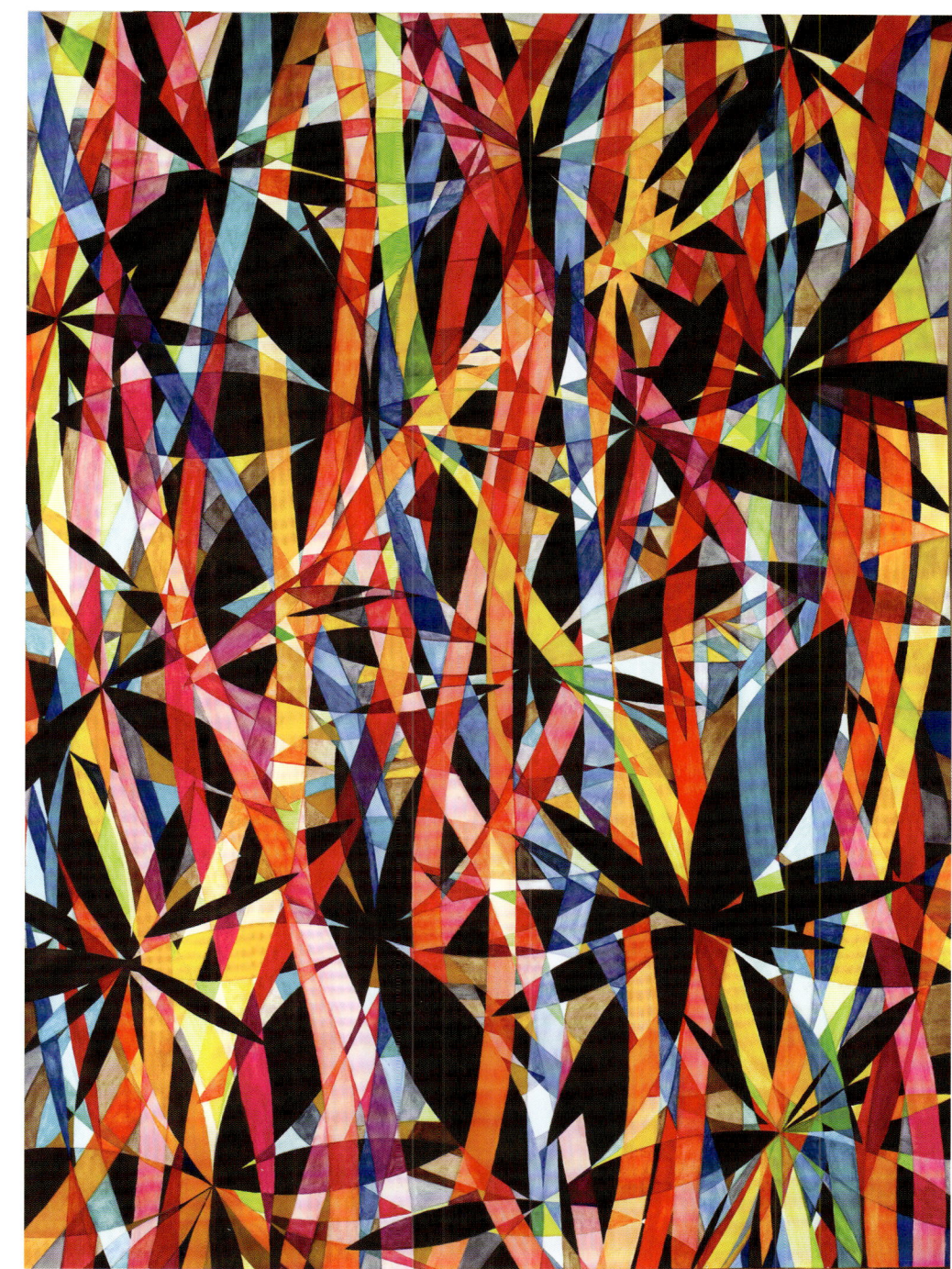

WHEEL WITHIN A WHEEL 48 *(LEFT)*

51 IN X 51 IN
WATERCOLOR/GOUACHE, 2007

WHEEL WITHIN A WHEEL 49

62 IN X 45 IN
WATERCOLOR/GOUACHE, 2007

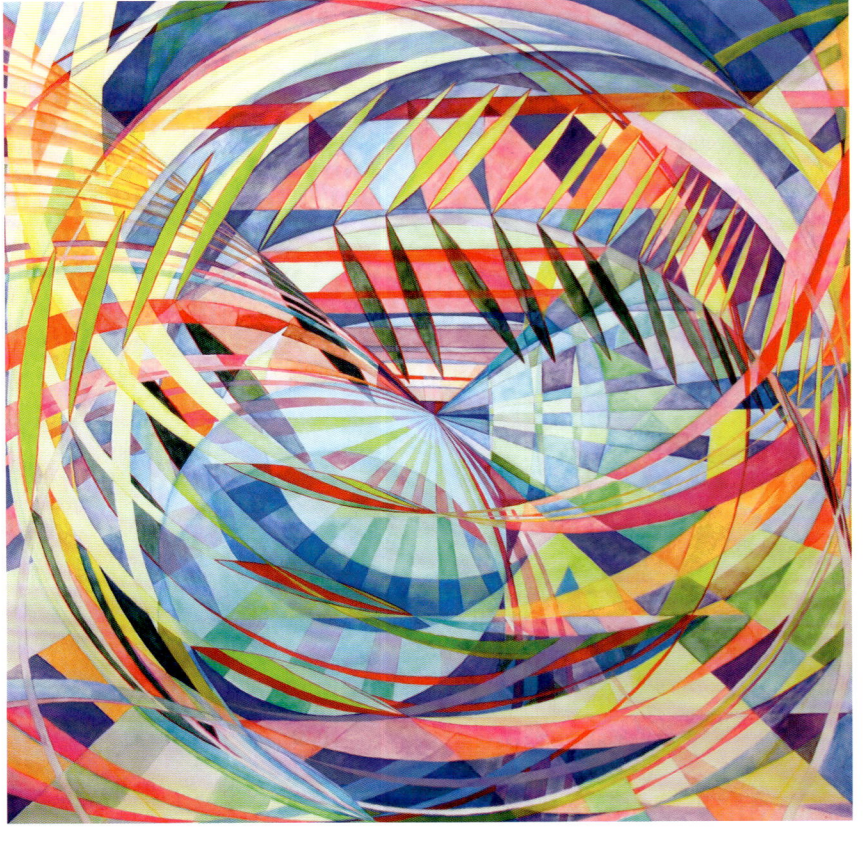

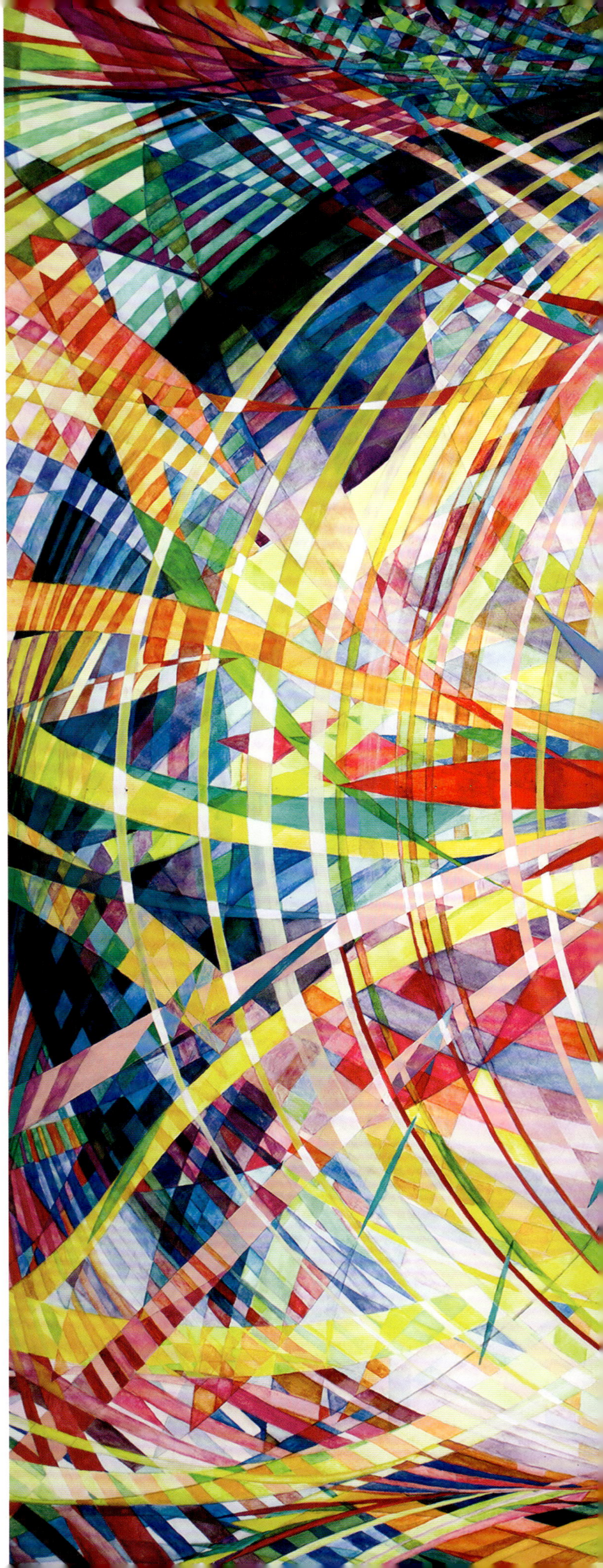

WHEEL WITHIN A WHEEL 49

45 IN X 45 IN
WATERCOLOR/GOUACHE, 2008

WHEEL WITHIN A WHEEL 50 *(RIGHT)*

62 IN X 45 IN
WATERCOLOR/GOUACHE, 2007

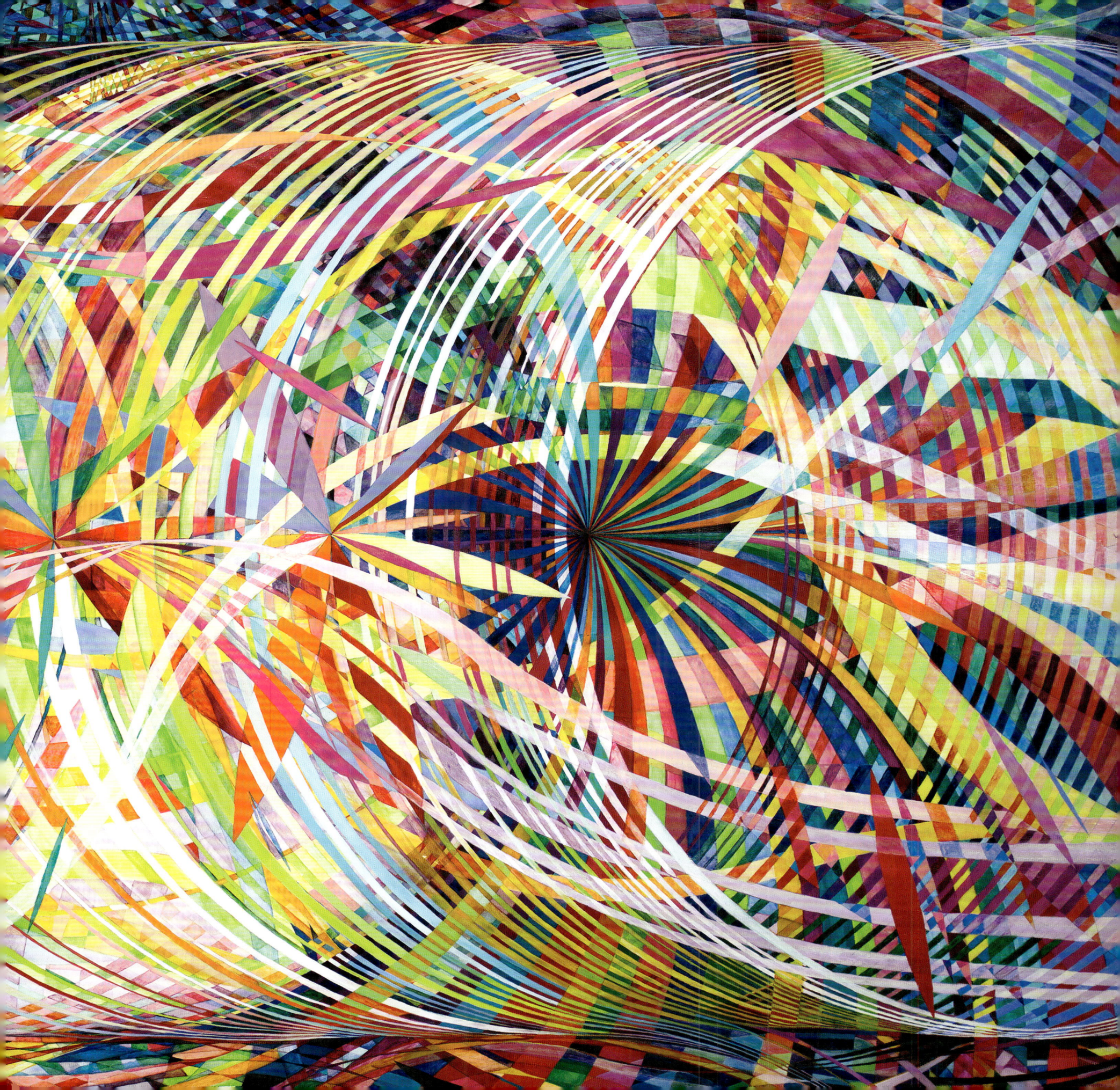

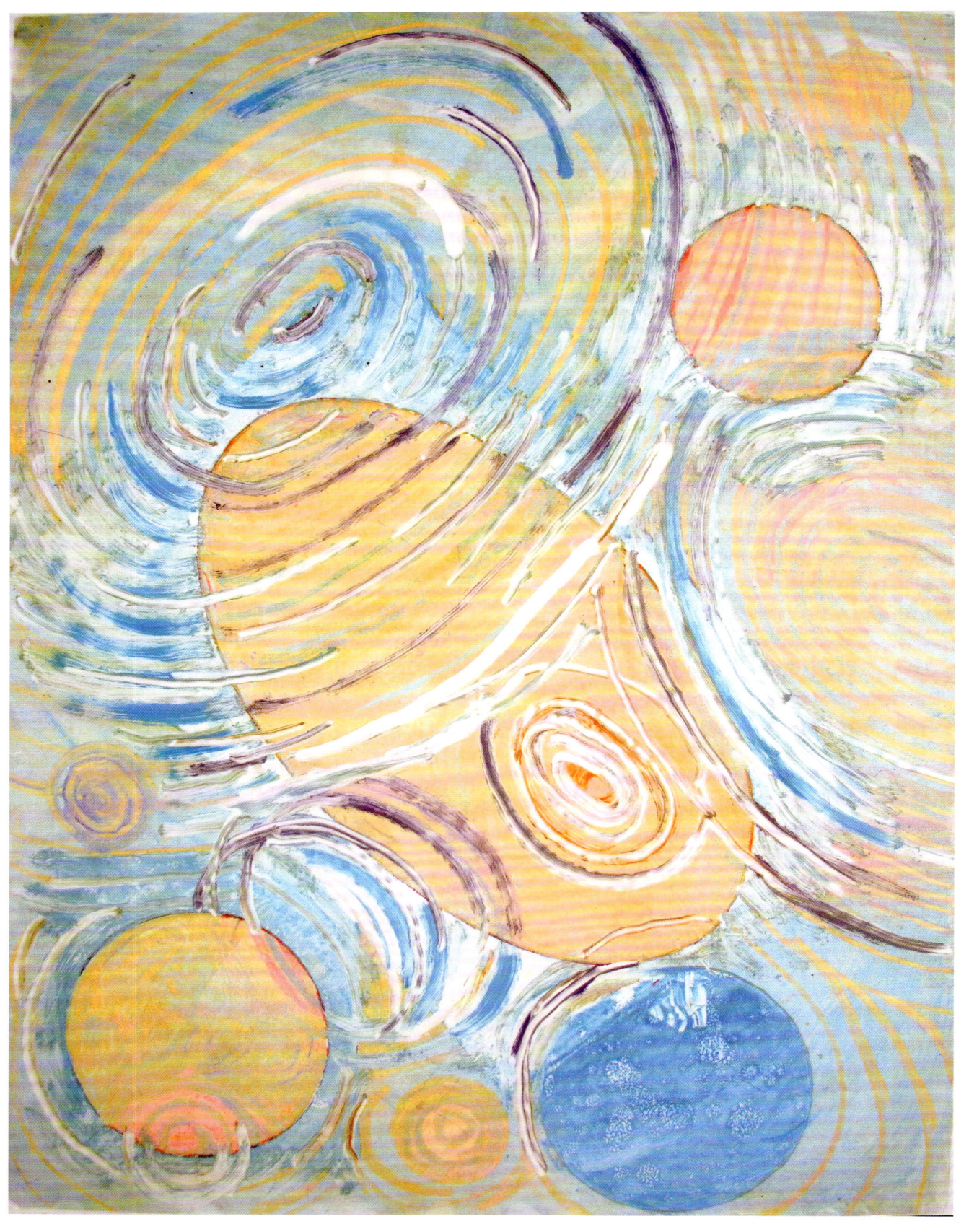

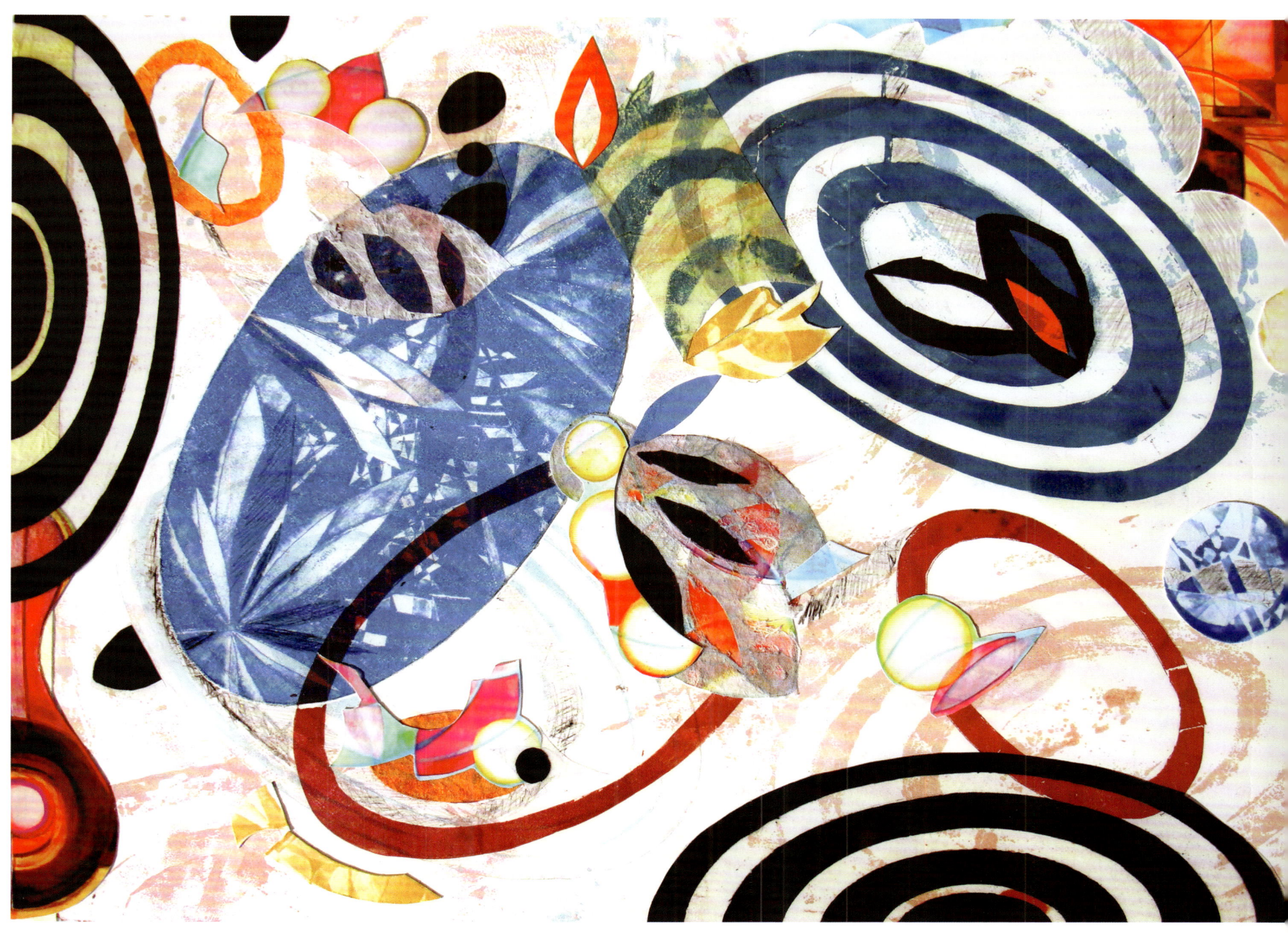

WHEEL WITHIN A WHEEL 53 *(LEFT)*

20 IN X 16 IN
MONOPRINT, 2007

WHEEL WITHIN A WHEEL 54

20 IN X 16 IN
MONOPRINT, 2007

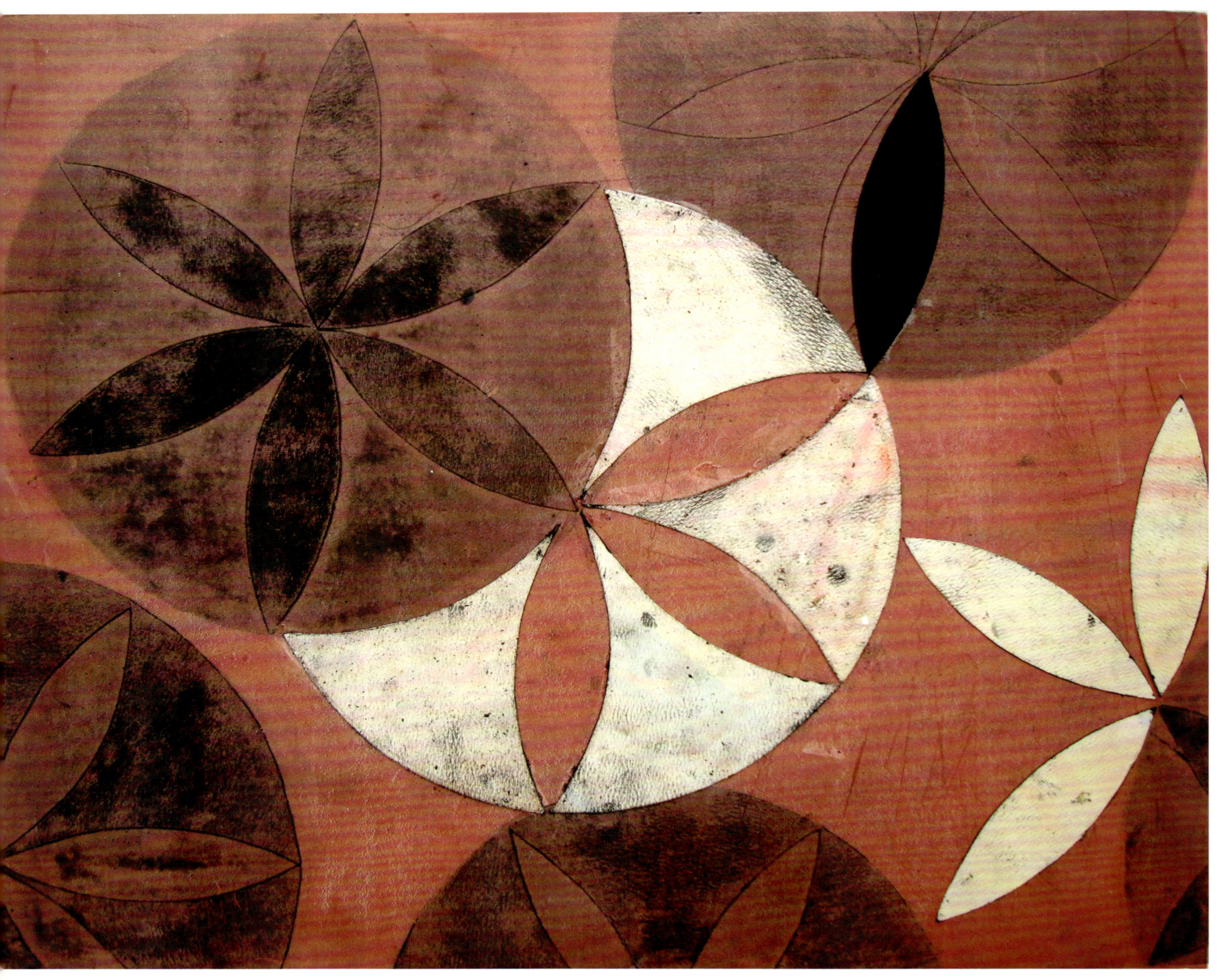

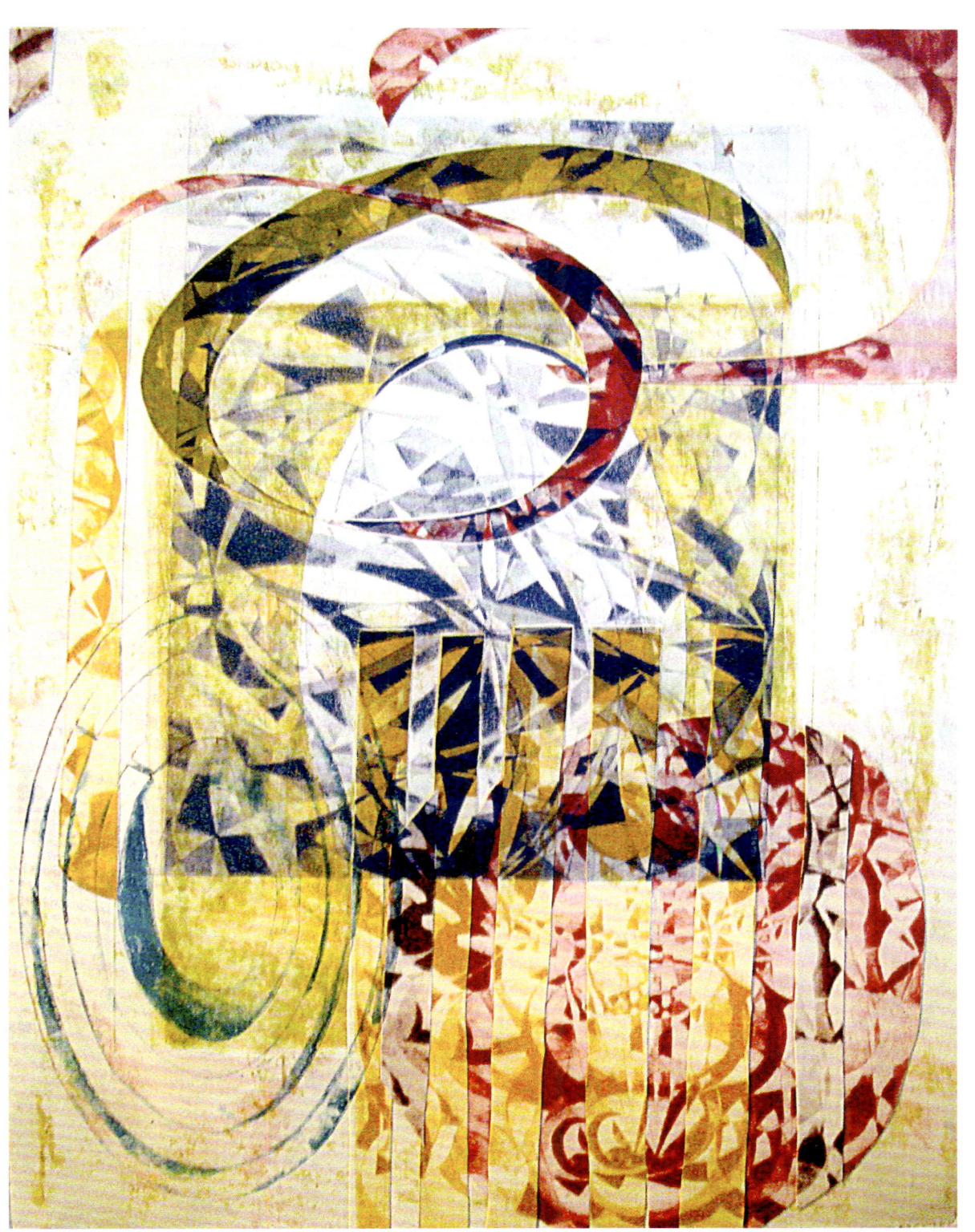

WHEEL WITHIN A WHEEL 55
(LEFT)

20 IN X 16 IN
MONOPRINT, 2008

WHEEL WITHIN A WHEEL 57

20 IN X 16 IN
MONOPRINT, 2008

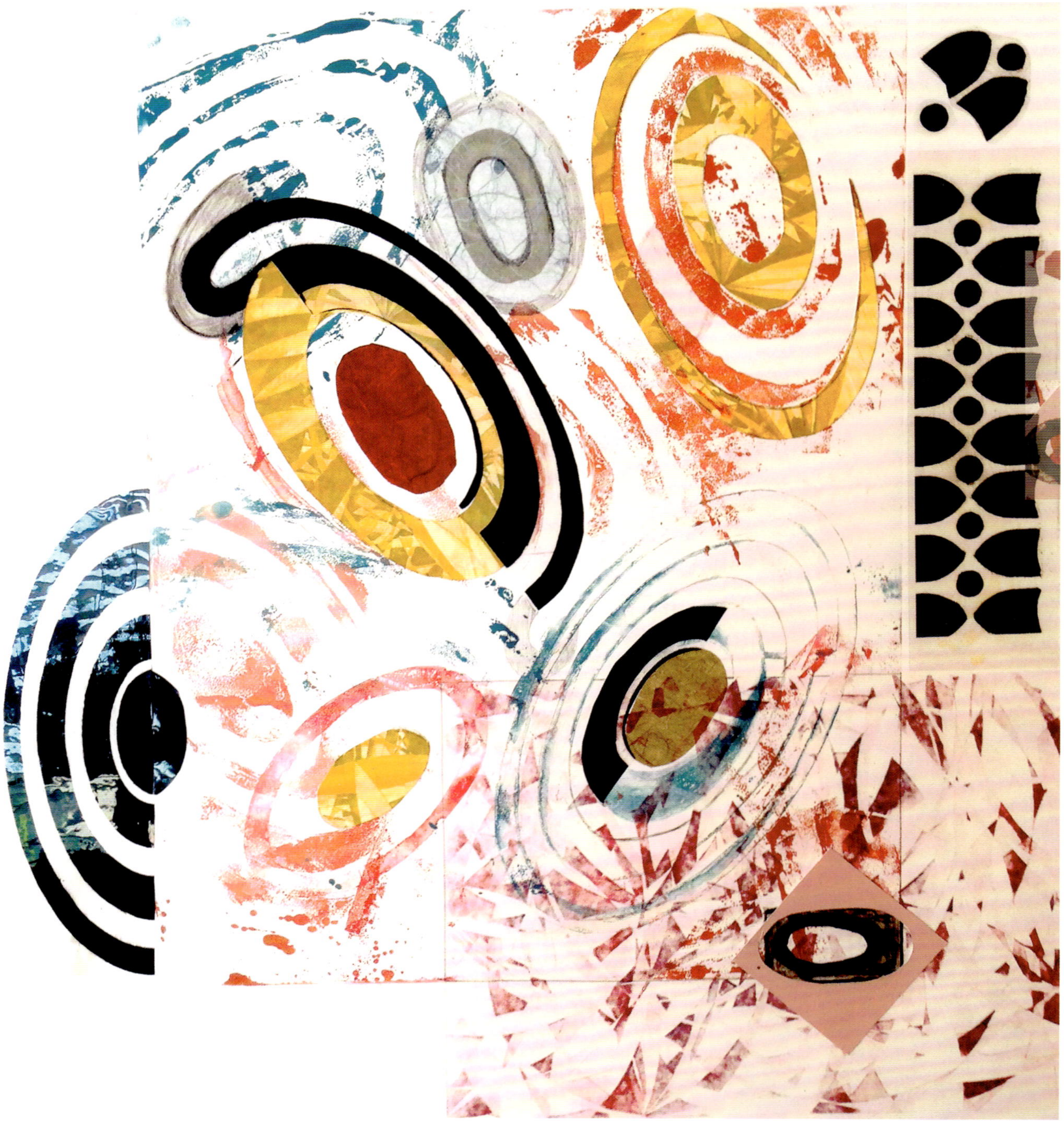

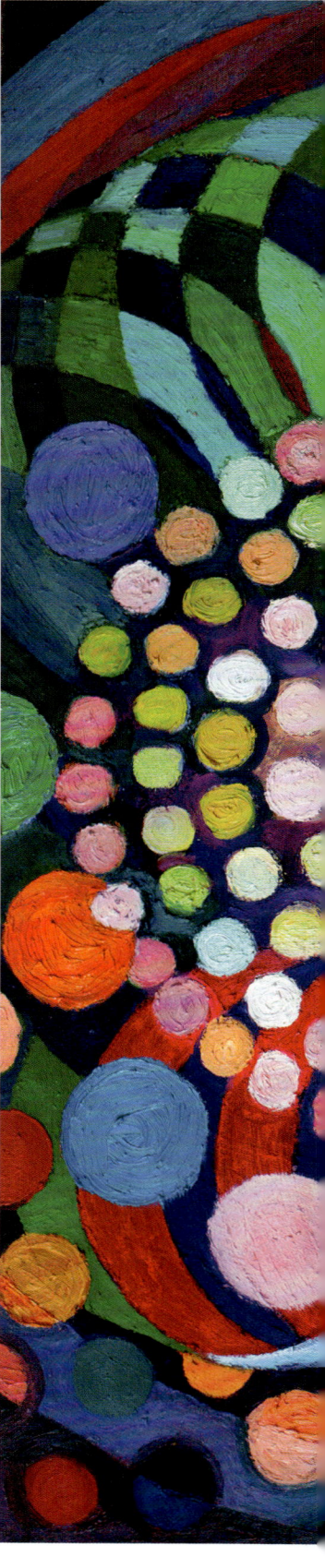

WHEEL WITHIN A WHEEL 59

20 IN X 20 IN
MONOPRINT, 2008

WHEEL WITHIN A WHEEL 60 *(RIGHT)*

30 IN X 40 IN
OIL ON CANVAS, 2009

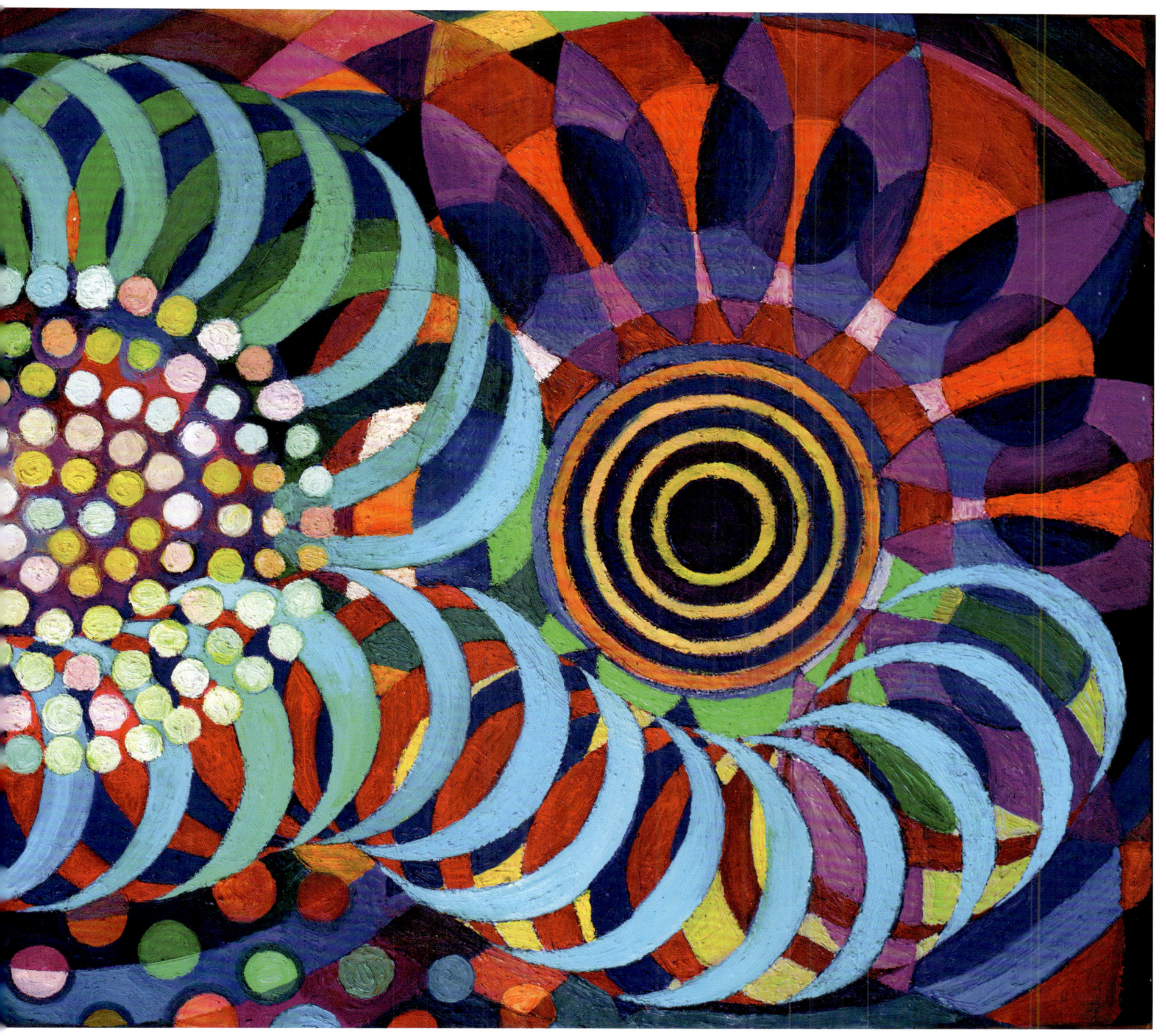

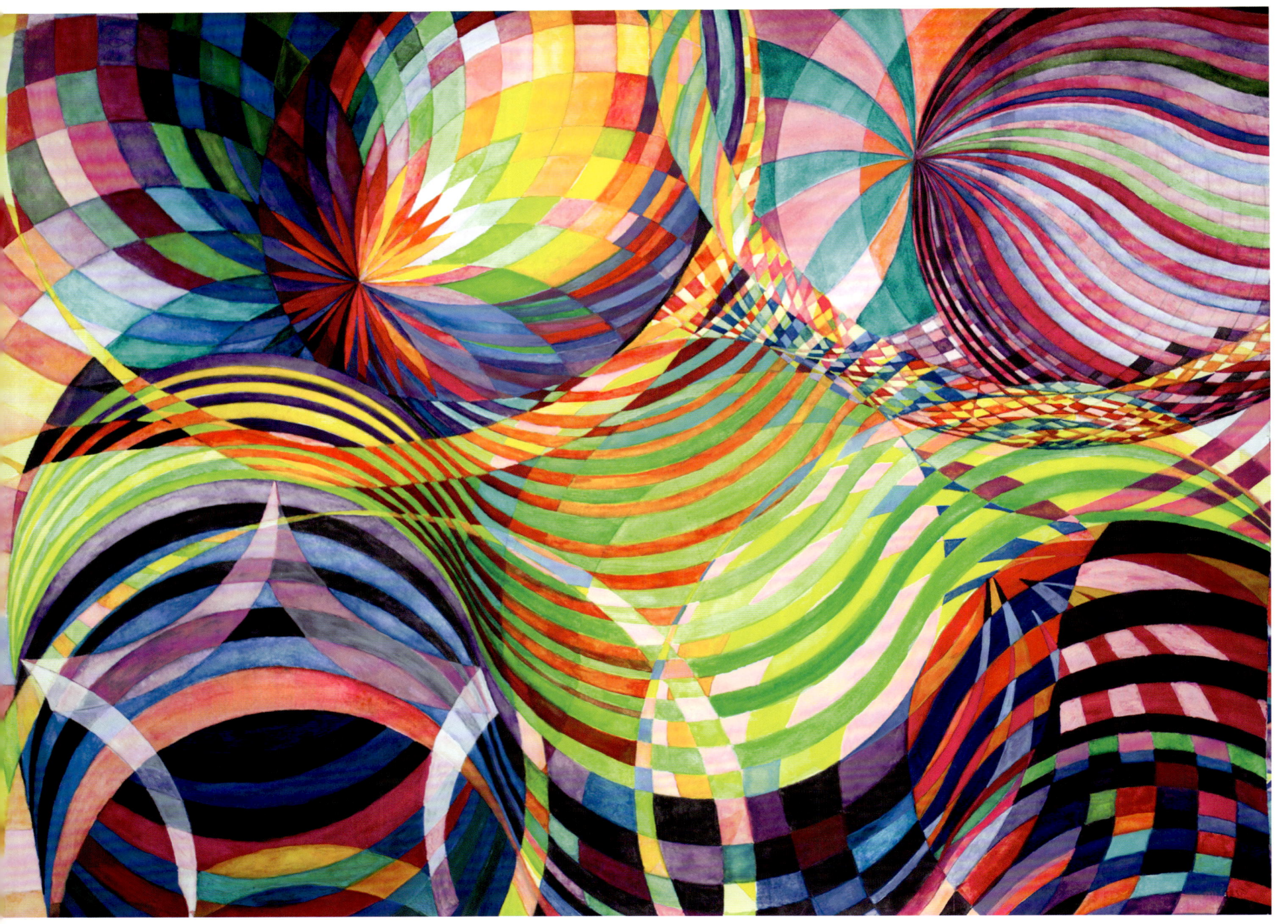

WHEEL WITHIN A WHEEL 61

22 IN X 30 IN
WATERCOLOR/GOUACHE, 2009

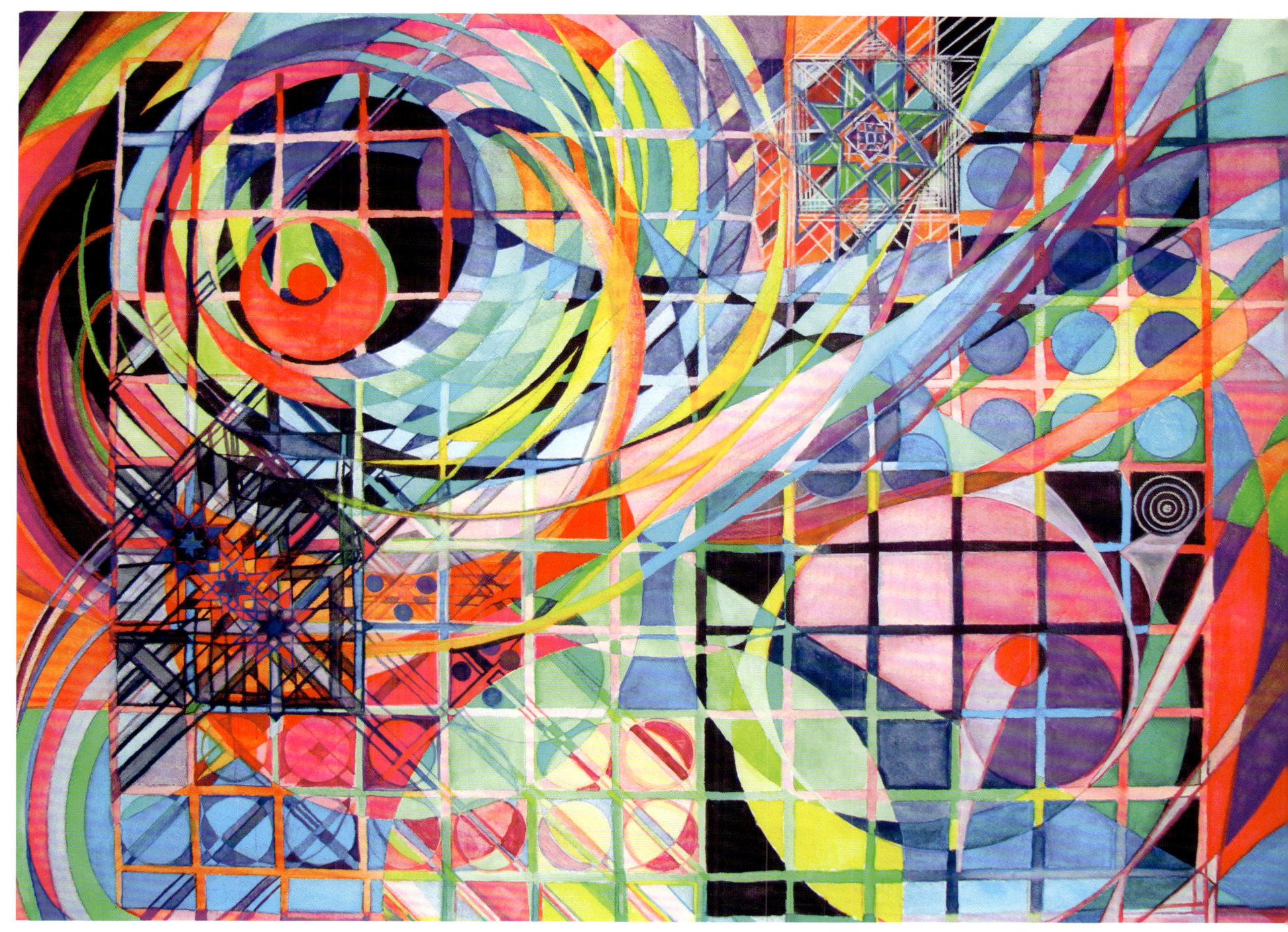

WHEEL WITHIN A WHEEL 66
18 IN X 24 IN
WATERCOLOR/GOUACHE, 2009

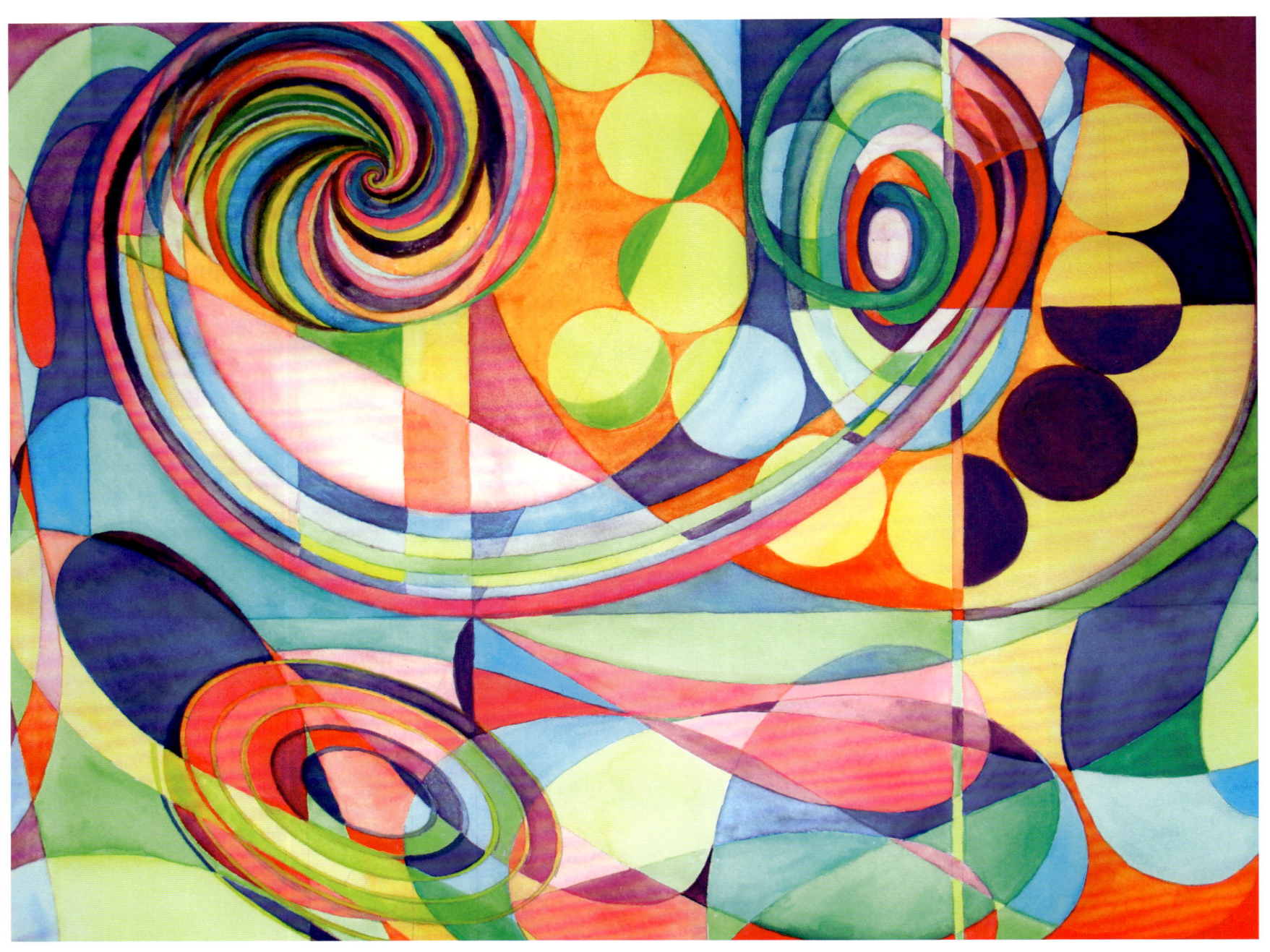

WHEEL WITHIN A WHEEL 64

18 IN X 24 IN
WATERCOLOR/GOUACHE, 2009

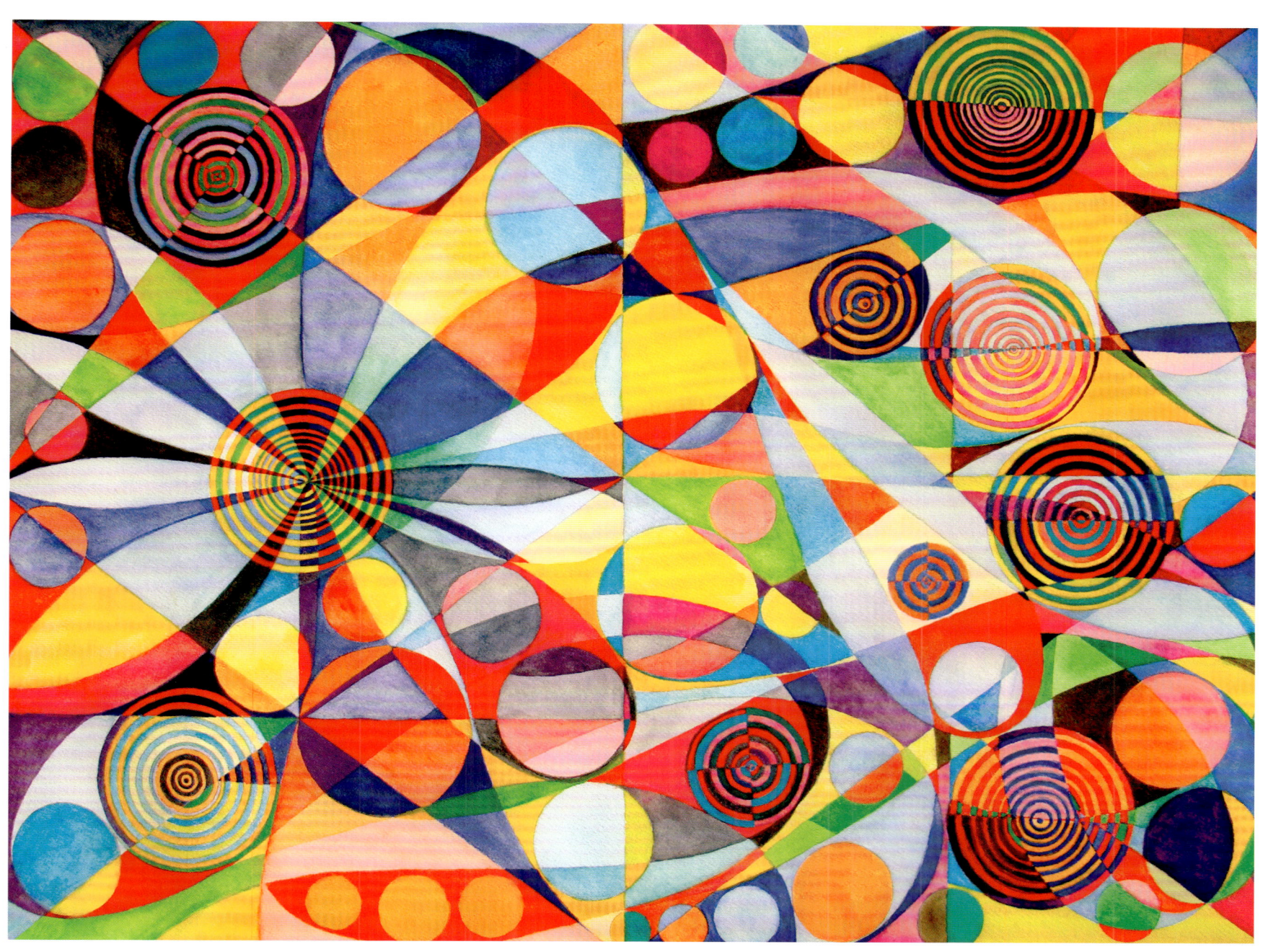

WHEEL WITHIN A WHEEL 65
18 IN X 24 IN
WATERCOLOR/GOLACHE, 2009

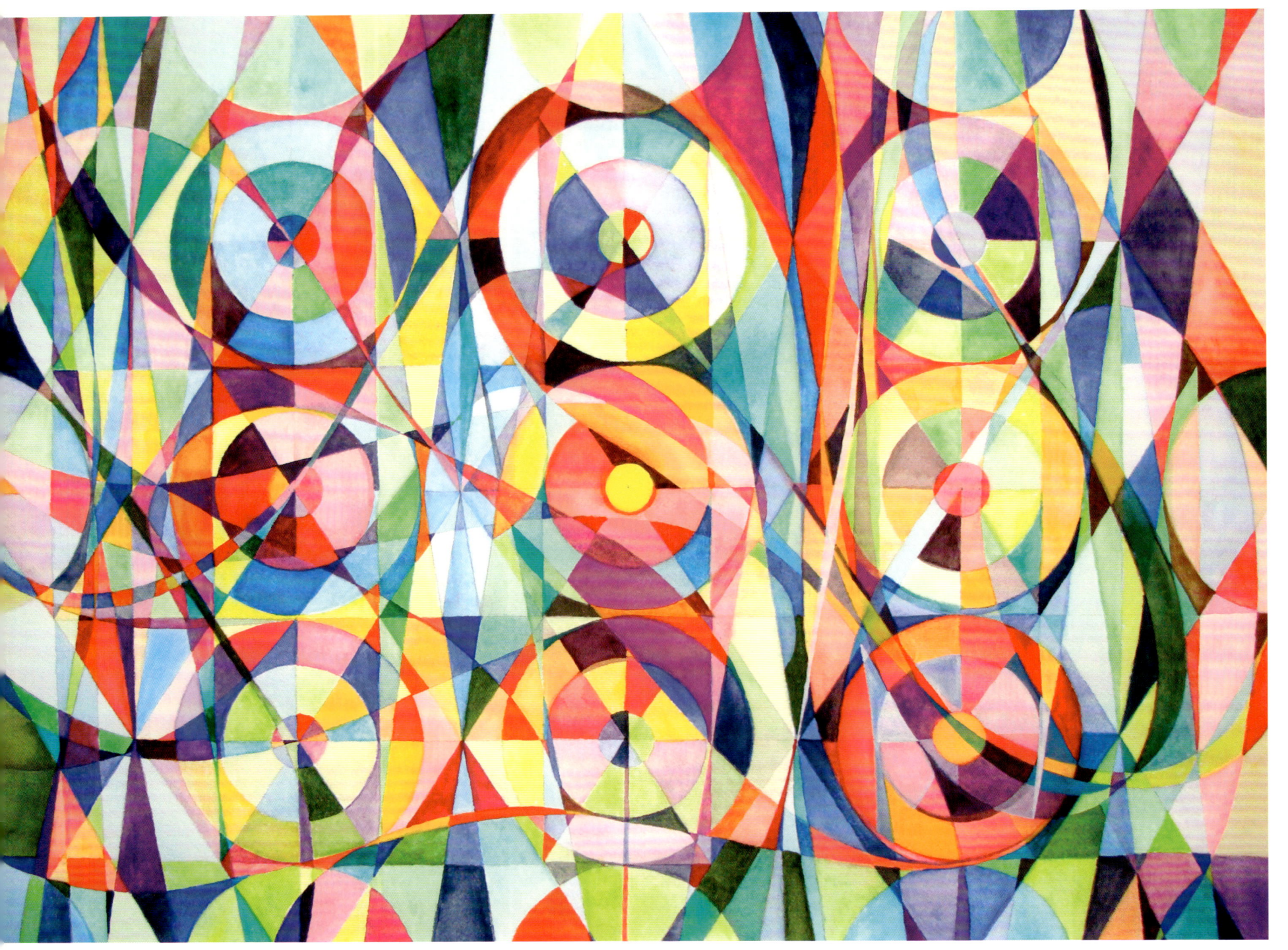

WHEEL WITHIN A WHEEL 67

18 IN X 24 IN
WATERCOLOR/GOUACHE, 2009

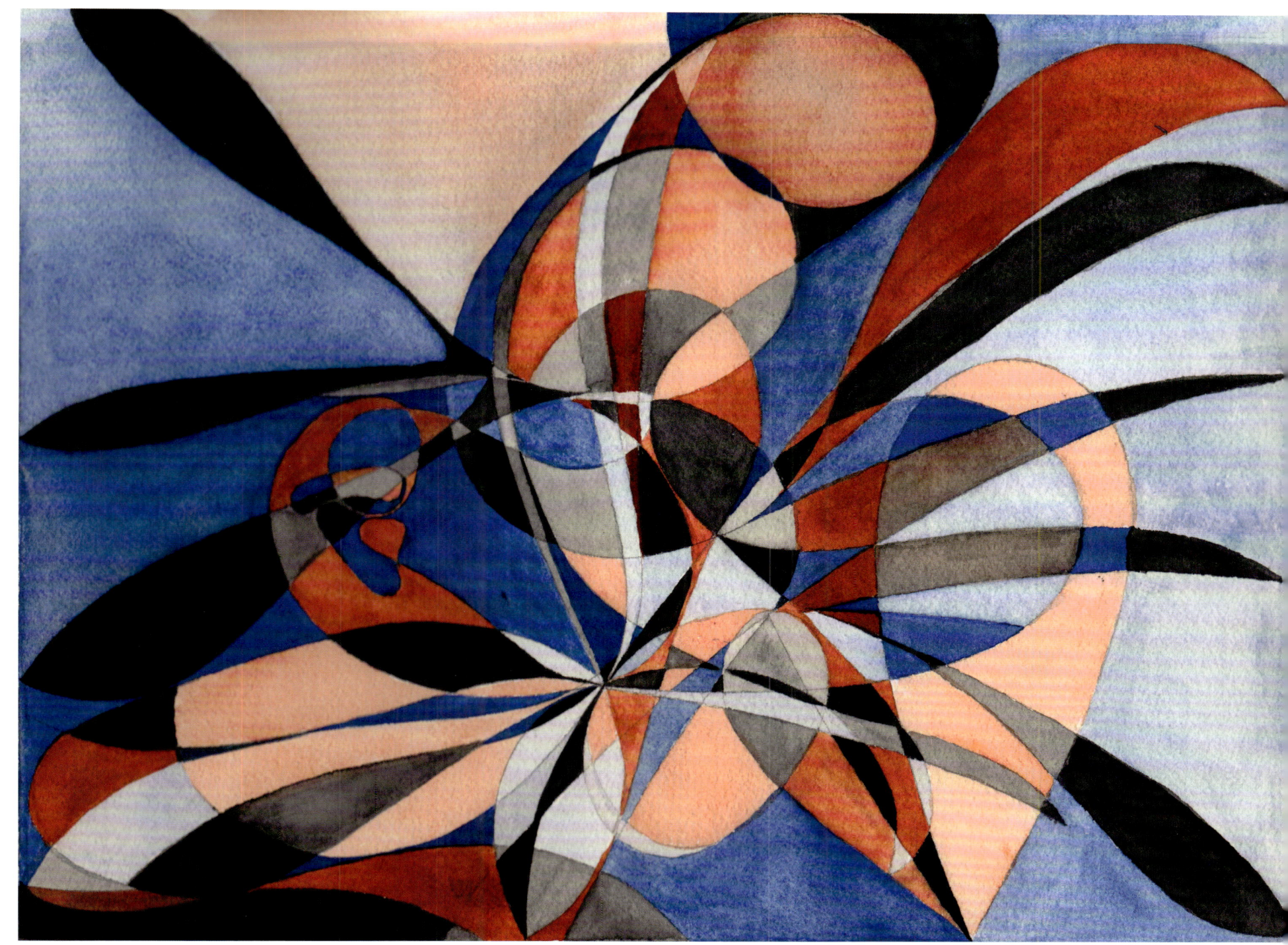

WHEEL WITHIN A WHEEL 68

9 IN X 12 IN
WATERCOLOR/GOUACHE, 2009

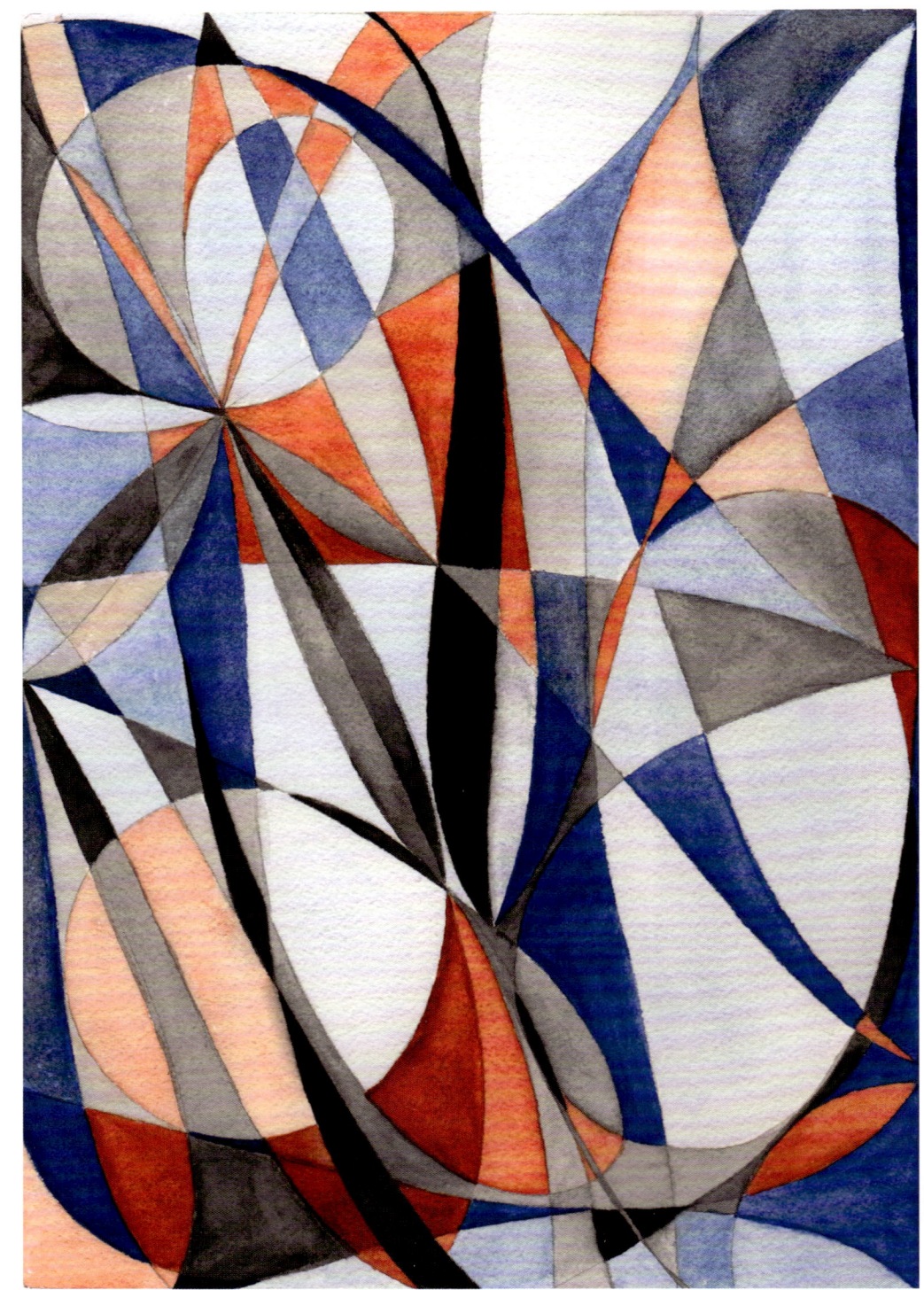

WHEEL WITHIN A WHEEL 69

12 IN X 9 IN
WATERCOLOR/GOUACHE, 2009

WHEEL WITHIN A WHEEL 70 *(RIGHT)*

9 IN X 12 IN
WATERCOLOR/GOUACHE, 2009

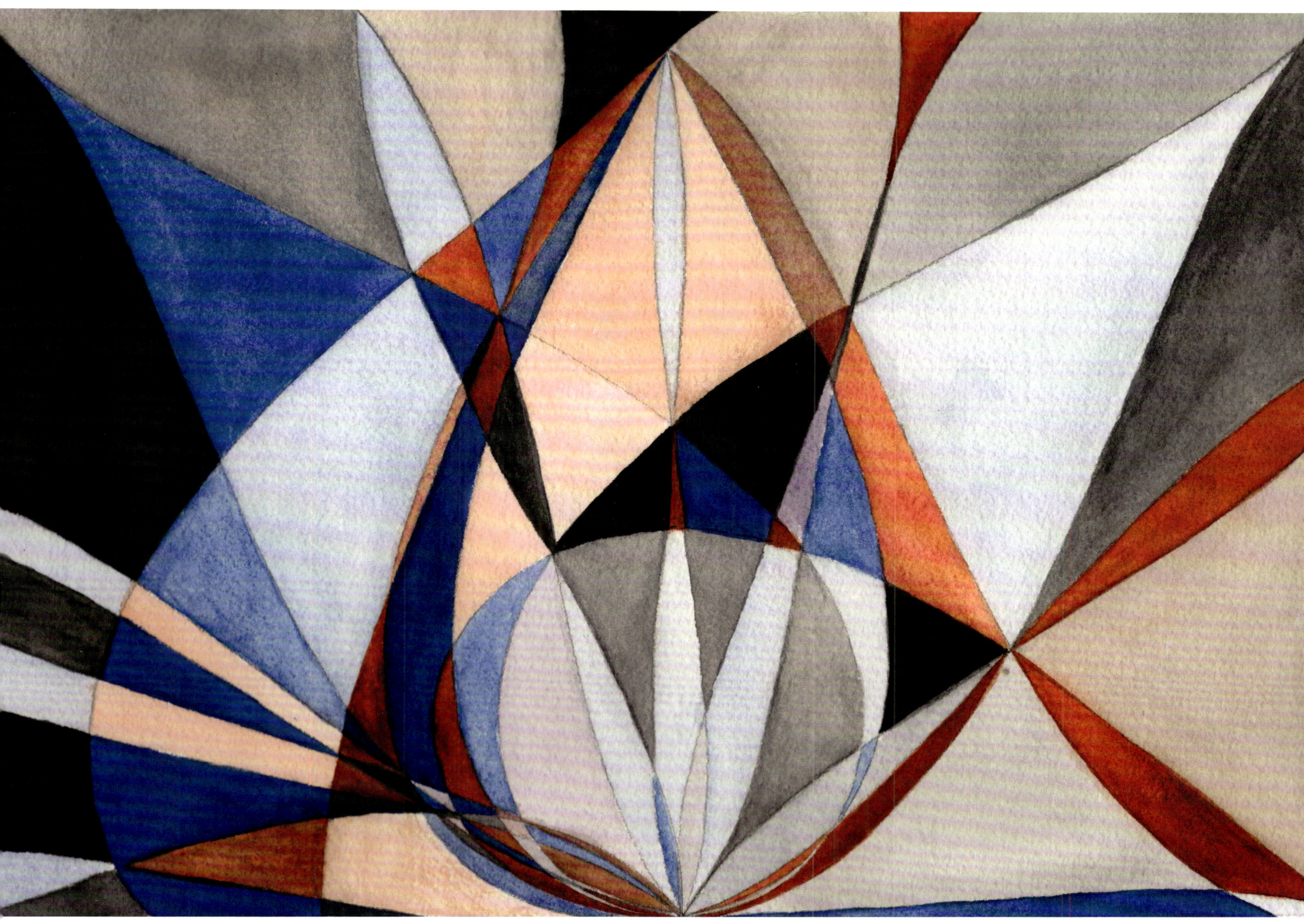

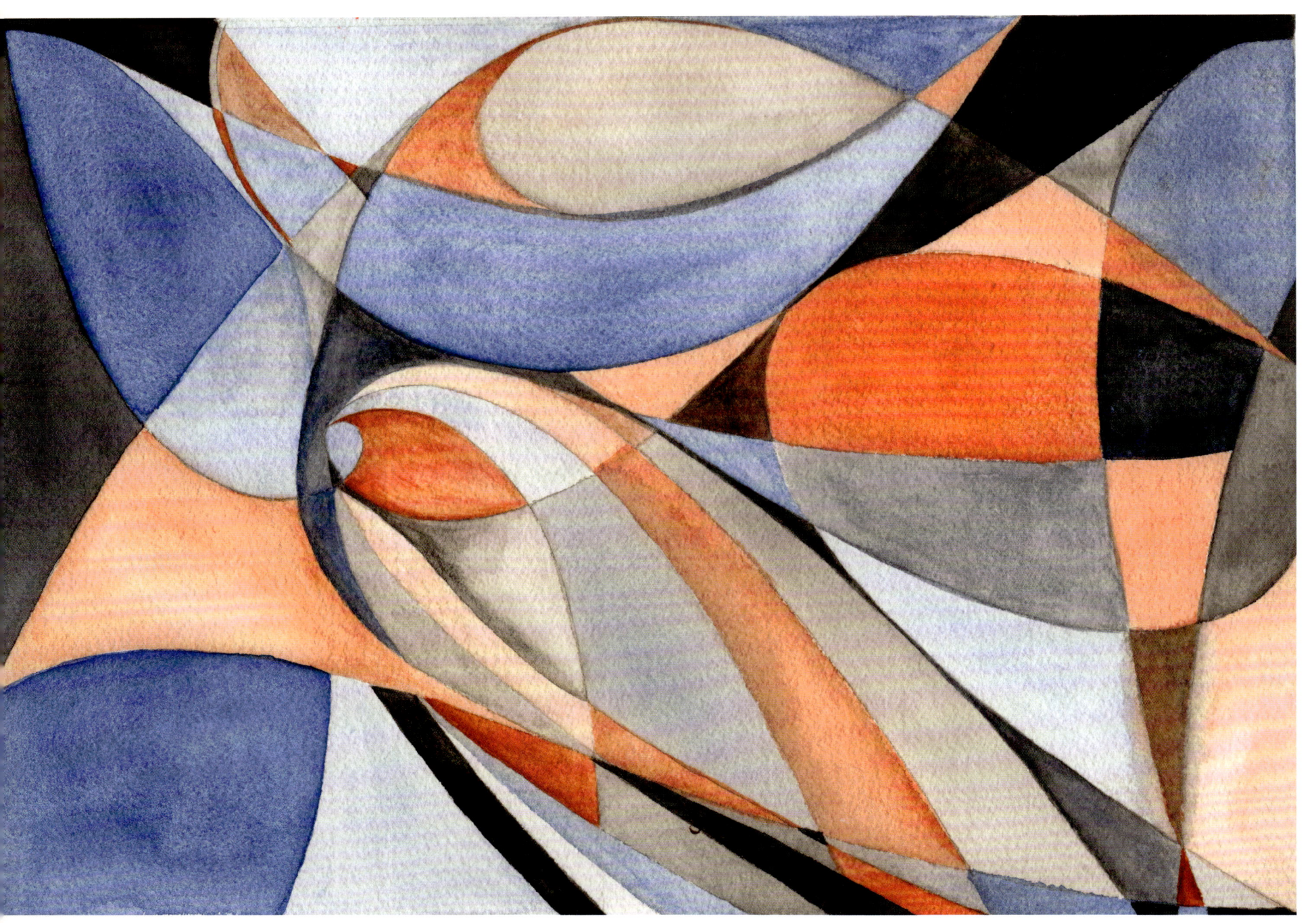

WHEEL WITHIN A WHEEL 71

9 IN X 12 IN
WATERCOLOR/GOUACHE, 2009

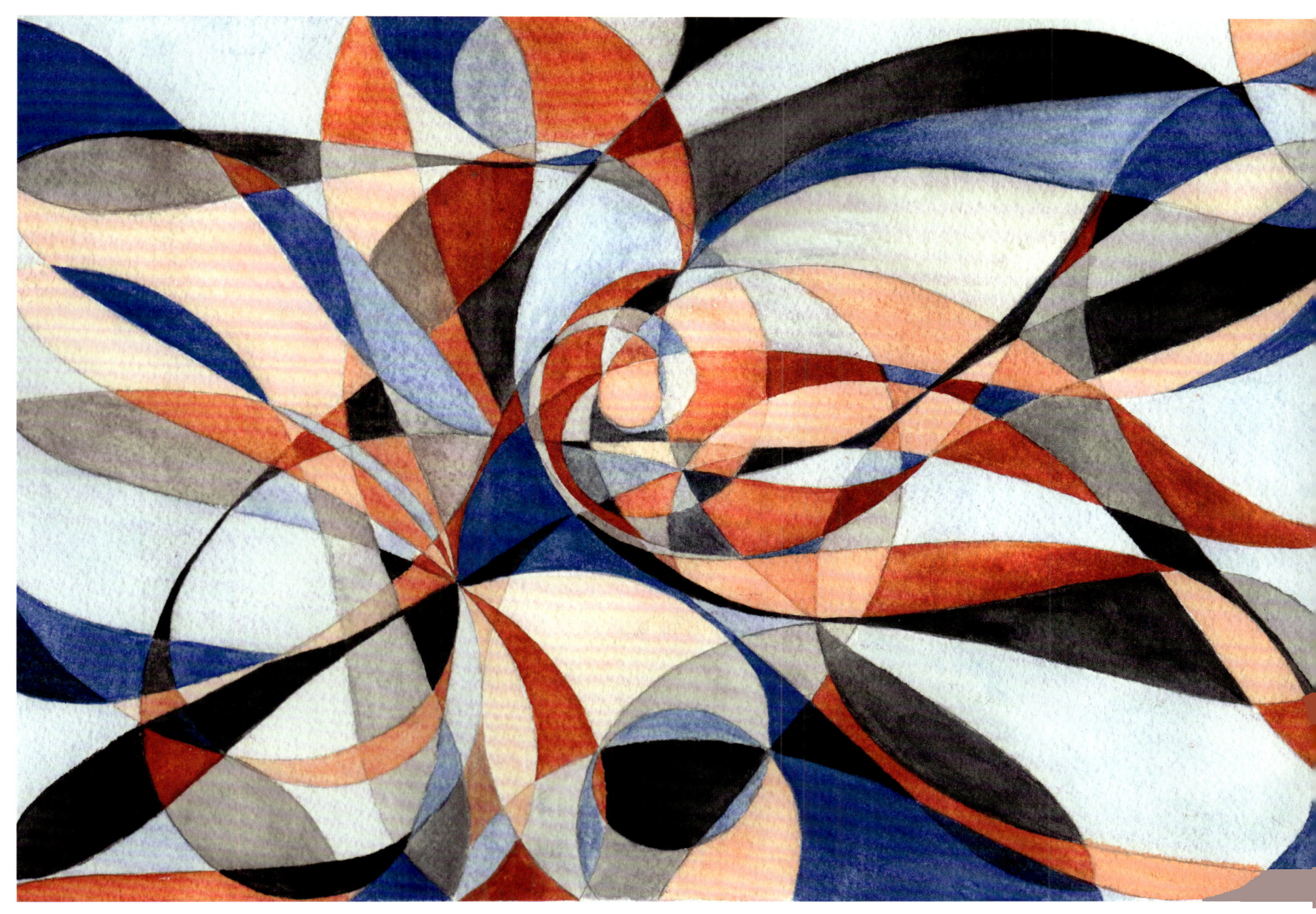

WHEEL WITHIN A WHEEL 72
9 IN X 12 IN
WATERCOLOR/GOJACHE, 2009

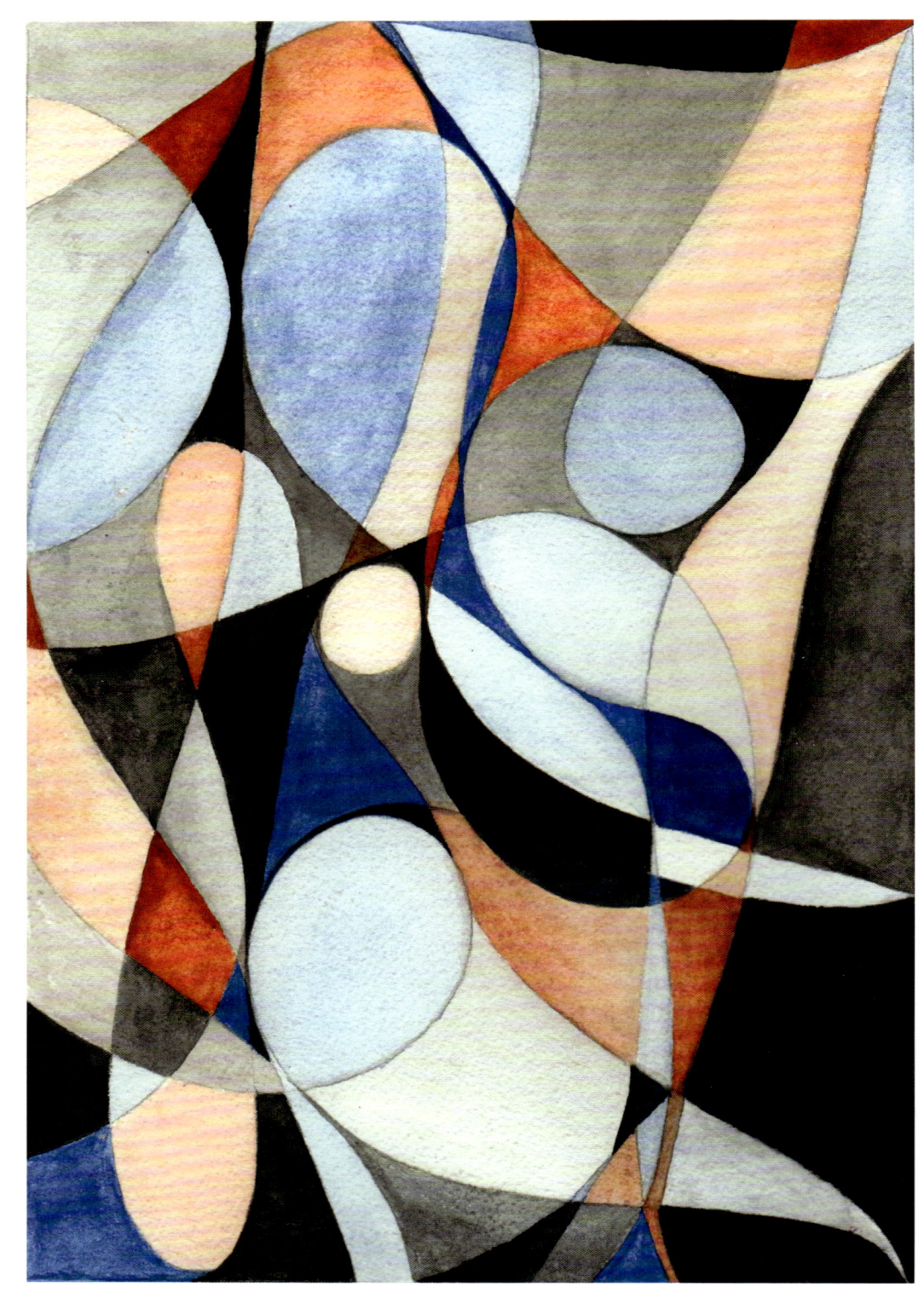

WHEEL WITHIN A WHEEL 74
12 IN X 9 IN
WATERCOLOR/GOUACHE, 2009

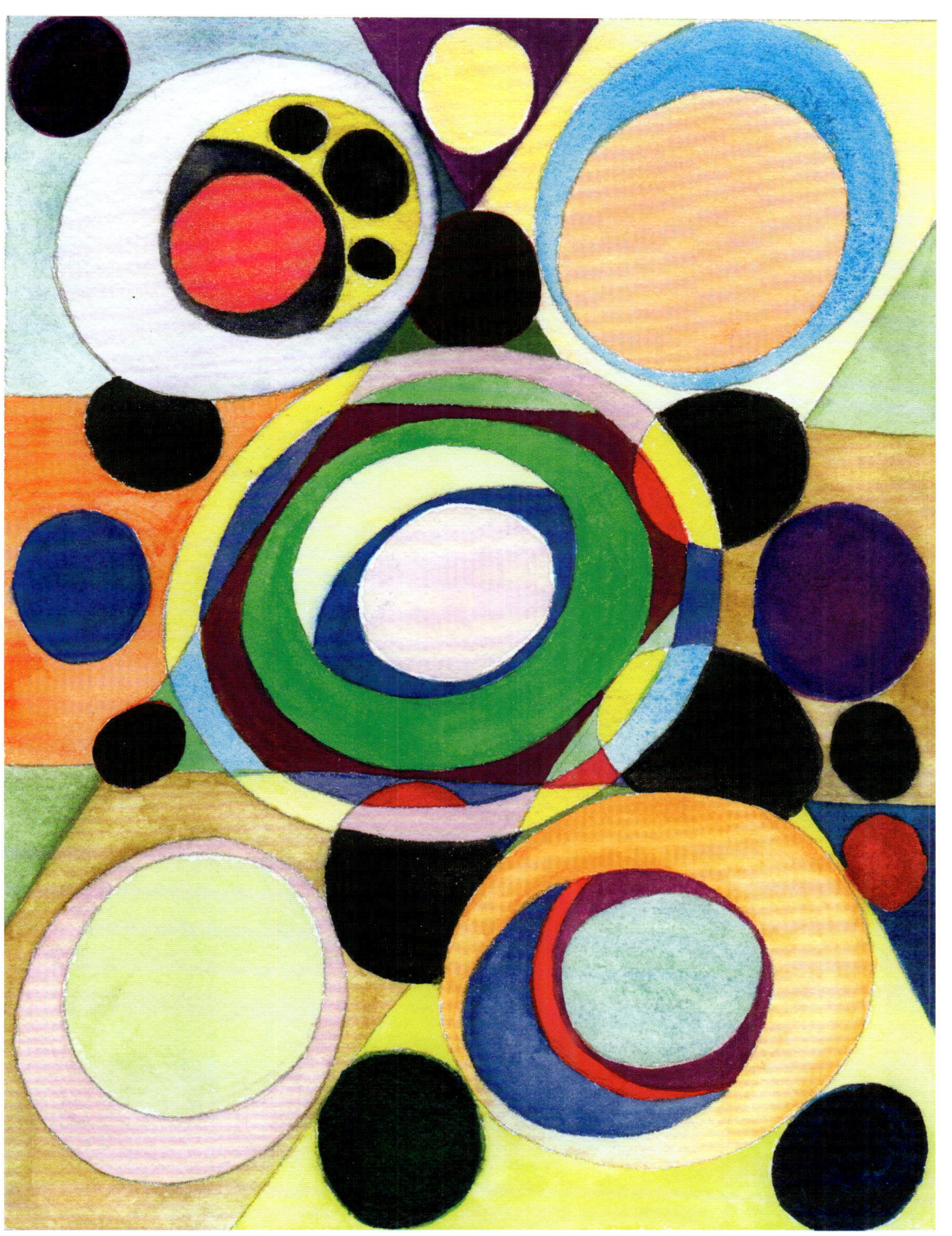

WHEEL WITHIN A WHEEL 80
8 IN X 5 IN
WATERCOLOR/GOUACHE, 2011

119

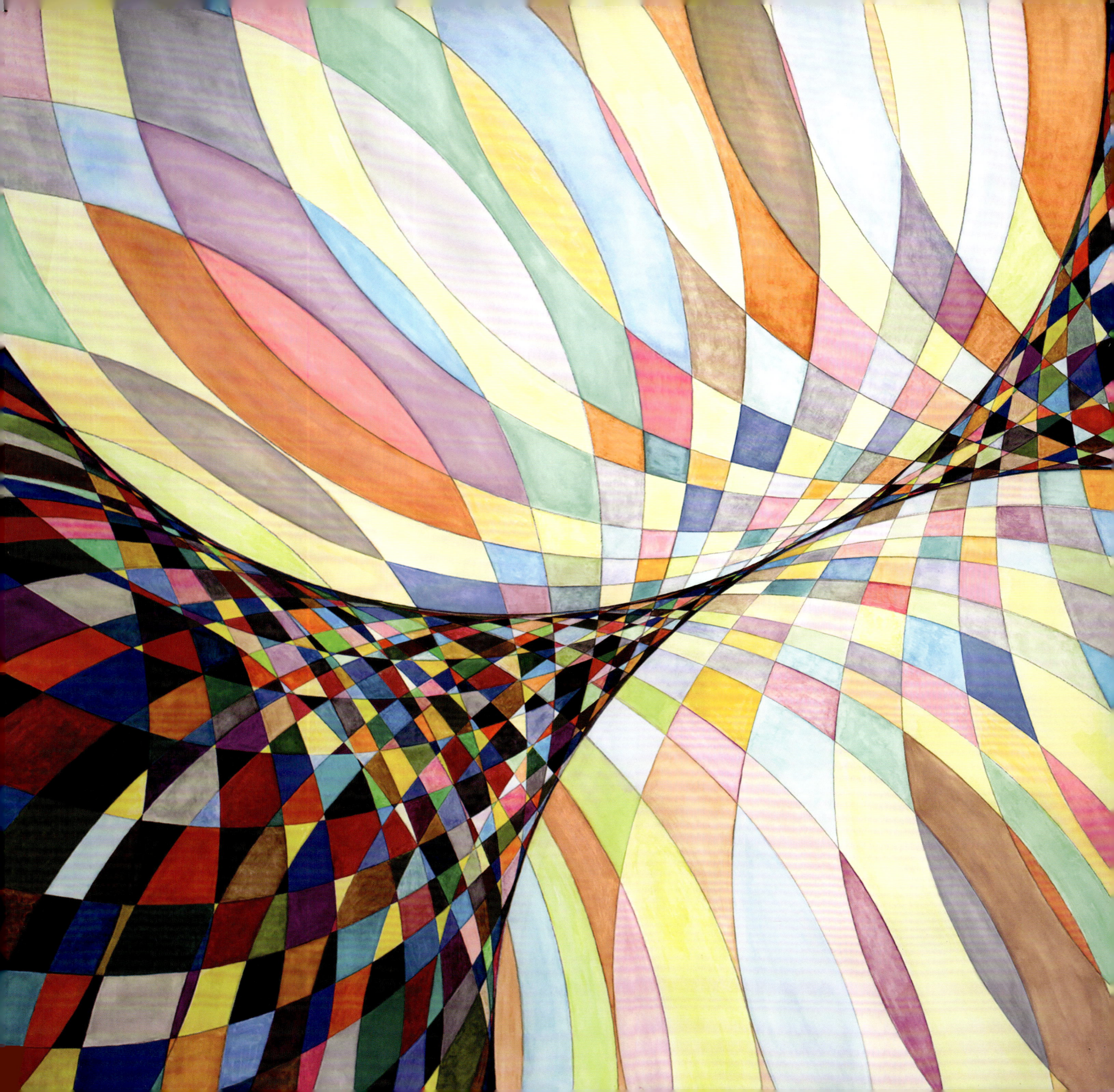

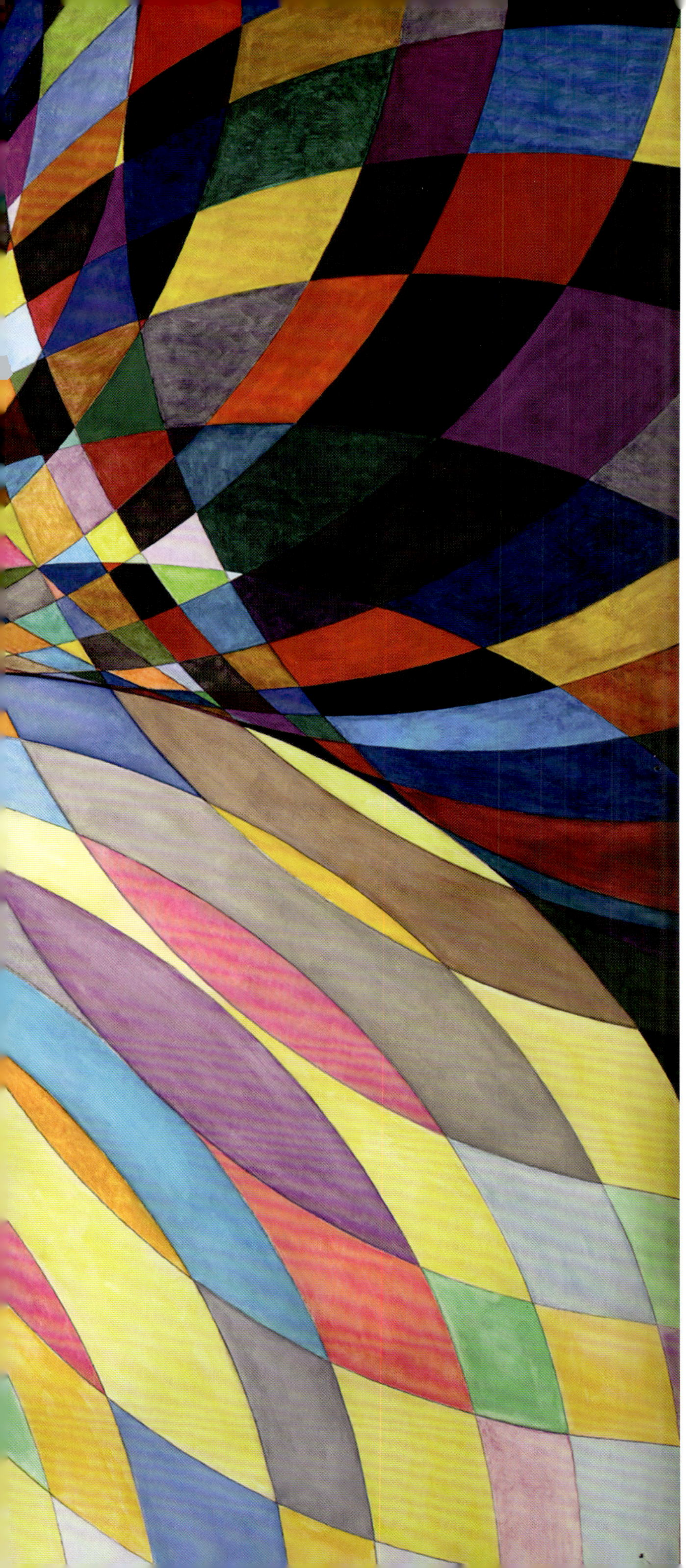

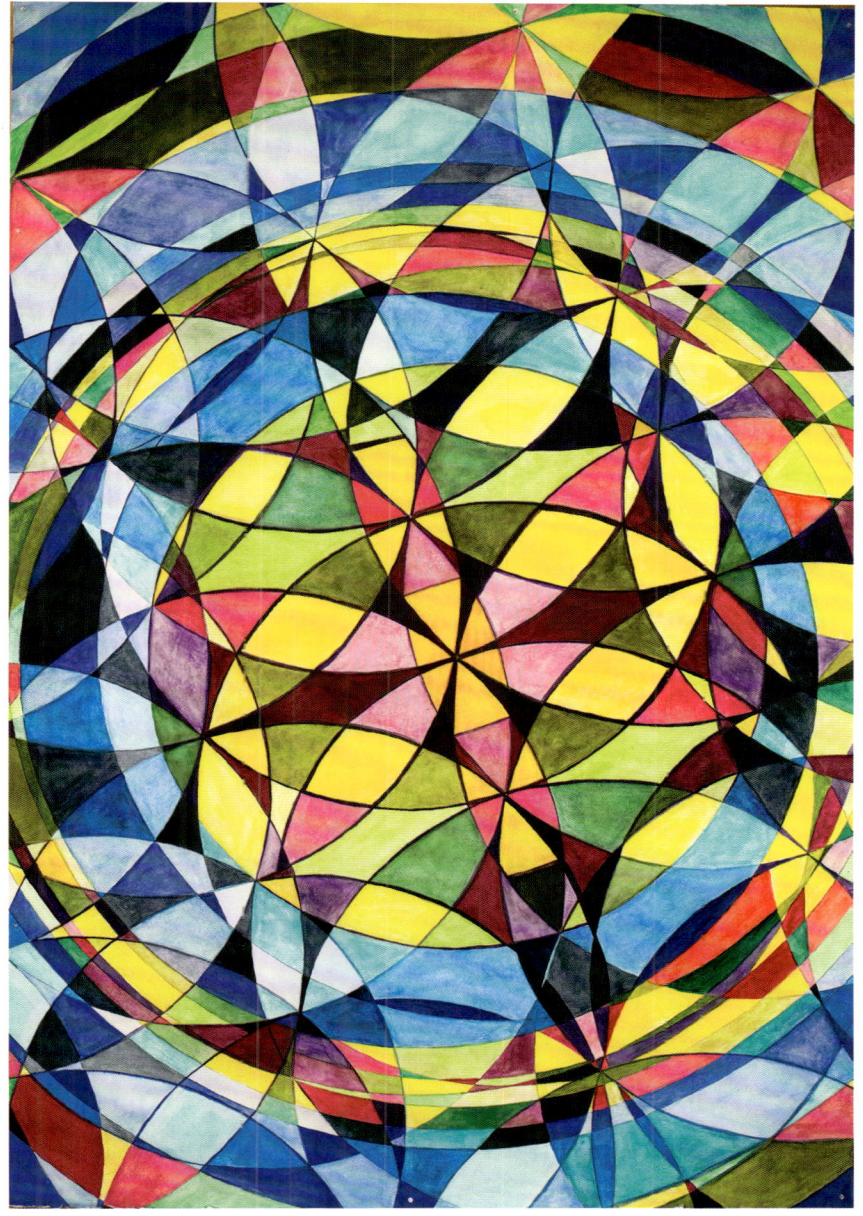

WHEEL WITHIN A WHEEL 81 *(LEFT)*

62 IN X 45 IN
WATERCOLOR/GOUACHE, 2010

WHEEL WITHIN A WHEEL 84

28 IN X 35 IN
WATERCOLOR/GOUACHE, 2011

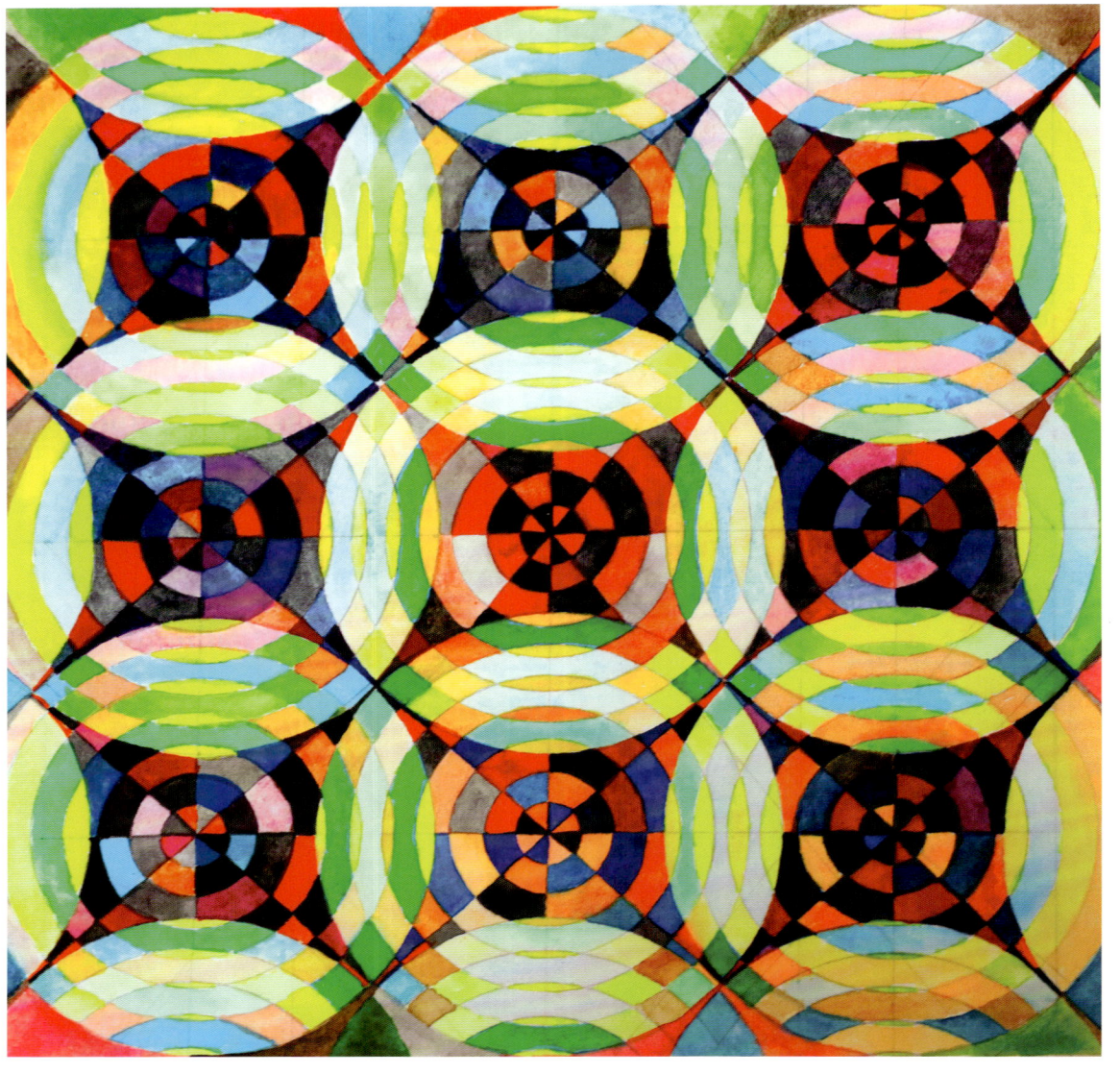

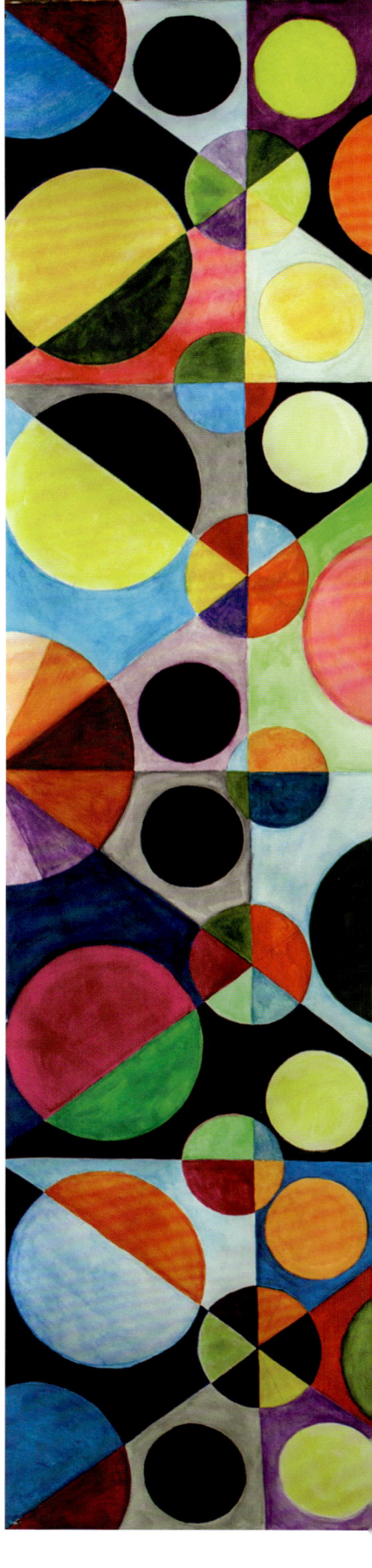

WHEEL WITHIN A WHEEL 88

11 IN X 11 IN
WATERCOLOR/GOUACHE, 2011

WHEEL WITHIN A WHEEL 87 *(RIGHT)*

45 IN X 60 IN
WATERCOLOR/GOUACHE, 2012

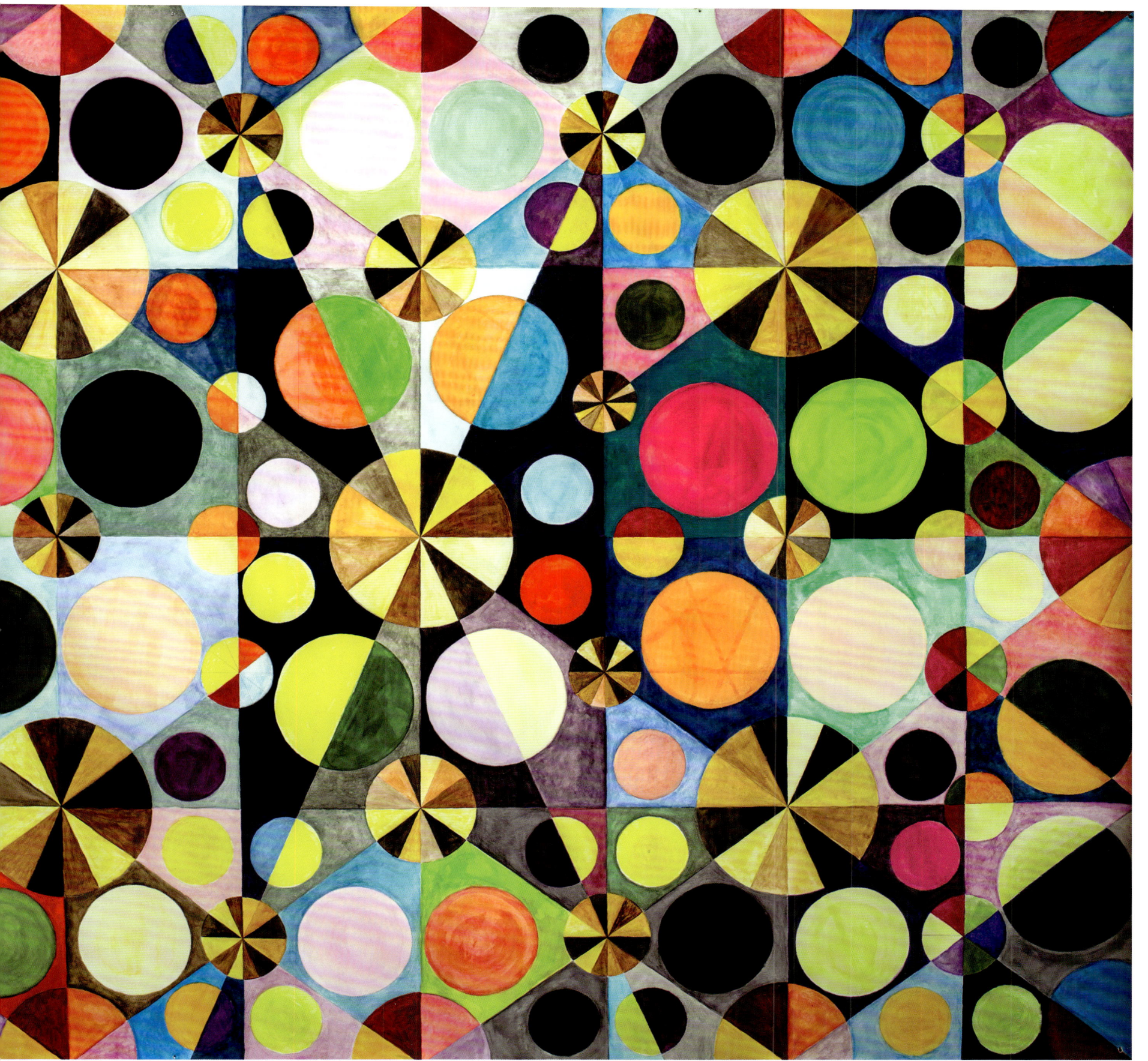

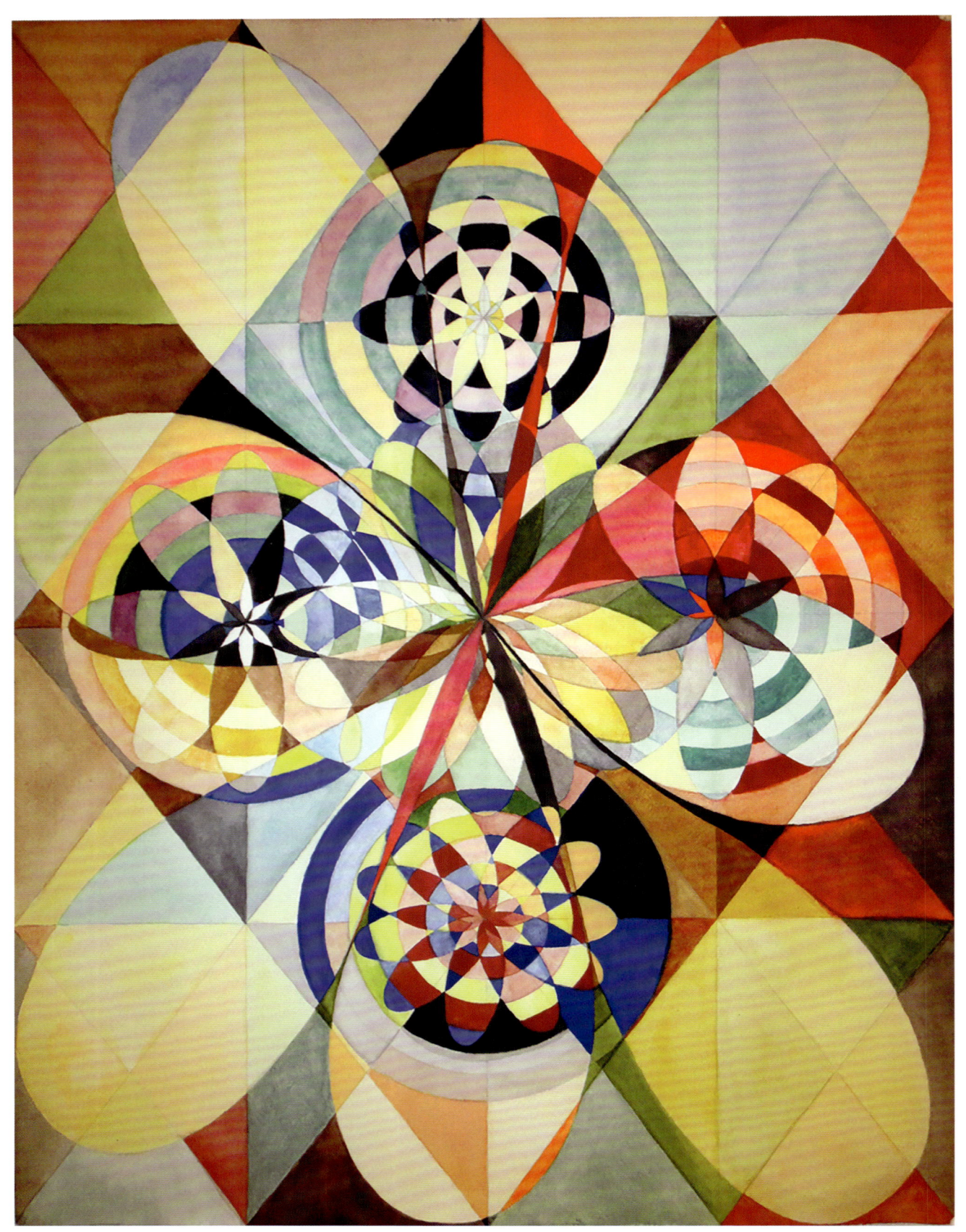

WHEEL WITHIN A WHEEL 89
24 IN X 18 IN
WATERCOLOR/GOUACHE, 2011

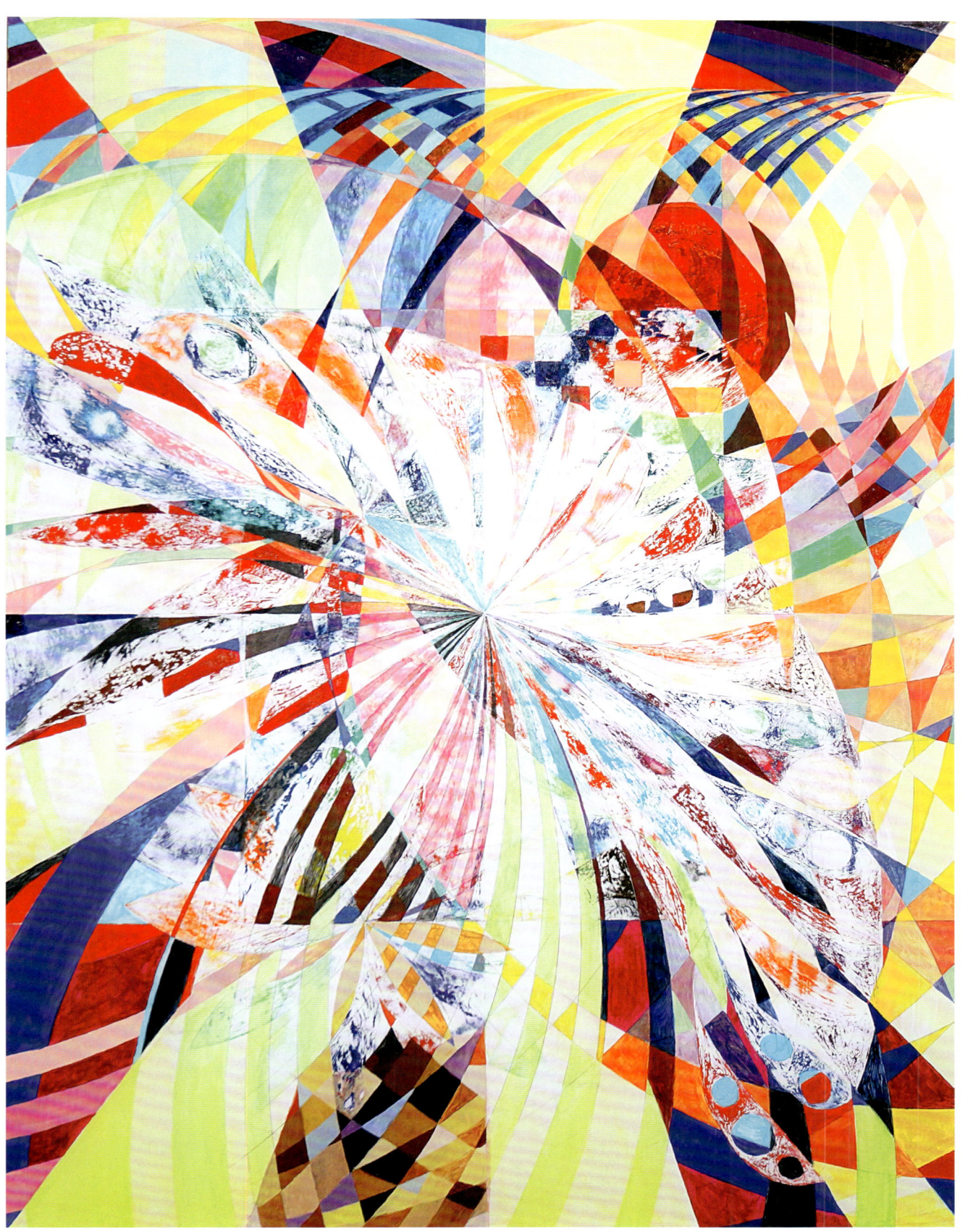

WHEEL WITHIN A WHEEL 92

48 IN X 36 IN
ACRYLIC, 2013

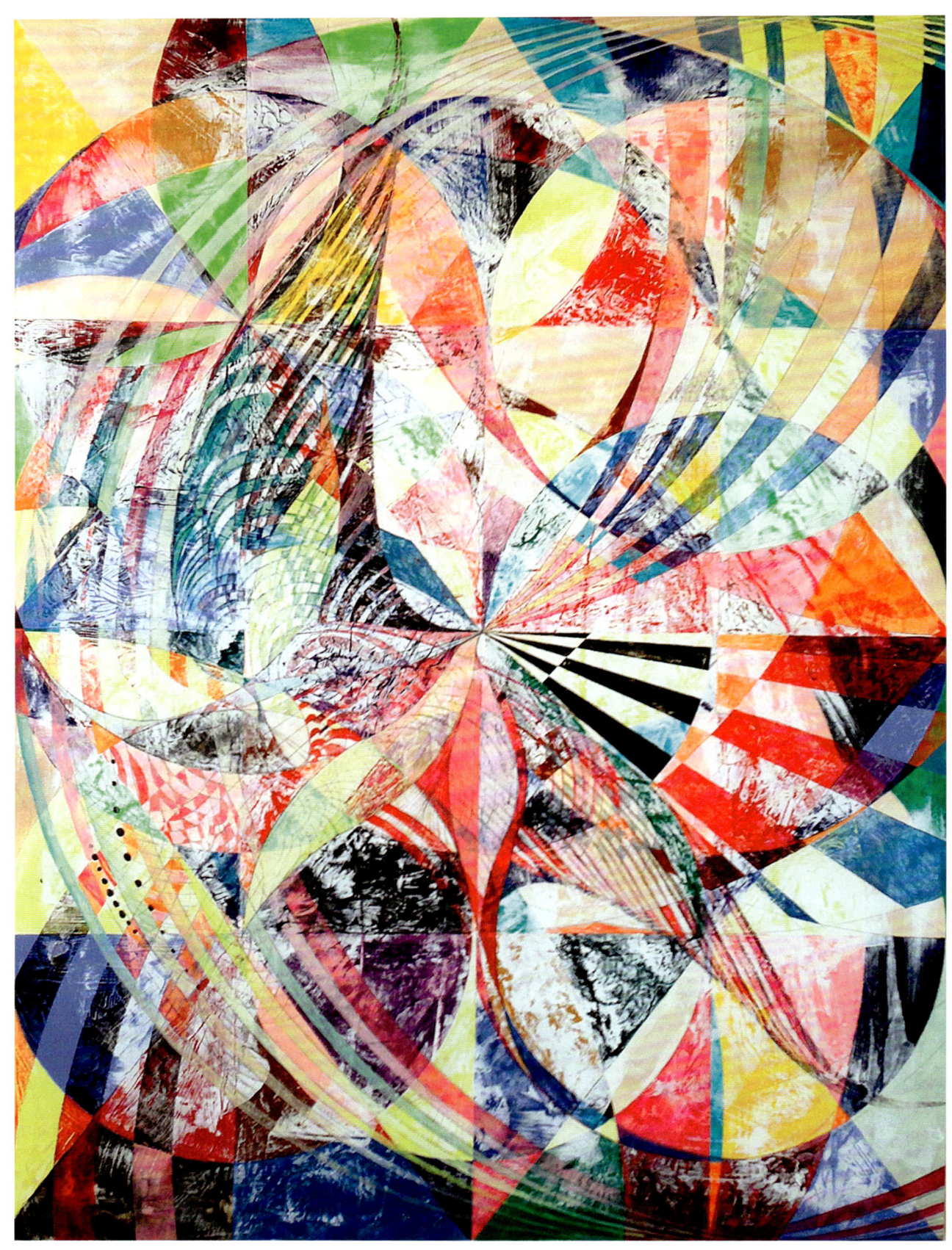

**WHEEL WITHIN A
WHEEL 93**

48 IN X 36 IN
ACRYLIC, 2013

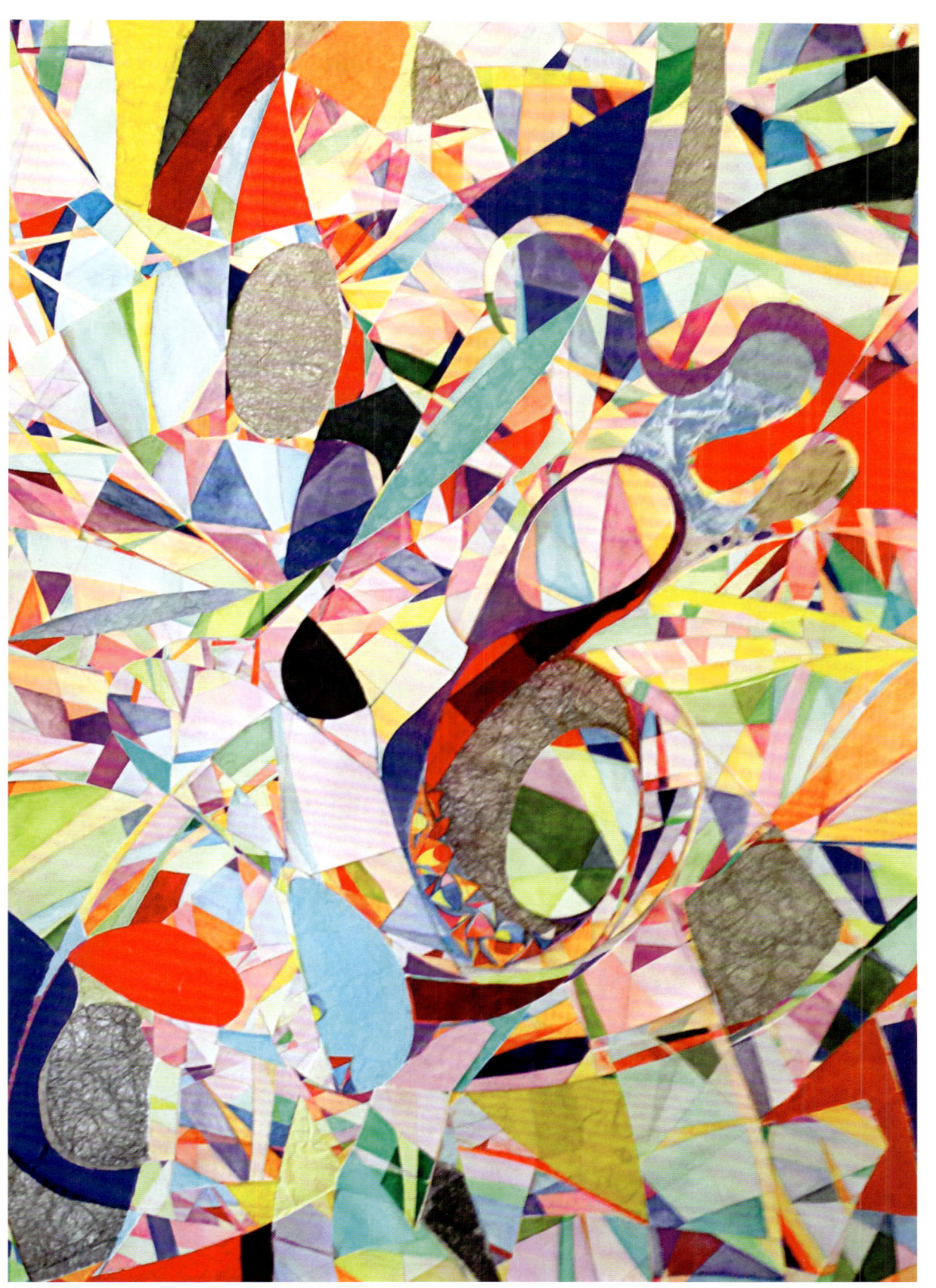

WHEEL WITHIN A WHEEL 96

48 IN X 36 IN
COLLAGE, 2013

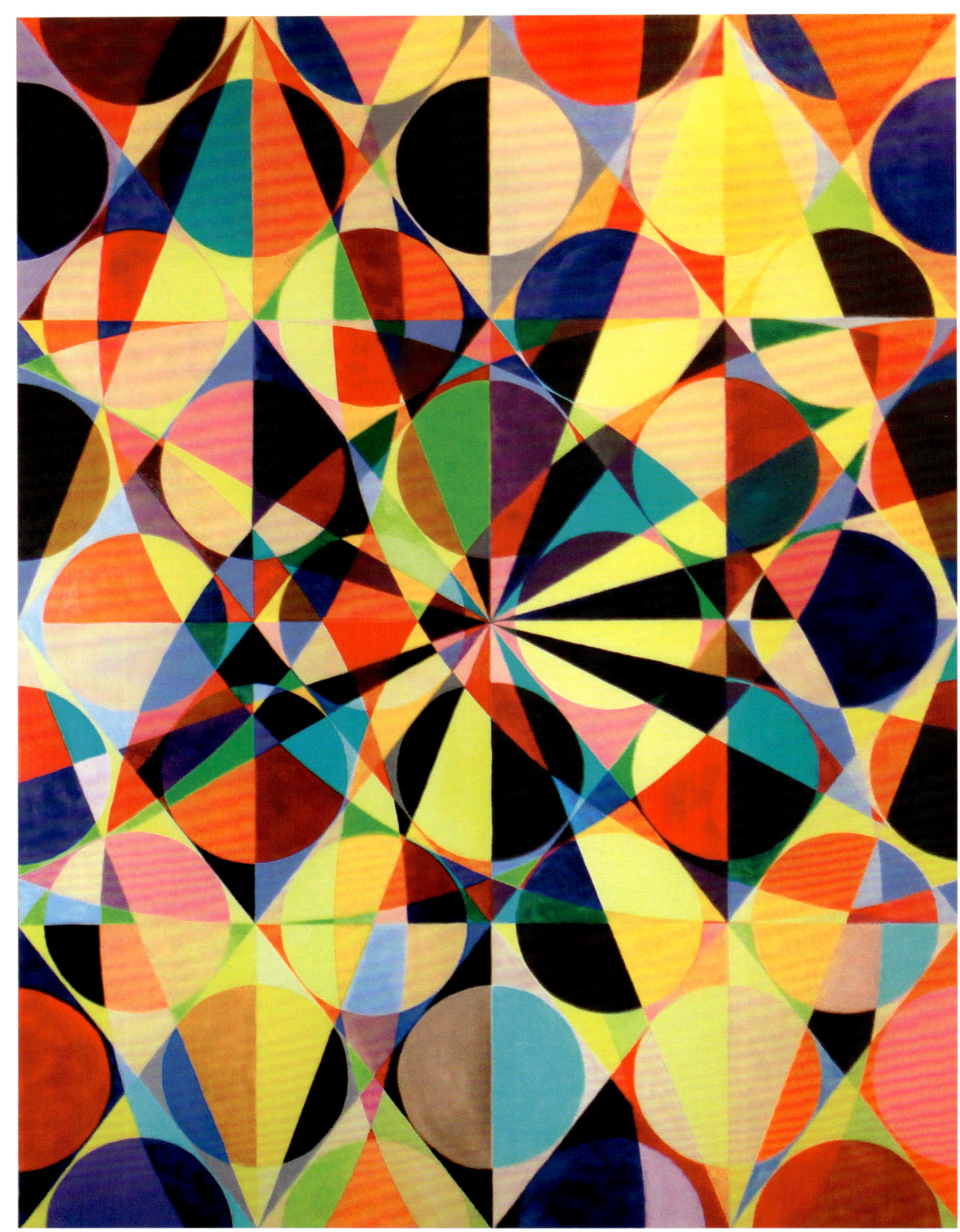

WHEEL WITHIN A WHEEL 95

48 IN X 36 IN
ACRYLIC, 2013

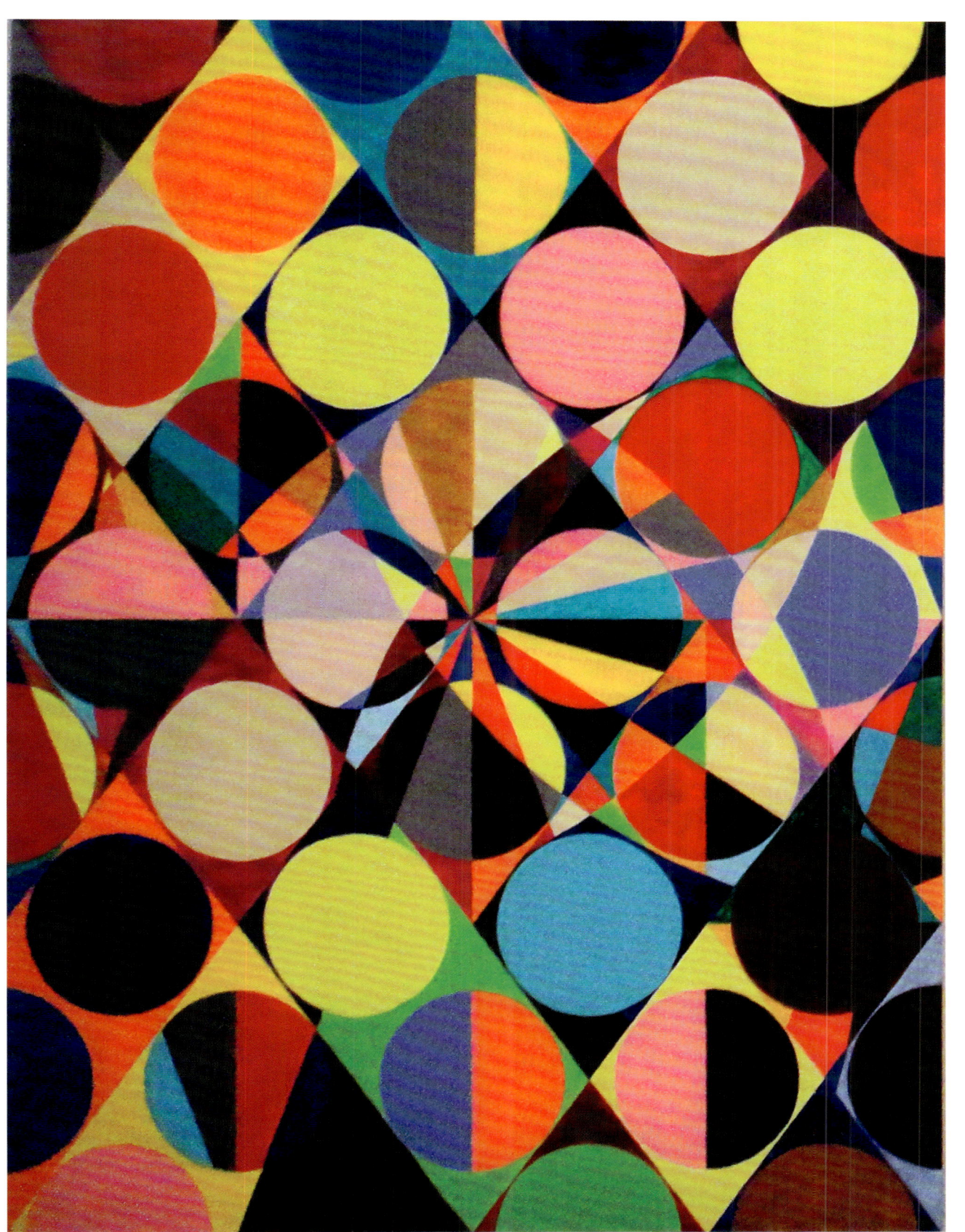

**WHEEL WITHIN A
WHEEL 94**

48 IN X 36 IN
ACRYLIC, 2013

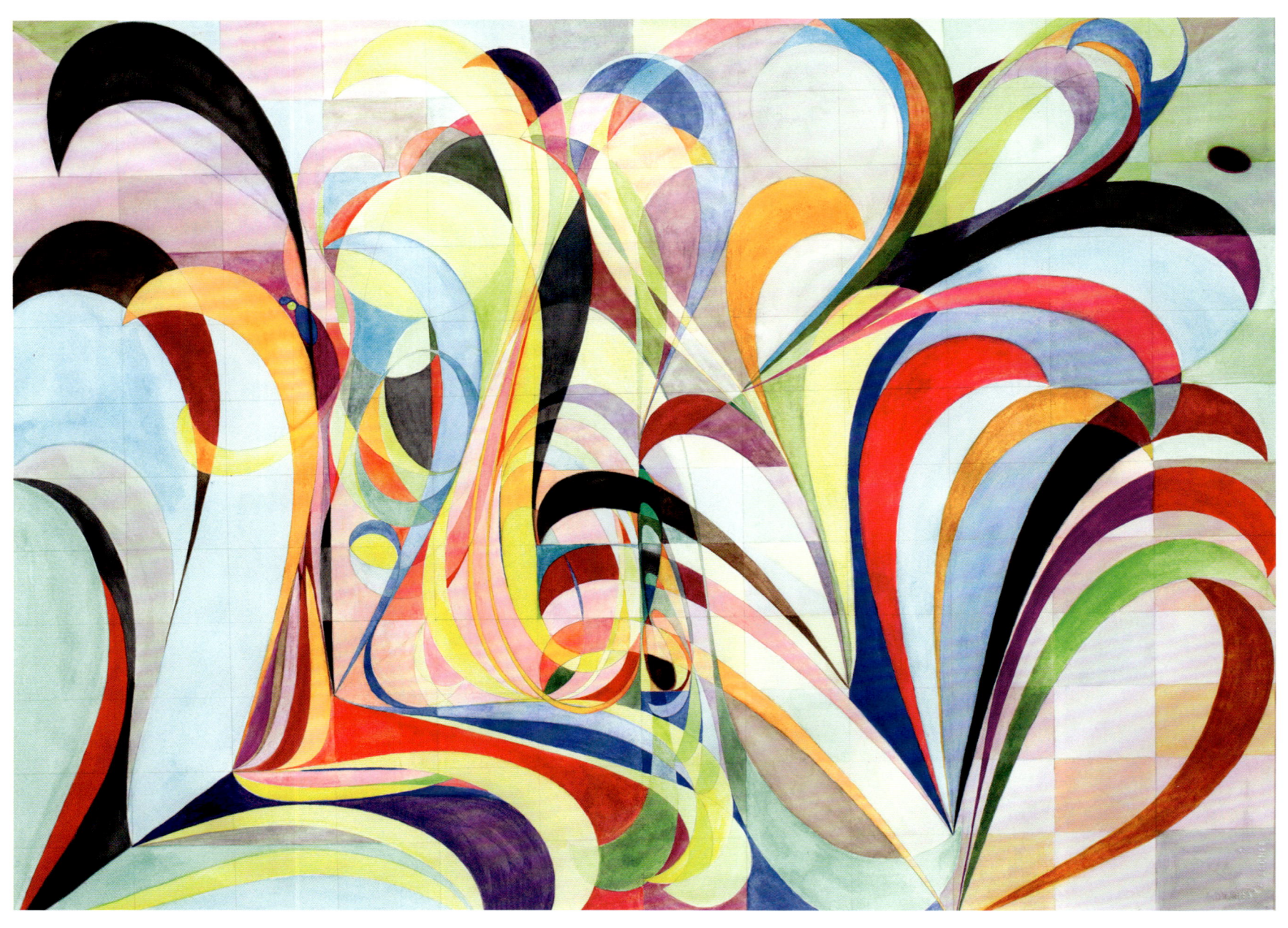

WHEEL WITHIN A WHEEL 98

22 IN X 30 IN
WATERCOLOR/GOUACHE, 2014

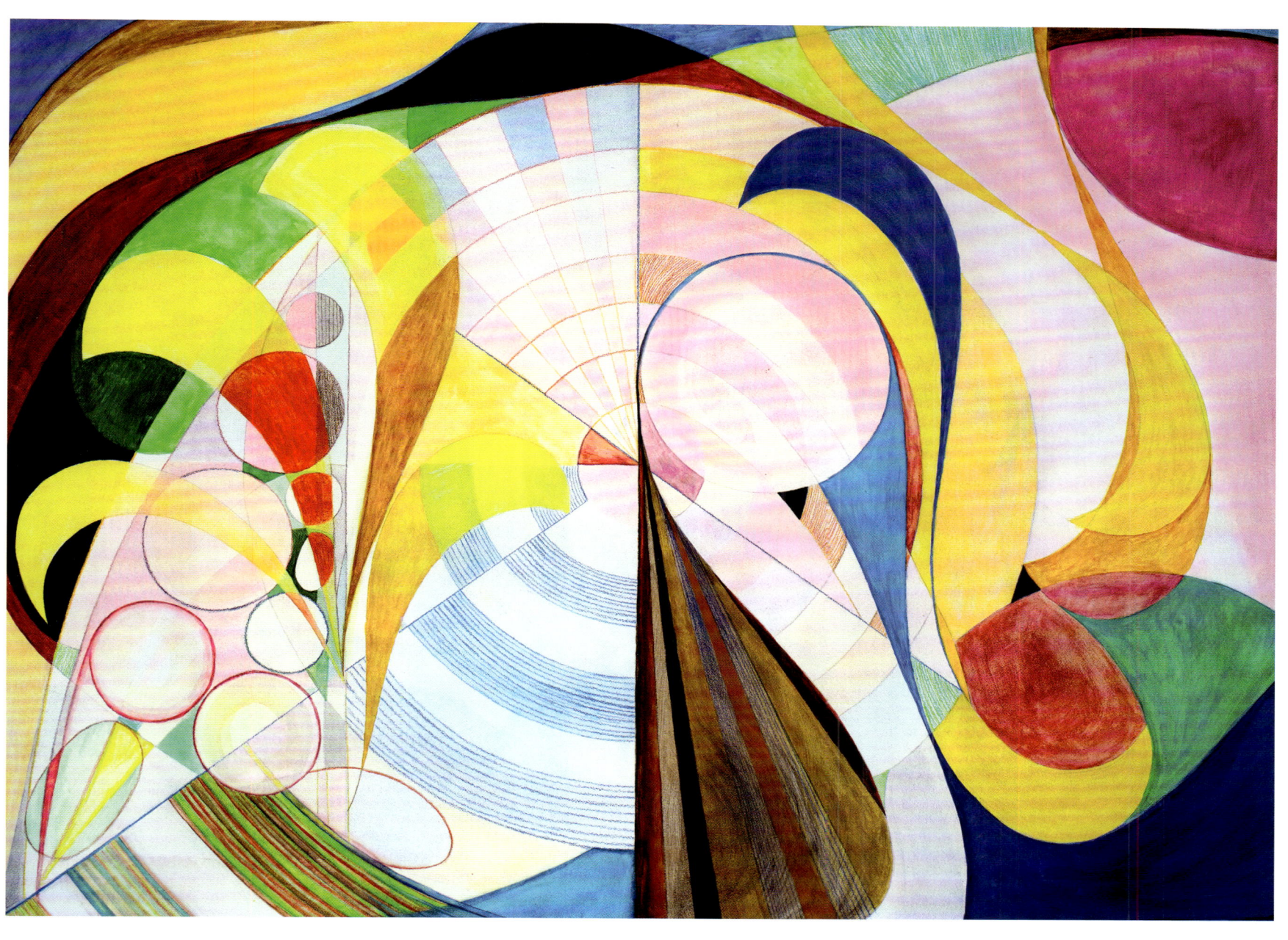

WHEEL WITHIN A WHEEL 100
22 IN X 30 IN
WATERCOLOR/GOUACHE, 2014

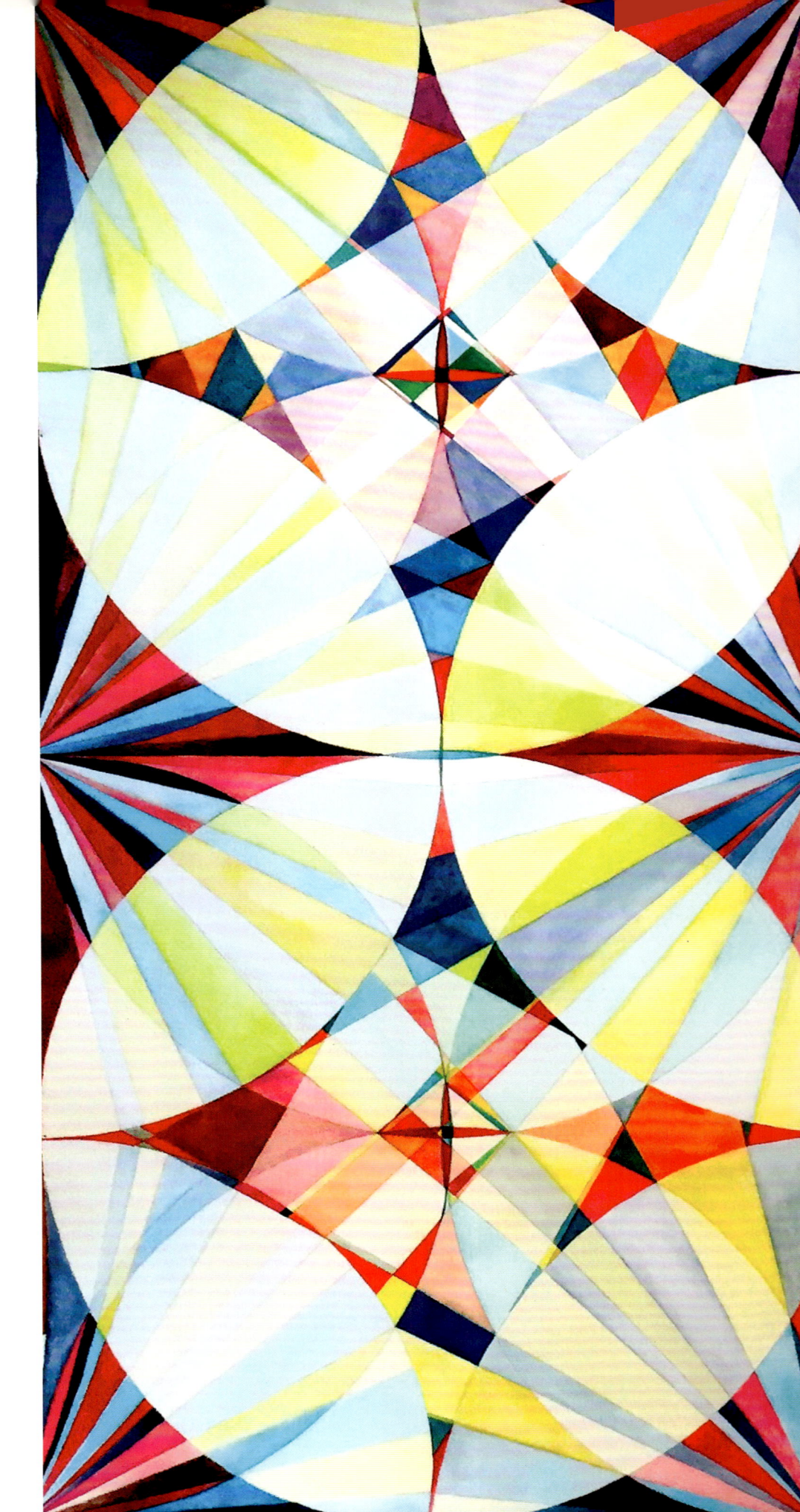

WHEEL WITHIN A WHEEL 112

60 IN X 40 IN
WATERCOLOR/GOUACHE, 2016

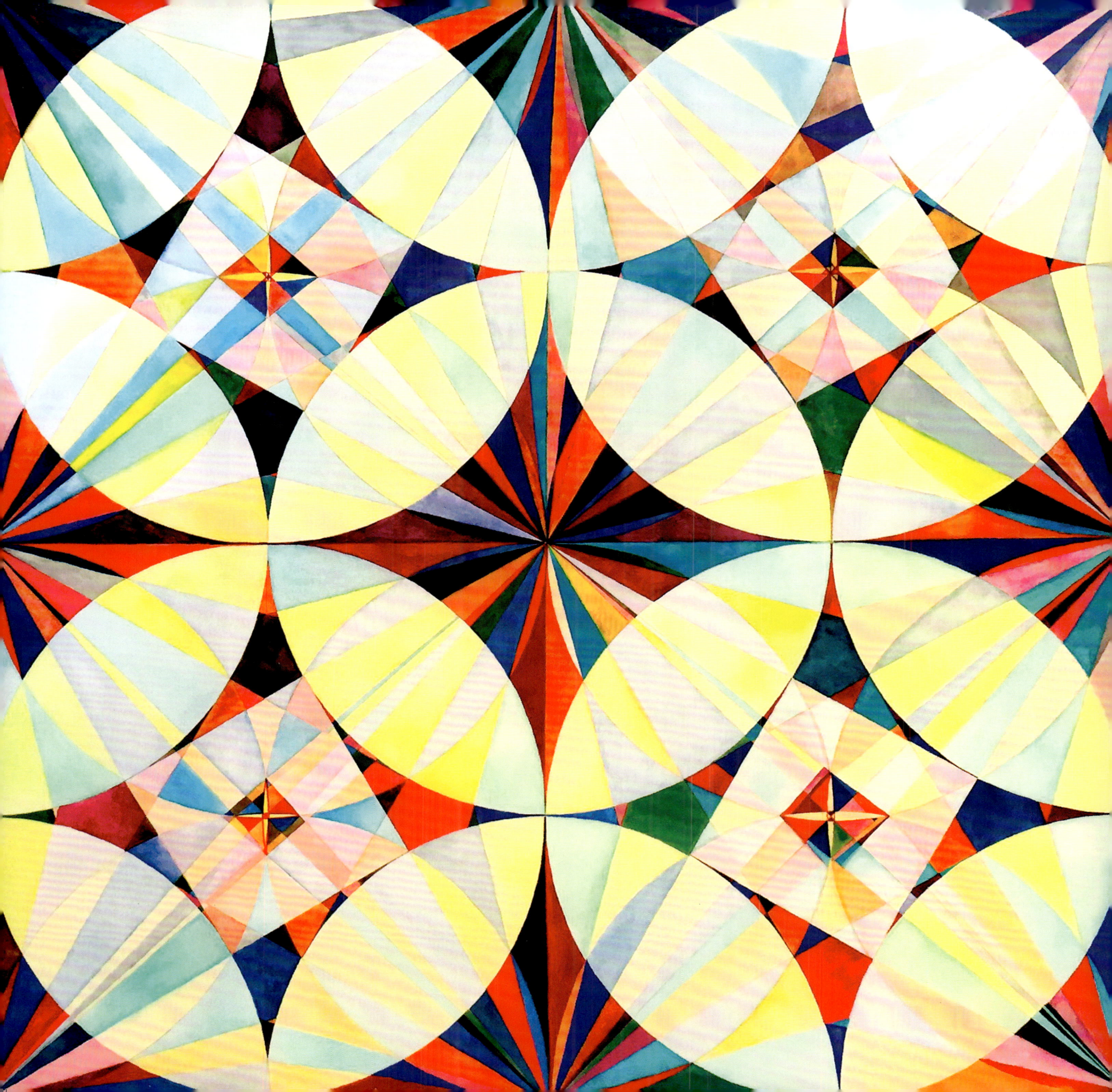

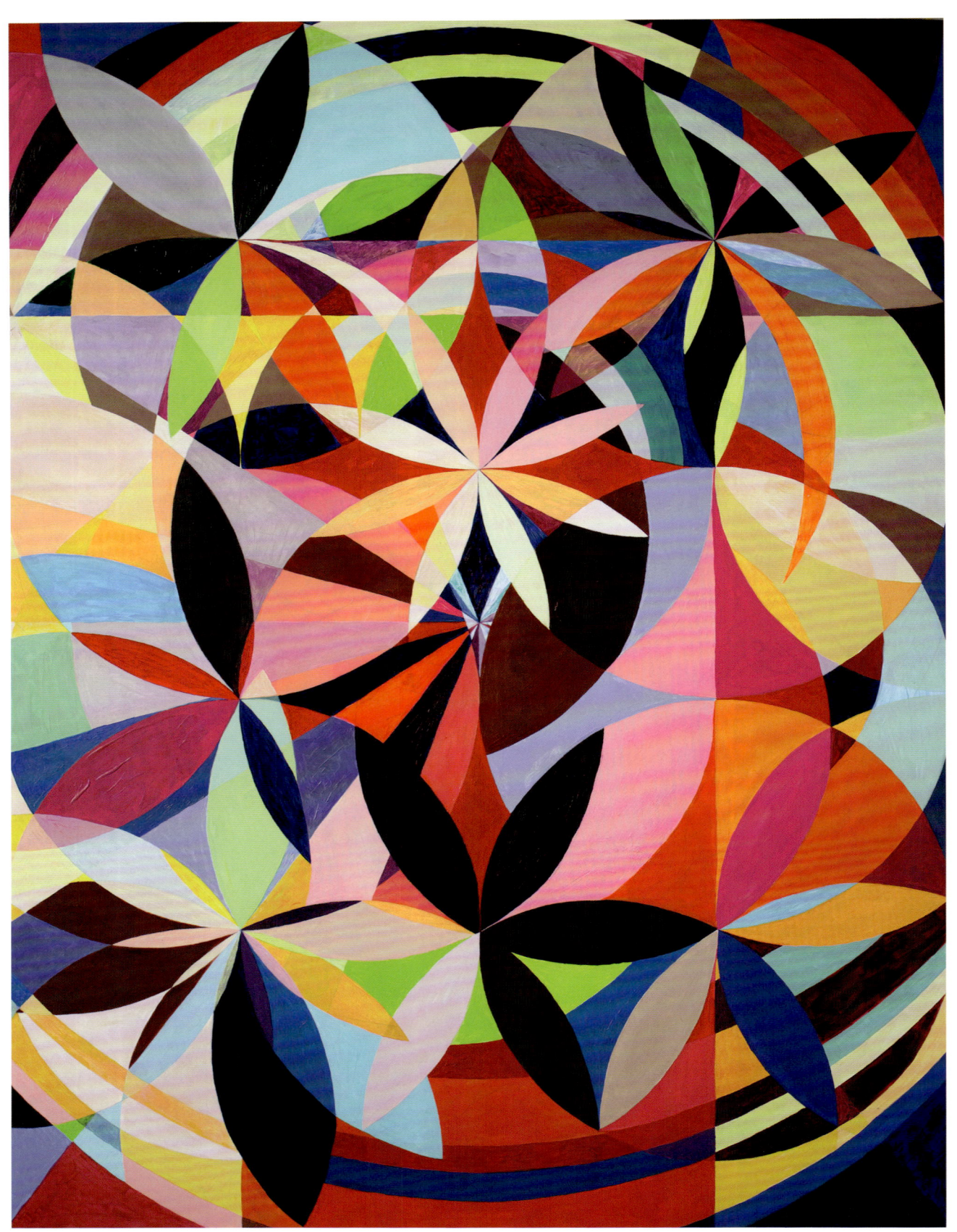

**WHEEL WITHIN A
WHEEL 113**

48 IN X 36 IN
ACRYLIC, 2017

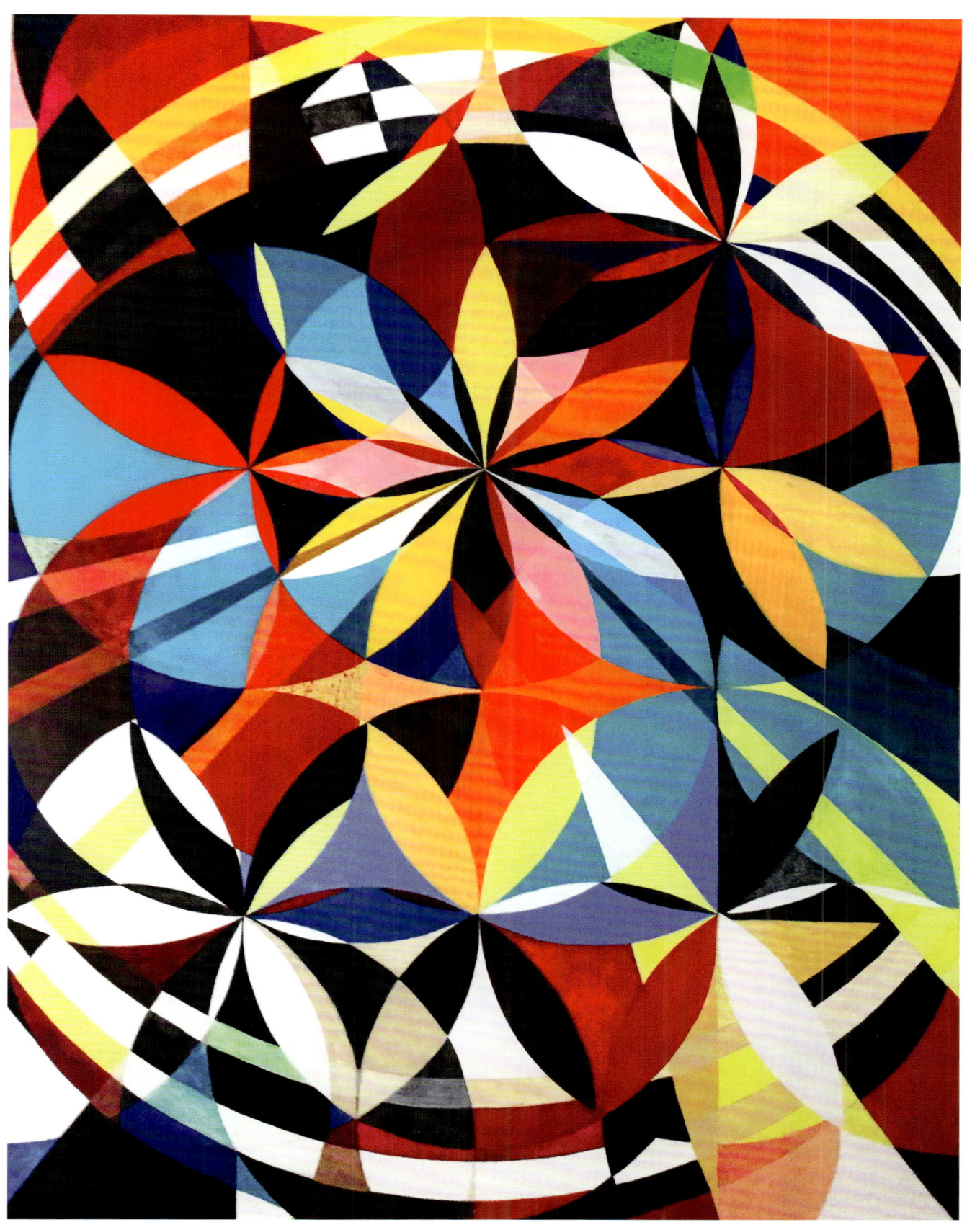

WHEEL WITHIN A WHEEL 115
48 IN X 36 IN
ACRYLIC, 2017

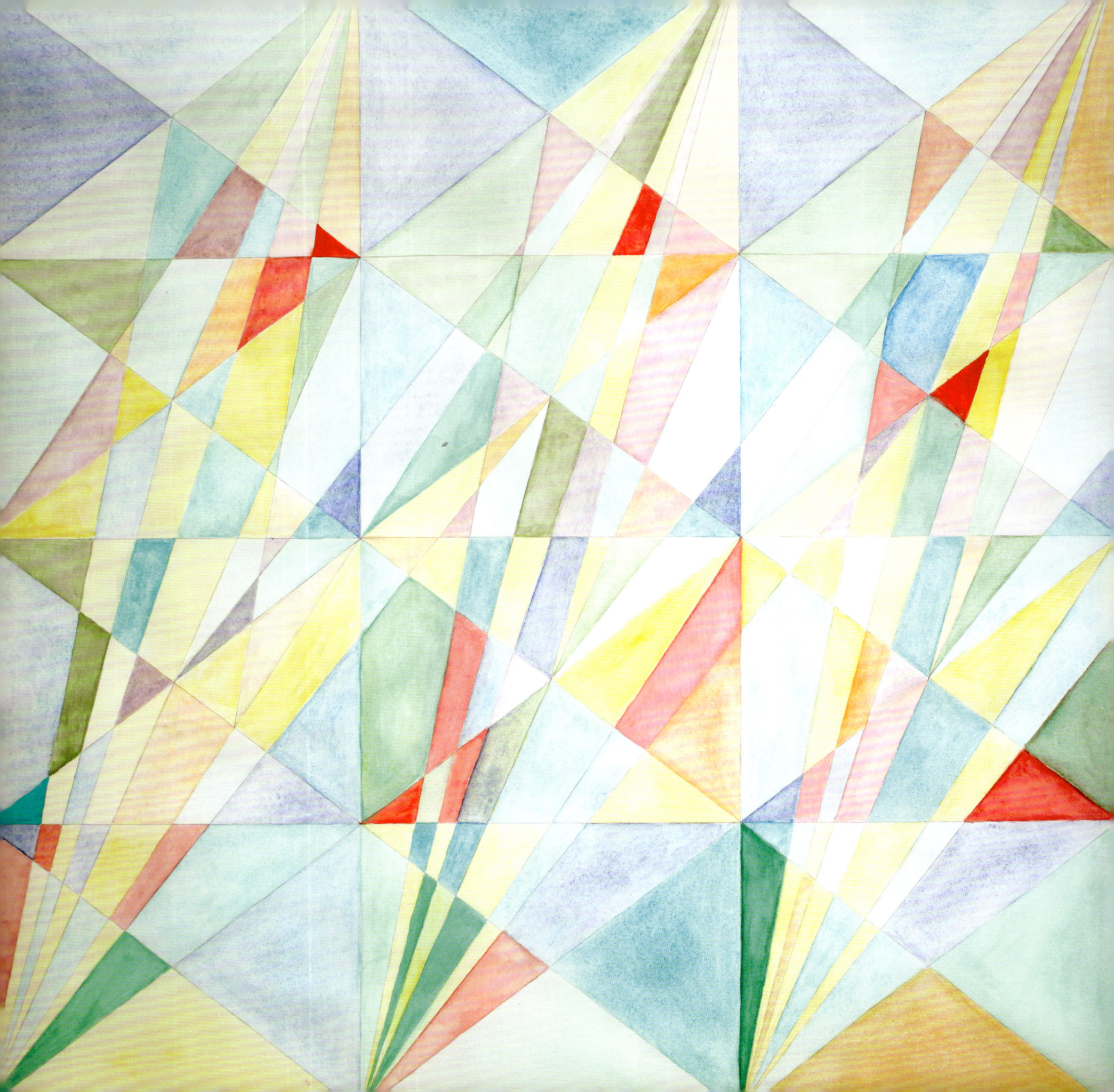

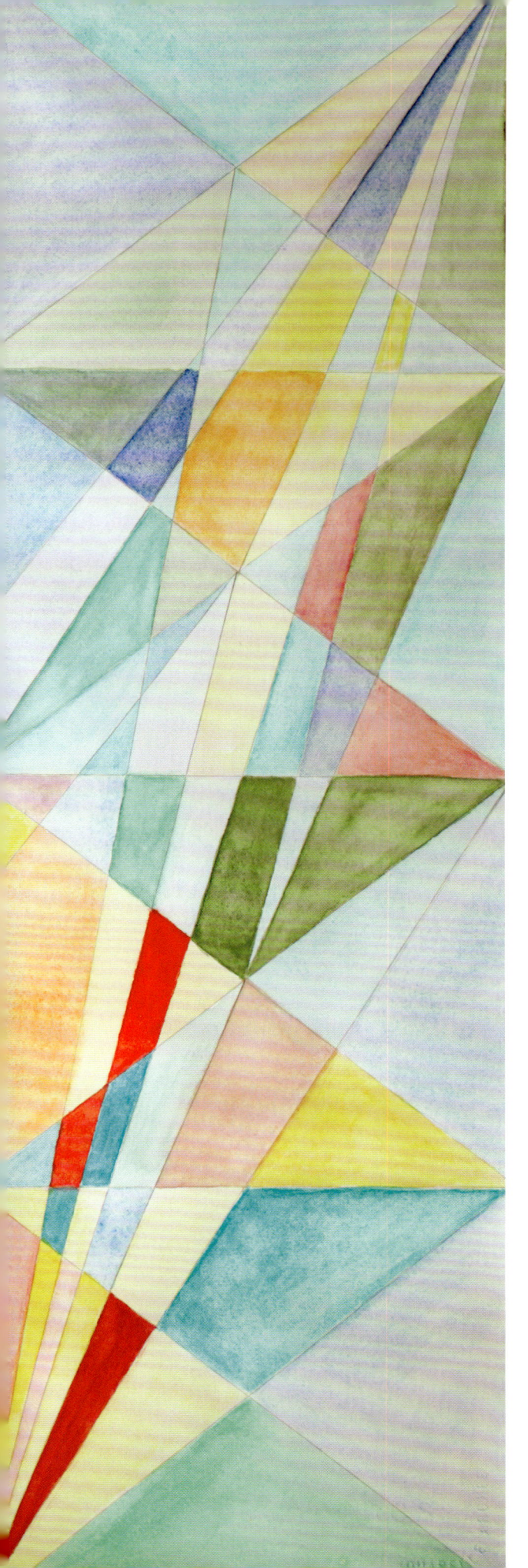

WHEEL WITHIN A WHEEL 111
30 IN X 22 IN
WATERCOLOR/GOUACHE, 2016

REFLECTIONS: A DYNAMIC ARRANGEMENT OF PARTS AMONGST THE WHOLE

TEN PANEL PAINTINGS BY LORIEN SUÁREZ-KANERVA

A naturally unfolding art making process in my studio turned into a rich period of inner awakening through an exploration of meditation and contemplation practices. The geometries in the paintings at that point became looser and more free-flowing.

(Panel Series "Initial Arrangement of 8 Panels", below)

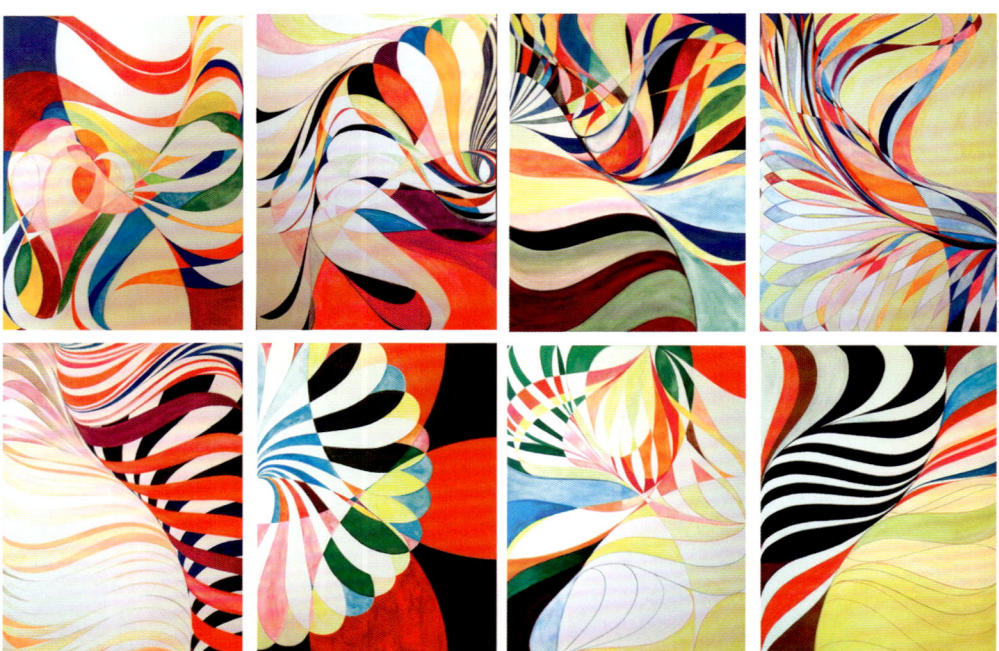

A quality these geometric works shared was a visual sense of expansion, movement and vibrancy. Many floral-plant-undulating and a life-like set of attributes, like leaves and petals with their interconnected lines and forms, combined and shared patterns that permeate the arrangement of parts amongst the whole in nature. The Fibonacci numerical sequence can be seen in the structure of leaves and branches on a tree or petals on a flower.

"Wheel within a Wheel" started in 2003 and by 2014 I had produced 100 paintings in this geometric abstract series. The fluidity in my designs began to arise through contemplation and a conscious recognition of my own sense of participation in the dance of life as the "Beloved."

"Being the Beloved expresses the core truth of our existence."

HENRI J.M. NOUWEN

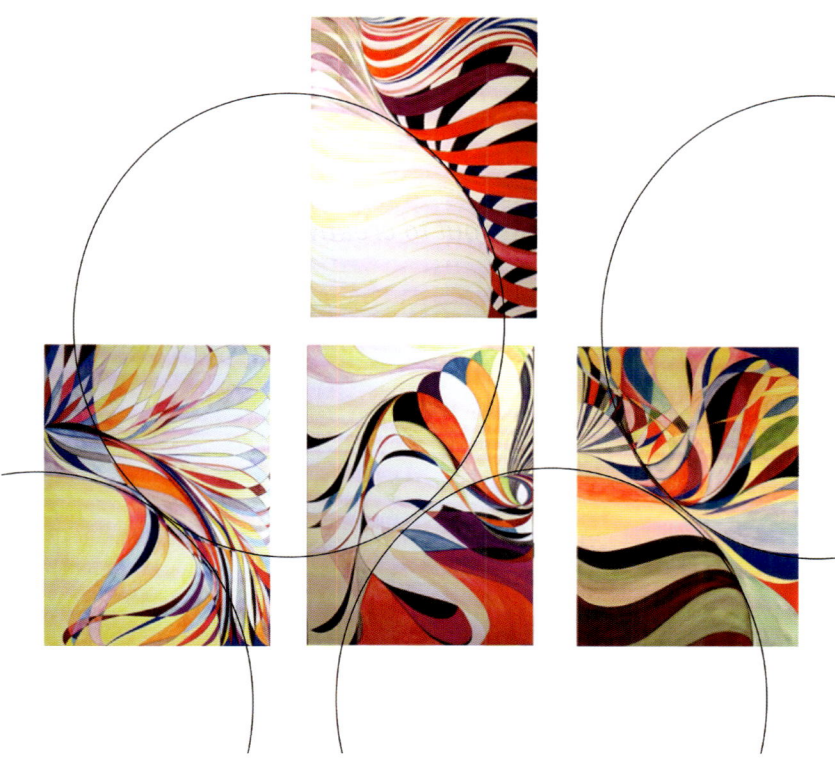

singularly. But, the intent was that these should be a part of a more expansive unified whole.

(Panel Series "Schematic of Design", left)

"Energy, then, becomes Presence.
And so the possibility
is disclosed for,
opens out for,
humanity,
not only of believing and hoping but
(what is much more unexpected and
much more valuable)
of loving.
Co-existing
and co-organically with all the past,
the present and the future of the Universe
is in a process
of concentration upon itself."

TEILHARD DE CHARDIN, THE HEART OF MATTER

It is worth noting that these paintings were themselves a progression within the scope of my contemplative intent to be still and observe the inner promptings for the design of each singular panel. To accomplish this, I didn't want to reject or cling to any one particular artwork or concept.

This was not straightforward since there was one particular artwork that just did not want to "fit in" chromatically with the rest. I thought seriously of replacing it with another as an anomaly but opted to keep it as its own signpost of the nature of "imperfection" within the harmonizing efforts of an aesthetic seeking of perfection.

Because we are born
and live in the very heart of

This spiritual search led to a fascination with a mystical envisioning of the interweaving of the "many into one".

"The success of humanity's evolution will not be determined by 'survival of the fittest' but by our own capacity to converge and unify."

TEILHARD DE CHARDIN, PHENOMENON OF MAN

Drawing loosely from my naive understanding of Teilhard de Chardin's reflections, I set about the task of creating a ten panel composition of artworks that would visually translate my experience with these mystical stirrings. To accomplish this overarching presentation, I selected to create each artwork as a panel that would be fashioned

this thing that is happening,
we still find it
quite natural not only to think with ourselves
but also, inevitably,
to think with all other persons at the same time:
in other words, we can't move a finger
without finding ourselves involved in the construction
of a total human act that includes what we see
and what we make.

TEILHARD DE CHARDIN, THE HEART OF MATTER

During this time, I came across Thich Nhat Hanh's calligraphy of "No Mud, No Lotus" at my doctor's office. I asked her about it. For her it spoke of noble purposes that spring forth from humble grounds. I considered that from our shared aspiration to draw forth higher purposes from our day to day activities we can lose sight of experiencing the immediate moment for its own sake. The challenge can rest on our perception – can we see the present moment just as it is with wonder, including the mud, while also knowing it signals the unfolding of nobler moments to come?

These artworks evolved from my daily sojourn with the beauty (and the mud) that surrounds me. Art-making draws me towards a transformative journey of welcoming the immediate moment. With curiosity, I enter my studio with the prospect of discovering the artwork that's yet a mystery at that precise moment. The process is enigmatic, fascinating and captivating. While painting, I set aside readymade notions and look for the response that grows within me. Art is like that "lotus" that grows from the grounds and "mud" of day to day life.

Up until now,

to adore has meant
to prefer God to things by referring them to God
and by sacrificing them to God.
Now adoration means
the giving of our body and soul to creative activity,
joining that activity to God
to bring the world to fulfillment
by effort
and intellectual exploration.

TEILHARD DE CHARDIN, CHRISTIANITY AND EVOLUTION

The concept of "adoration" includes all forms of creative envisioning – especially in this instance, an artist's aim to bring into being something that had not been perceived prior to the artwork's creation. Chardin's expectation is that the unfolding of perception through our work and study to satisfy the creative process is what our inherent role is to be as creators "bringing the world to fulfillment." In this vision and through our dedicated efforts, we become pioneers with creative pursuits that sustain the world.

Before I plunge into my exploration of perception as a form of seeing alongside creativity through the use of my own artwork, as a basis of study, I think it important to go back to the first statement I quoted from Teilhard de Chardin's concerning how "adoration" is itself a form of creative fulfillment.

The whole of life lies in the verb seeing.

TEILHARD DE CHARDIN

The unfolding of perception and the creative process itself as a journey takes on the language of color as poetic imagery and wording in Teilhard de Chardin's mystical writings – it is "beyond" the "familiar" to a "threshold of another universe" with "colours...in full growth." In this vision, we become the authors of a creative pursuit.

The truth is, indeed, that love is the threshold of another universe. Beyond the vibrations with which we are familiar, the rainbow-like range of its colours is still in full growth.

TEILHARD DE CHARDIN, TOWARD THE FUTURE

Similarly, and much like the contemplative path, I am learning to welcome the unexpected changes of the creative journey. Each development of the design builds on what's still unresolved in the prior creative undertaking. During the construction of these intermediate design steps, in the making of the multiple panel composition, I was keenly conscious of the creative process at work.

Teilhard de Chardin reflects on a life long process where creative activity includes an inner struggle between what is longed for and what is attained at each moment in time.

"How can it be that 'when I come down from the mountain' and in spite of the glorious vision I still remain, I find that I am so little better a person, so little at peace, so incapable of expressing in my actions, and thus adequately communicating to others, the wonderful unity that I feel encompassing me?"

TEILHARD DE CHARDIN, THE HEART OF MATTER

An answer to this question found in Chardin's writings, would connect this matter of creative effort with being and seeing with faith. From my own intuition, I consider that for the artist to make what is to be perceived through an art-form is itself an act of creative trust in the process – that is, faith.

I have found that my art suffers when I allow myself to doubt or to reject the process that a creative journey calls

for. Basically, I have to allow for what has not been to be, while building, until it reaches fruition.

"I begin to think that most of our weaknesses are due to the fact that our 'belief' is to narrow, and that we don't believe enough to the end. To stop believing a second too soon, or not to believe enough, is sufficient to ruin the whole structure we are building.'

TEILHARD DE CHARDIN, LETTER TO ZANTA

Both at the point of the insight - the creative spark and/or the "glorious vision" - and following through the composition's building process, to be creative is to embark on a journey of discovery – making art then becomes an act of faith.

As I began envisioning a more premeditated design framework that would serve to unify and interrelate a multiplicity of designs amongst as of yet emerging artworks, the design plans became more elaborate and structured. Here, the geometric core of my artwork is evident in the layering of circular patterns. The designs suggest an encircling movement to embrace, enclose and enfold the many parts of the whole.

The challenge was to allow each of the new paintings that I completed to intertwine and coordinate with one another in a multiplicity of rotations and combinations. My aim for the artwork still held as a constant that over time these could be inter-related to achieve the desired unity despite the diversity reflected in each of the artworks.

A person cannot disappear
by passing into another person;
for by nature we can only give ourselves as people
so long as we remain self-conscious units,
that is to say distinct.

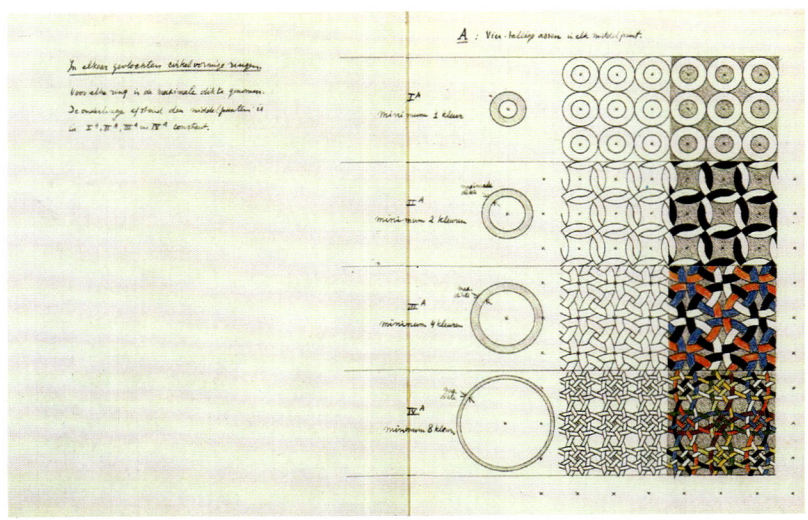

Entwined circular rings

For each ring, the maximum thickness is taken.
The distance between centers [of the circles] is constant
in I^A, II^A, III^A, and IV^A.

A: Four-fold axes at each center point.

I^A
minimum 1 color
II^A maximum thickness ⟶
minimum 2 colors
III^A max. thickness ⟶
minimum 4 colors
IV^A max. thickness ⟶
minimum 8 colors

Moreover,
this gift which we make of ourselves
has the direct result of reinforcing
the most incommunicable quality,
that is to say
the quality of superpersonalizing.
Union Differentiates.

TEILHARD DE CHARDIN, HUMAN ENERGY

And most importantly, each artwork had to maintain its own intrinsic uniqueness. The unification was not intended to draw forth uniformity but the opposite – greater diversity and more differentiation. The effort of engagement with the design process of this series had its own leaps of faith in the mix as well.

While doing research, I discovered M.C. Escher's writings. In his notebooks with drawings and studies of the geometric design work at the Alhambra and La Mesquita in Córdoba, I found a particular drawing (one with circular decorative patterns and the growing complexity of "hidden" circular interweaving layers) – along with his reflections on the general adaptability of geometric designs.

(Escher Notebook 1, left)

"The regular division of the plane can, for aesthetic purposes, be applied to decorate an arbitrary surface. In the regular division of the plane the drawing surface is infinite in all directions...Usually, however, the surface is bounded on all

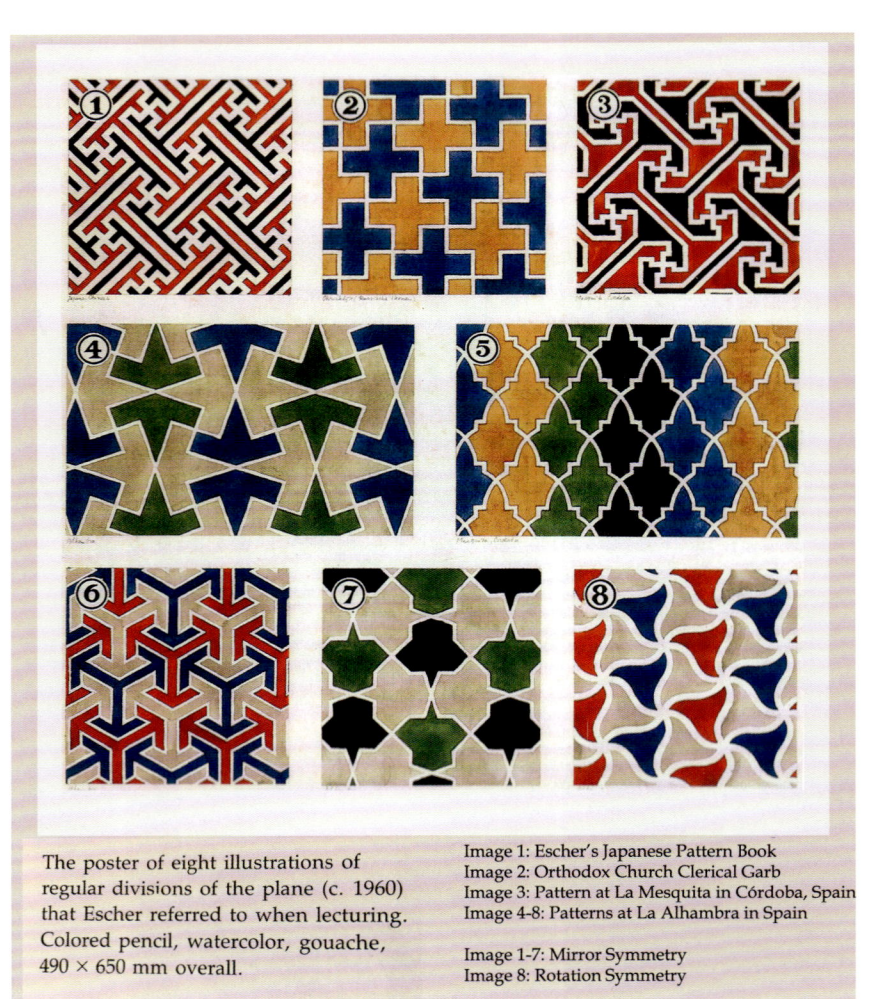

The poster of eight illustrations of regular divisions of the plane (c. 1960) that Escher referred to when lecturing. Colored pencil, watercolor, gouache, 490 × 650 mm overall.

Image 1: Escher's Japanese Pattern Book
Image 2: Orthodox Church Clerical Garb
Image 3: Pattern at La Mesquita in Córdoba, Spain
Image 4-8: Patterns at La Alhambra in Spain

Image 1-7: Mirror Symmetry
Image 8: Rotation Symmetry

sides, namely in a rectangular way...When the form of the repeating motif, or motifs, is a purely geometric one, then the question of whether the drawing surface is to be placed horizontally or vertically may be important from an aesthetic point of view, but from a logical point of view it does not matter: a mathematical figure can be viewed aesthetically from whatever side one looks at it."

ESCHER NOTEBOOKS (1941):
THE REGULAR DIVISION OF THE PLANE, P. 30

(Escher Notebook 2, left)

Escher adopted a set of geometric forms as a structural framework for his designs. He employed the "*parallelogram, rectangle, square, triangle, rhombus, hexagon*" and a set of what he termed "*geometric motions that [would] preserve [an] exact shape: translation, rotation and glide reflection. These three motions and no others, are those that can be used to move a given motif to an adjacent congruent motif in a regular division of the plane.*"

DORIS SCHATTSCHNEIDER, "M.C. ESCHER: VISIONS OF SYMMETRY"

(Escher Notebook 3, next page)

Escher's work serves as a fascinating historical perspective on geometric designs and reveals how he devised his own structural approach. I appreciated anew the universality and constant principles that these mathematical figures and patterns, that I work closely with in my own design work, rest upon.

Clearly, while making some minor variations-alterations that I had to improvise upon, I re-adapted the artworks and the framework as the project evolved. Still, though striving to remain open to a process of exploration, the artworks I had been fashioning all drew from a selective vision

enveloped in a "subjective" symbolic design building process that gives my work its distinctiveness – as it does for most if not all artists.

At this time while reading about Matisse and his writings, I discovered a tad more about his own personal "philosophy" or refusal to have one as an artist. I agree with this artist c approach, although it contains the paradox that Jack Flam, the specialist who created the anthology of Matisse's work, noted. I mention it since it seems to me to be an inherent aspect of abstract art itself and addresses the artistic subjective selective envisioning at the heart of creative expression.

"Matisse, like Cèzanne, stands apart from the schools and systems that were contemporary with him...Matisse's extreme emphasis on self-expression is also very paradoxical in that it defines, reality by describing one's own reaction to it, suggesting that an artist's production is the somewhat involuntary result of his temperament, from which it follows that the artist must simply believe that he has painted what he has seen, "even when he deviates from it in order better to express it" Notes of a painter, 1908. This creates a kind of circular relationship between the self and nature, and between expression and copying, that results in a kind of theoretical impasse. But it is not a paradox Matisse wanted to resolve; rather, he absolutely needed to leave it unresolved and open in order to permit himself to act. For as Matisse states it, the artist must find his own signs, through which his deeply subjective responses to the world can be given form...because the true artist's work must emanate from the true self."

MATISSE ON ART, INTRODUCTION BY JACK FLAM, 1995.

The problem or paradox is itself, in my opinion, one that endows art with the value it holds for society. As artists

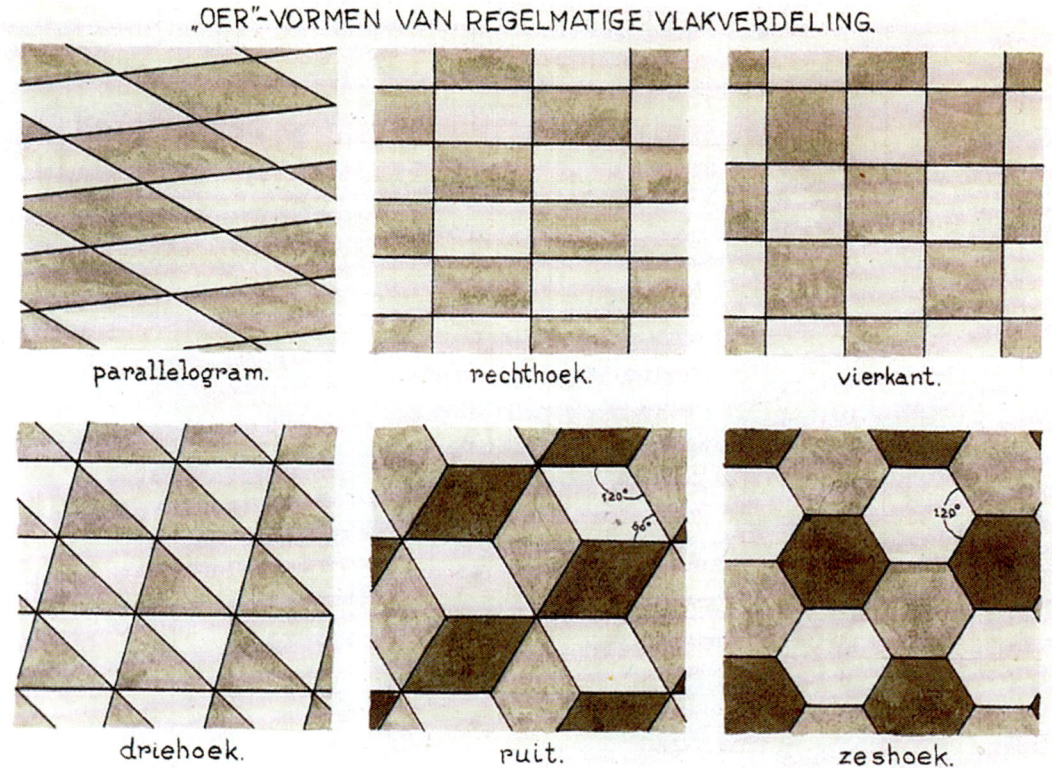

„OER"-VORMEN VAN REGELMATIGE VLAKVERDELING.

parallelogram.   rechthoek.   vierkant.

driehoek.   ruit.   zeshoek.

Second illustration that Escher used in his lectures to explain the theory of regular division of the plane, c. 1960. Watercolor and ink, 220 × 292 mm. Escher's title reads "'Fundamental' forms of regular division of the plane." The examples in the top row are labeled "parallelogram, rectangle, square," and in the bottom row "triangle, rhombus, hexagon."

we endeavor to articulate a mystery that is continually unfolding before us. And as Matisse (and other spiritual teachers) concludes, it is most perceivable through a child-like openness.

If an artist is true to the vision he/she holds of reality, and expresses it truthfully in his/her artwork, it clearly does not follow, that its "truth" should have to be discernible, in exactly the same terms, to someone else as its viewer, in order for it to be meaningful and hold value in itself. Abstract art is a perfect example.

I think it is precisely because the artwork does reach us with a truth beyond the realm of the purely rational and evident, that it is so compelling. In creating his/her work, the artist follows a similar perceptive journey of receptivity as the viewer experiences as he perceives the artwork.

Here are Matisse's words, "*To sum up, I work without theory. I am conscious only of the forces I use, and I am driven by an idea that I really only grasp as it grows with the picture.*"
NOTES OF A PAINTER ON HIS DRAWING, MATISSE 1939

Matisse creates a space of artistic freedom for himself and others. He arrives at this freedom by means of creating a unique notion of how the artist is to go about seeing – A notion that the viewers' of the artwork may adopt as well.

"*The effort needed to see things without distortion demands a kind of courage; and this courage is essential to the artist, who has to look at everything as though he were seeing it for the first time: he has to look at life as he did when he was a child and if he loses that faculty, he cannot express himself in an original, that is, a personal way...The work of art is thus the culmination of a long process of development. The artist takes from his surroundings everything that can nourish his internal vision, either directly, as when the object he draws is to appear in his composition, or by analogy. In this way he puts himself into a state of creativity. He enriches himself internally with all the forms he has mastered and that he will one day set within a new rhythm.*

It is in the expression of this rhythm that the artist's work will be really creative. To achieve it, he will need to sift rather than accumulate details, selecting in drawing, for example from all possible combinations, the line that will be most fully expressive and carry the most life; he will have to seek equivalences through which elements of nature are transposed into the realm of life.

It is in this sense, it seems to me, that art may be said to imitate nature: by the quality of life that creative work confers upon the work of art. The work will then appear as fertile and as possessed of this same inner vibration, of this same resplendent beauty, that we find in the products of nature.

Great love is needed to inspire and sustain this continuous striving towards truth, this concurrent generosity and profound laying bare that accompany the birth of any work of art. But isn't love at the origin of all creation?"

LOOKING AT LIFE WITH THE EYES OF A CHILD, MATISSE 1953

While thoroughly enjoying the openness of Matisse and his creative vision, I embrace with a kind of joy the freedom he achieves as an artist. He was absorbed in the creative discovery process and openly shared it through his correspondence and writings. It was a relief to learn that he was a bit of a compulsive correspondent and writer, something I can also readily identify with to a fault. It's estimated that throughout his lifetime he spent at least an hour a day writing letters and reflections in his journals.

My hope is that as the viewer, you find as much joy in the sight of the artworks, as I have discovered through the creative journey itself.

I conclude with Kandinsky's thoughts about Matisse's work:

"He paints "pictures" and through these "pictures" he seeks to reproduce the "divine."

KUNST AND KÜNSTLER, KANDINSKY 1909.

That is a wonderful aspiration to hold as an artist, and it is one I will continue to seek through my own efforts.

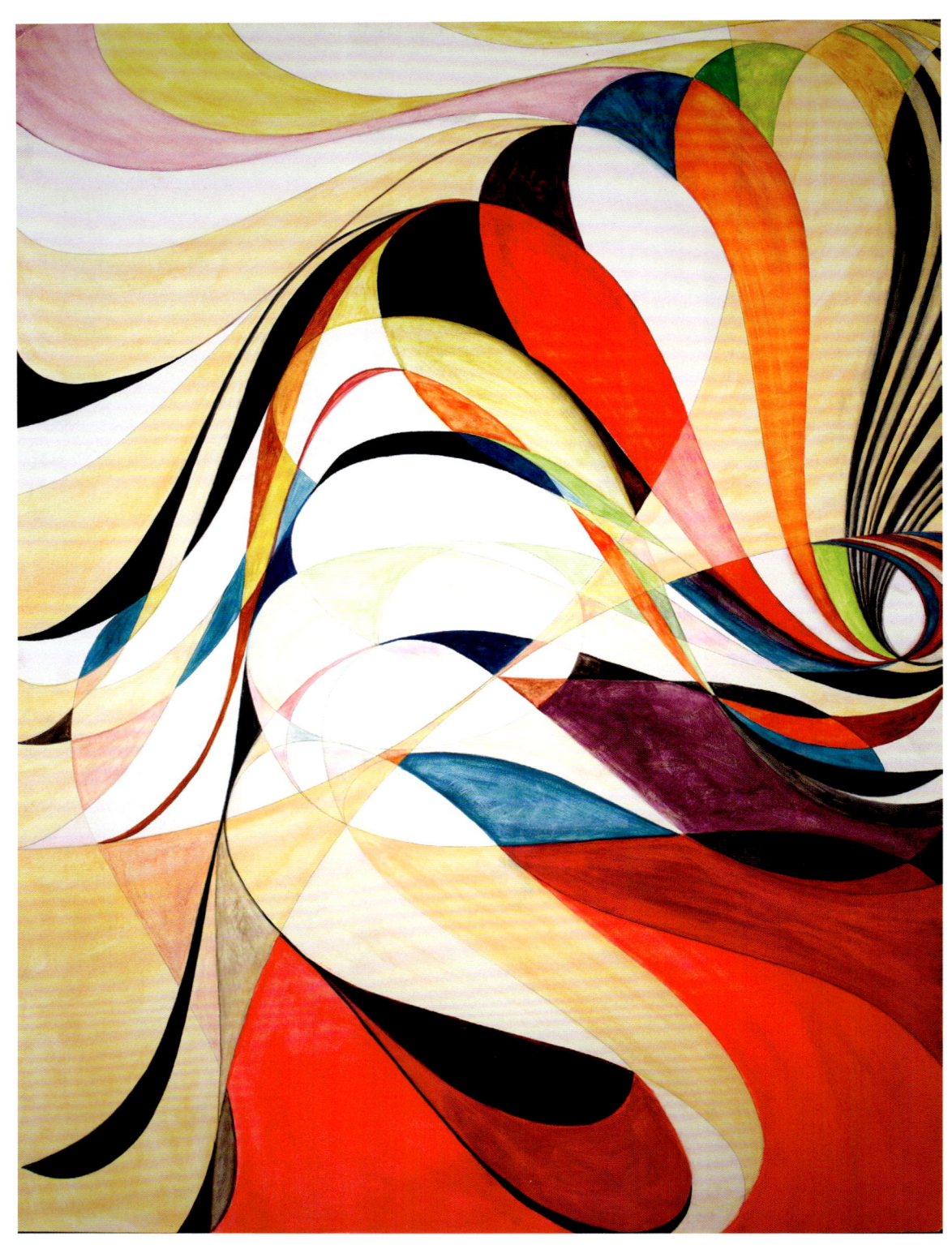

WHEEL WITHIN A WHEEL 101
30 IN X 22 IN
WATERCOLOR/GOUACHE, 2014

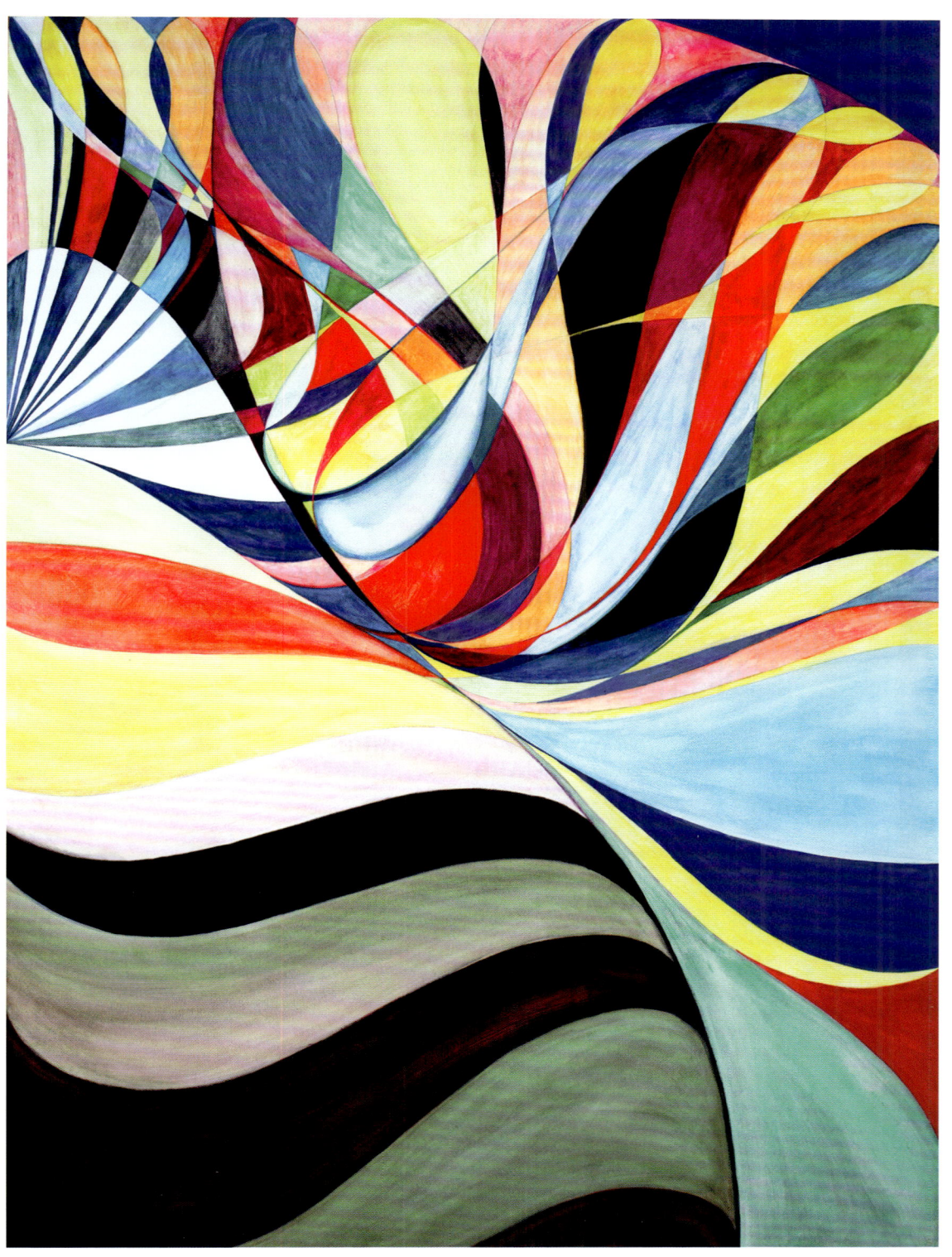

WHEEL WITHIN A WHEEL 102
30 IN X 22 IN
WATERCOLOR/GOUACHE, 2014

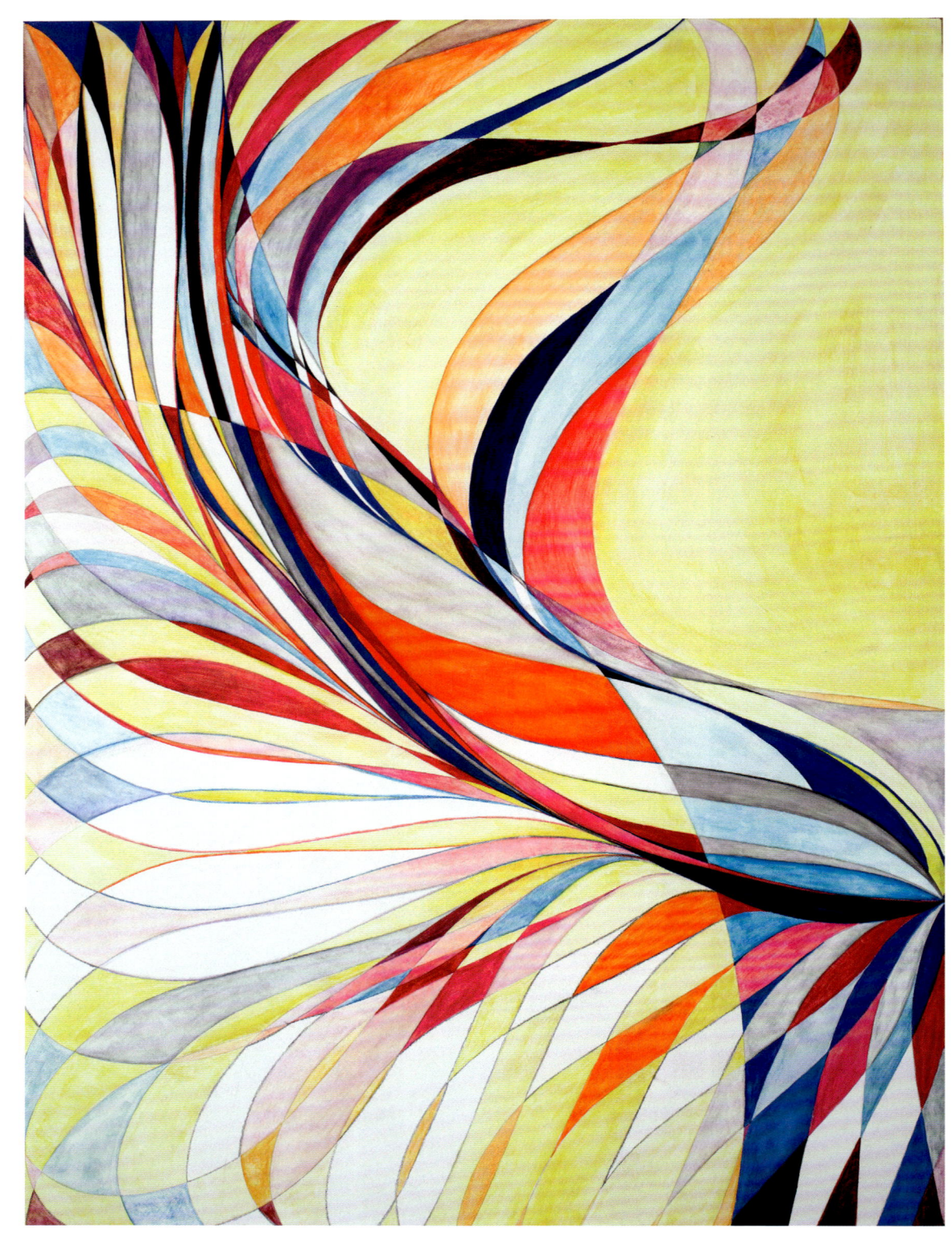

WHEEL WITHIN A WHEEL 103
30 IN X 22 IN
WATERCOLOR/GOUACHE, 2014

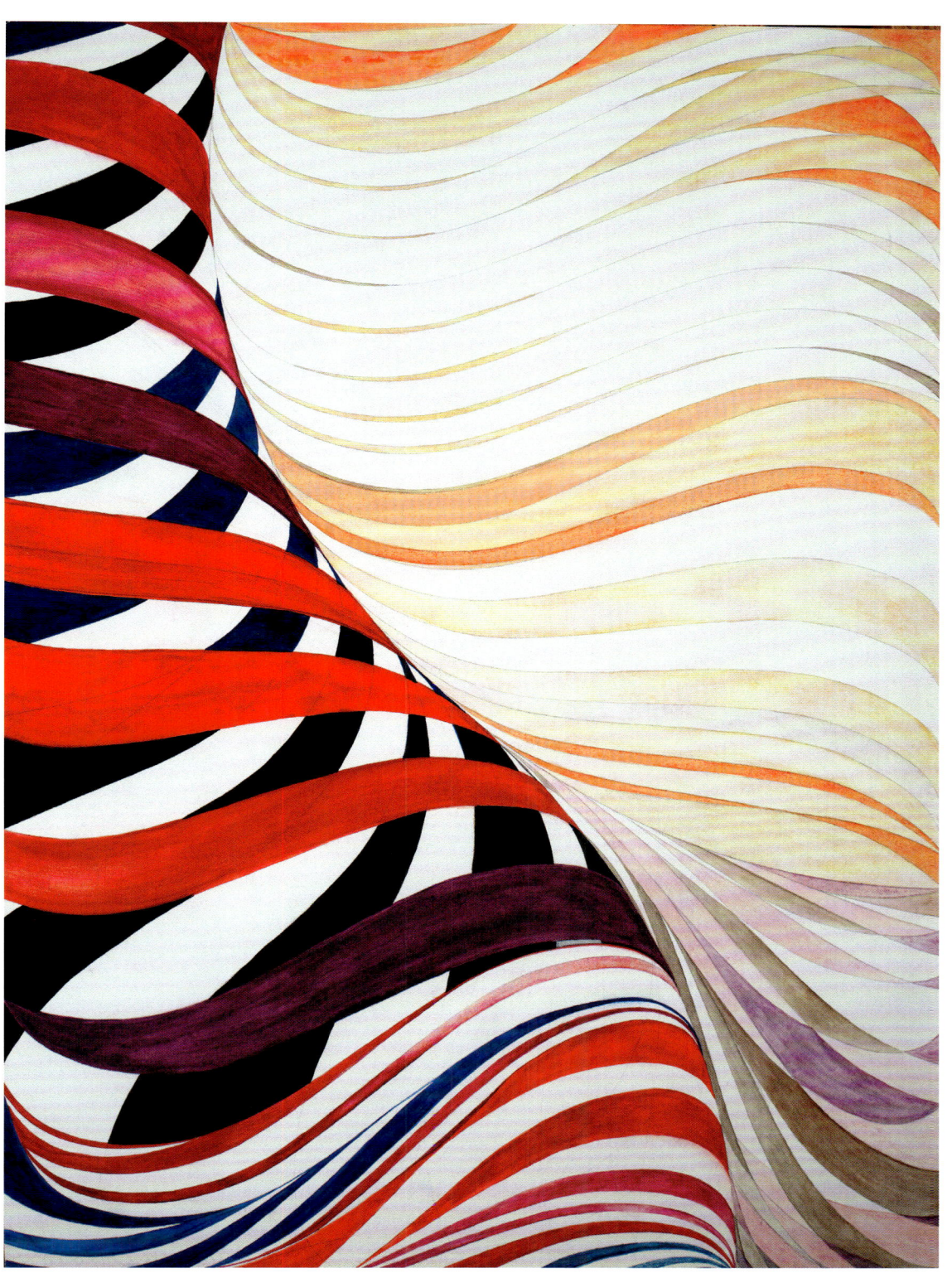

WHEEL WITHIN A WHEEL 104
30 IN X 22 IN
WATERCOLOR/GOLACHE, 2014

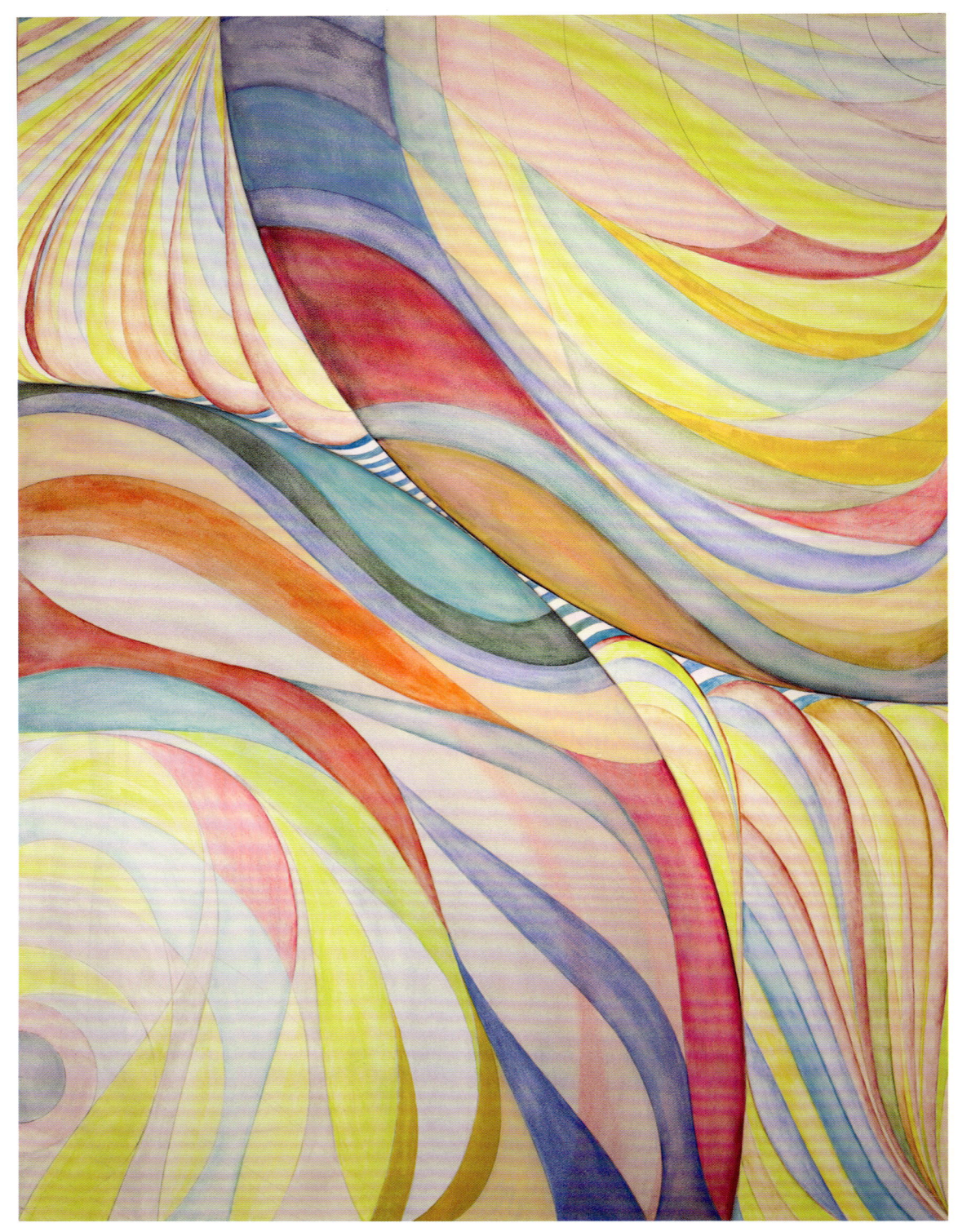

WHEEL WITHIN A WHEEL 105
30 IN X 22 IN
WATERCOLOR/GOUACHE, 2014

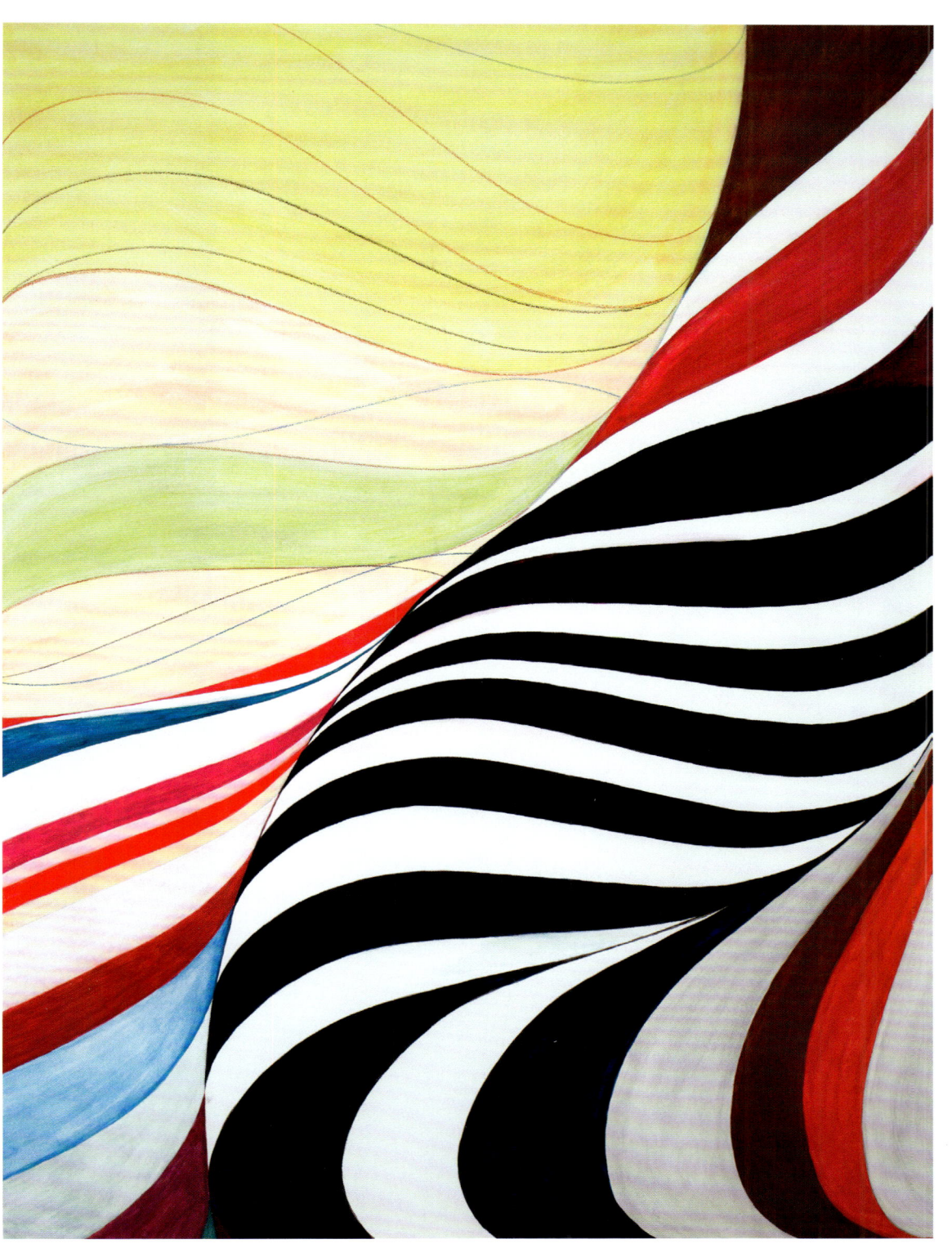

WHEEL WITHIN A WHEEL 106
30 IN X 22 IN
WATERCOLOR/GOUACHE, 2014

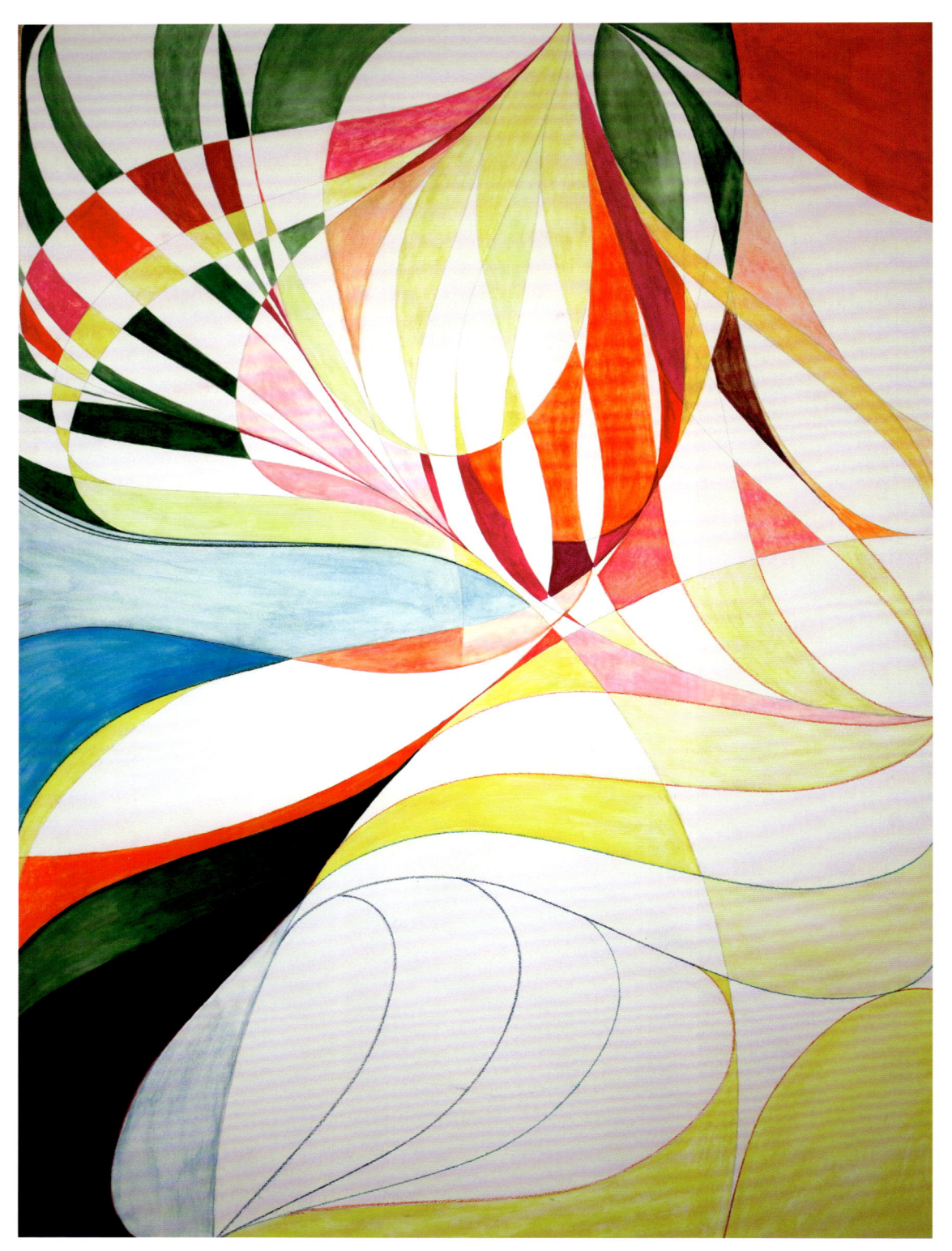

WHEEL WITHIN A WHEEL 107
30 IN X 22 IN
WATERCOLOR/GOUACHE, 2014

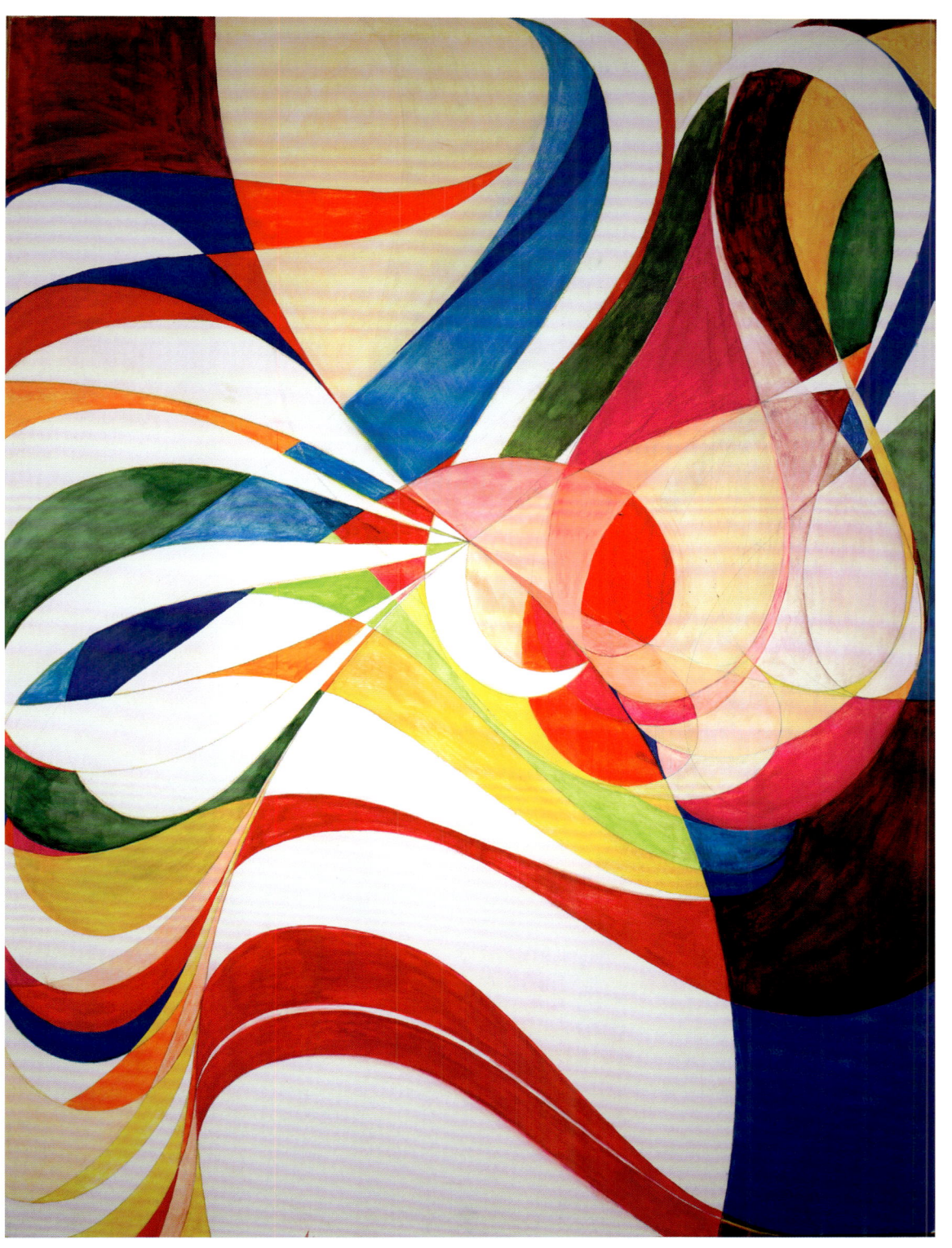

WHEEL WITHIN A WHEEL 108
30 IN X 22 IN
WATERCOLOR/GOUACHE, 2014

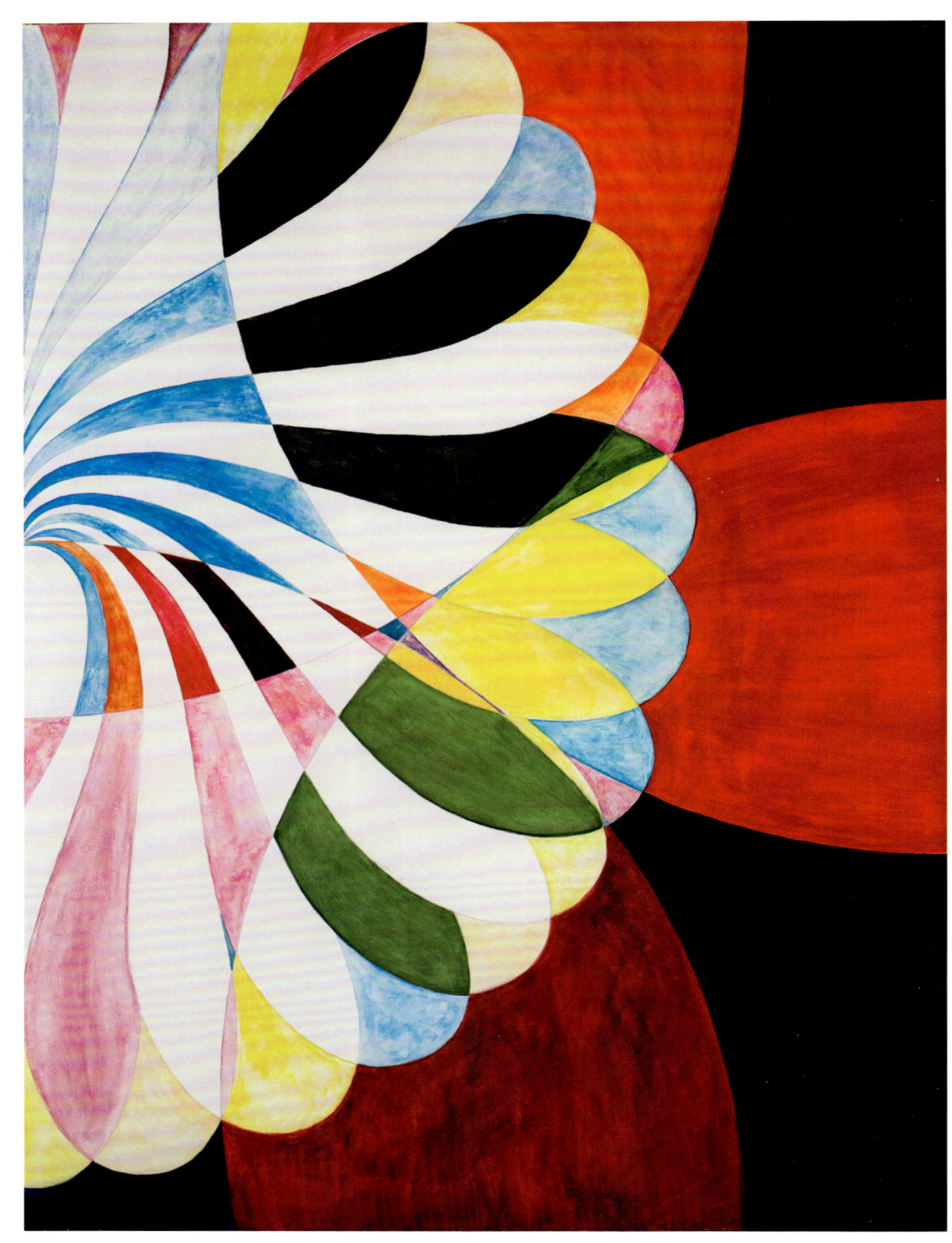

WHEEL WITHIN A WHEEL 109

30 IN X 22 IN
WATERCOLOR/GOUACHE, 2014

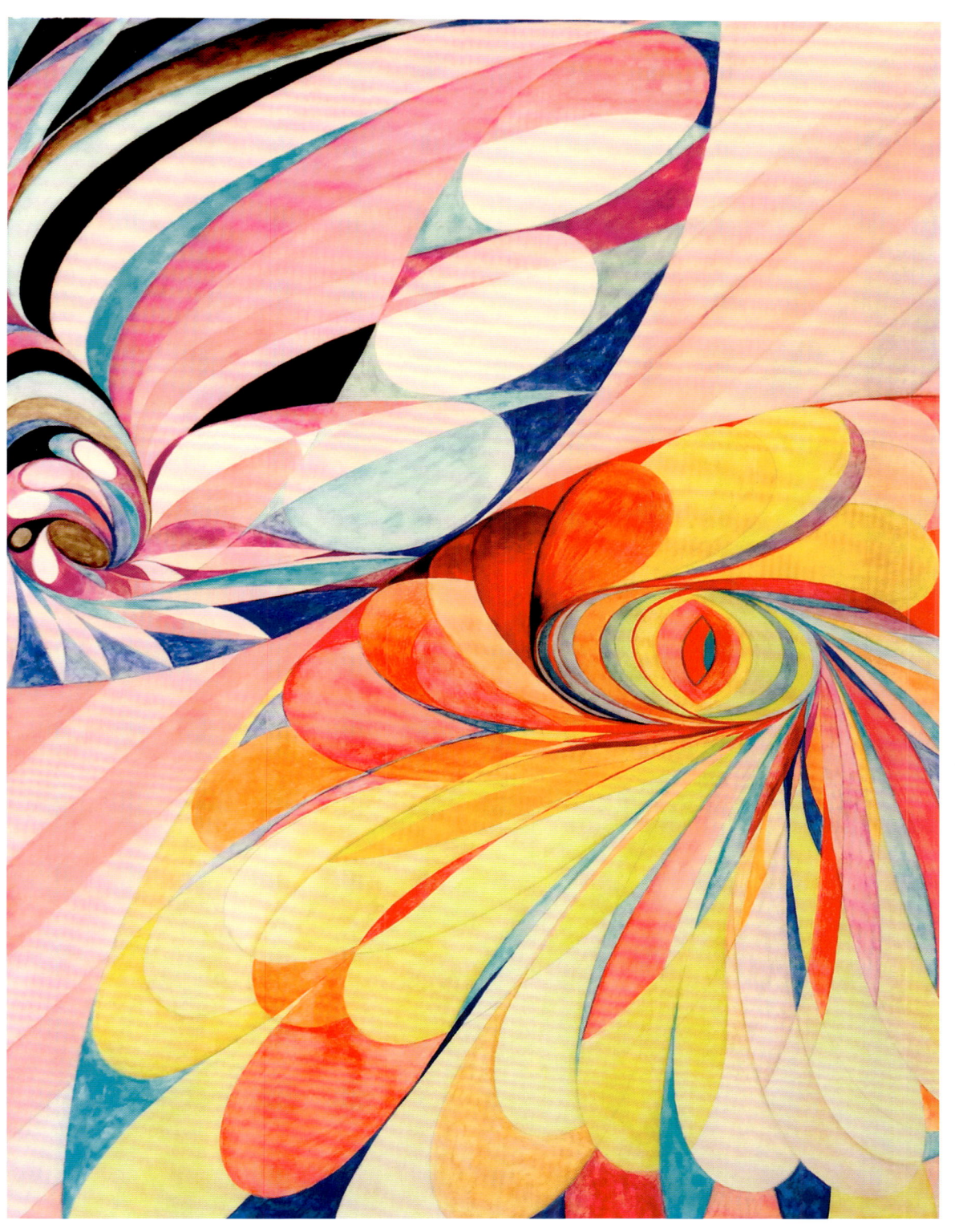

WHEEL WITHIN A WHEEL 110
30 IN X 22 IN
WATERCOLOR/GOUACHE, 2014

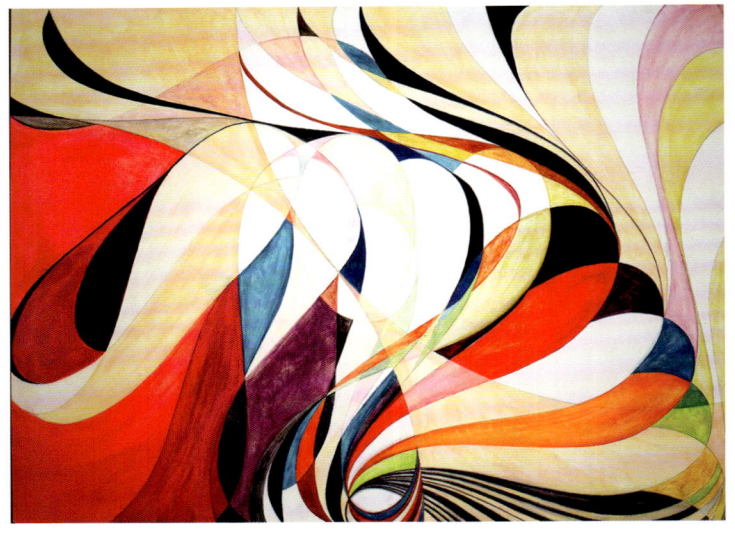
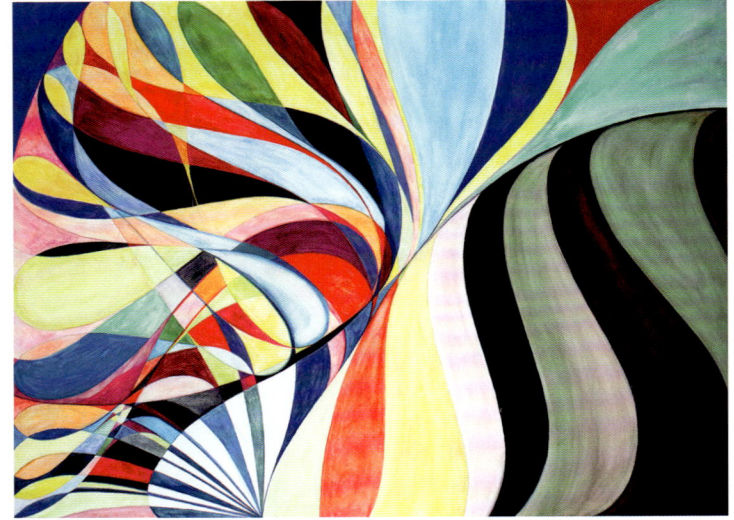
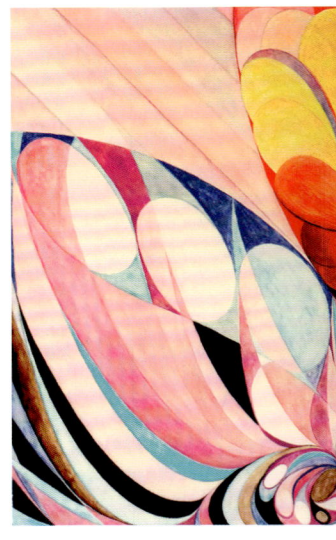
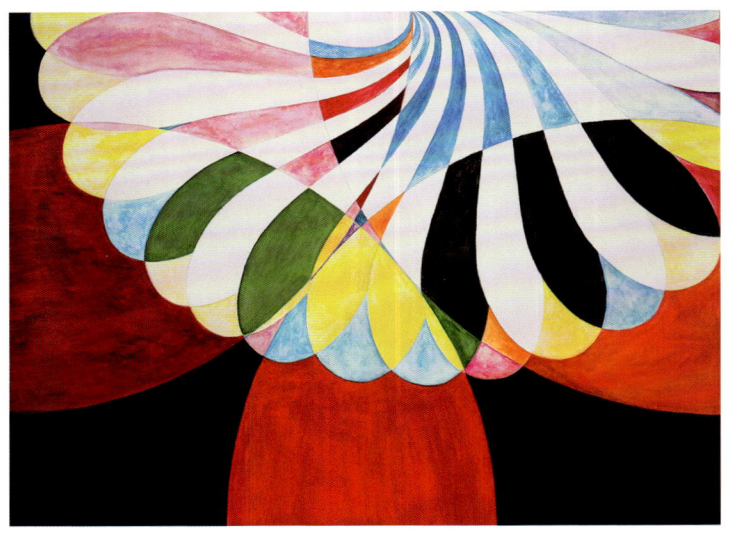
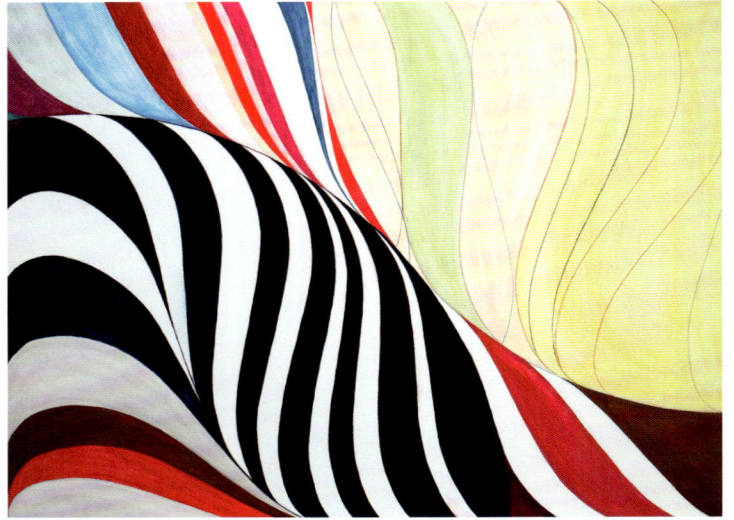
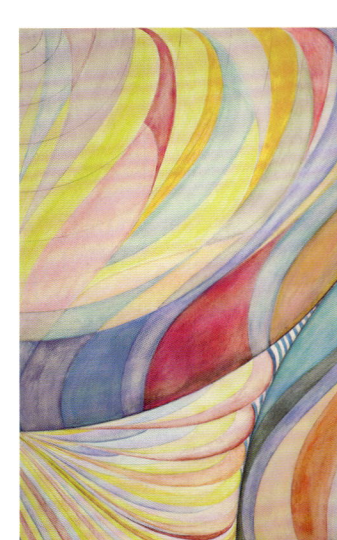

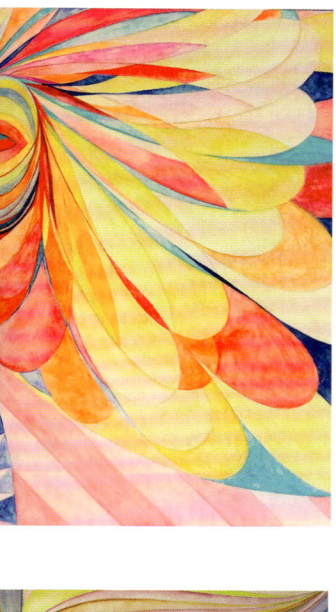
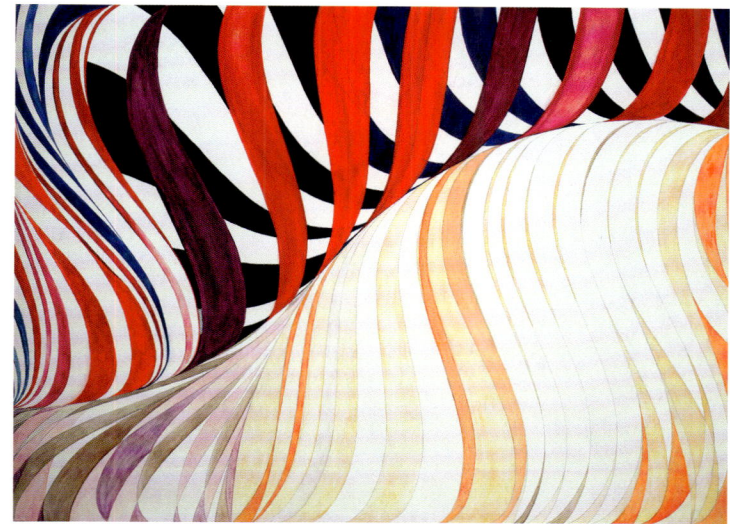
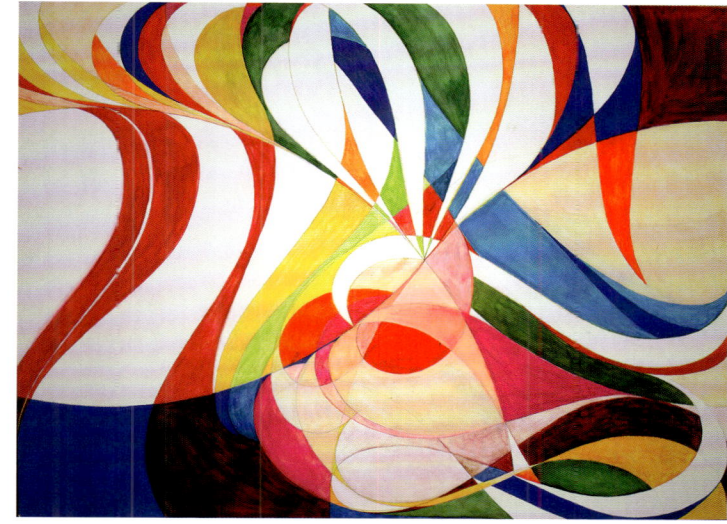
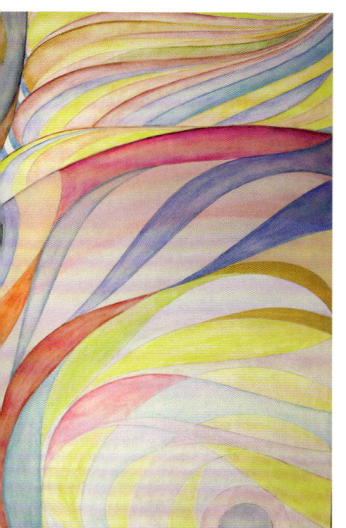
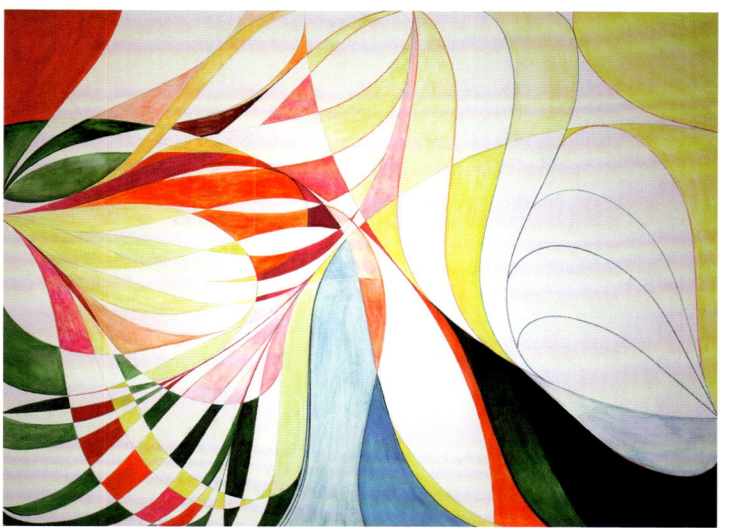
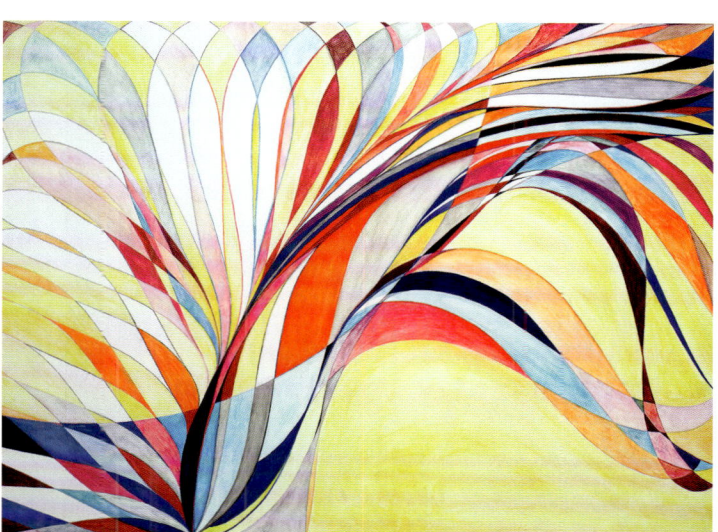

WHEEL WITHIN A WHEEL 101-110
30 IN X 22 IN (EACH PANEL)
WATERCOLOR/GOUACHE, 2014-2016

AN INSIDE EXAMINATION INTO THE MAKINGS OF THE PROCESS & PRACTICE

BY LORIEN SUÁREZ-KANERVA

THIS IS A BEHIND THE SCENES EXPLORATION OF AN ARTWORK'S EVOLUTION.

"Wheel within a Wheel" as a painting has a story that begins with geometry, metaphysics, memoir writing and book discoveries. The painting was shown at the Biennale in Venice in May of 2017.*

As a painter, I have discovered the meditative undertones of making brushstrokes on canvas. Creating art is in essence a practice of being attentive and focused in the present moment. Creative insights come to light. Over time, intuitive spiritual expressiveness grows.

A class on Teilhard de Chardin's mystical writings fed my curiosity. Cynthia Bourgeault masterfully distilled the foundation of Teilhardian metaphysics to a neophyte. The essence of his writings was the non-dual concept of how "unity differentiates, differentiation unifies."

Two specific characteristics of this unifying differentiation are "enroulment" and "convergence." Both of these processes have some easily recognizable cultural examples that Cynthia pointed out. What is enroulment? Think of winding airport lines as an efficient form of crowd control. It is the process of the rolling in of itself that occurs under the pressures of forced proximity due to a constricted space.

Convergence refers to the ever-evolving perspective that springs from an educated hope for world-wide mutual understanding. Cynthia describes it as a process where "in the long range, things come together in a point of completion which produces satisfaction in all dimensions: political, spiritual and aesthetic." An example would be the internet aiding an ongoing globalization.**

While studying, painting, working and writing, I discovered that these nebulous concepts were coming together subtly and meaningfully through the right-side of my brain especially as I painted a new work in the "Wheel within a Wheel" series.

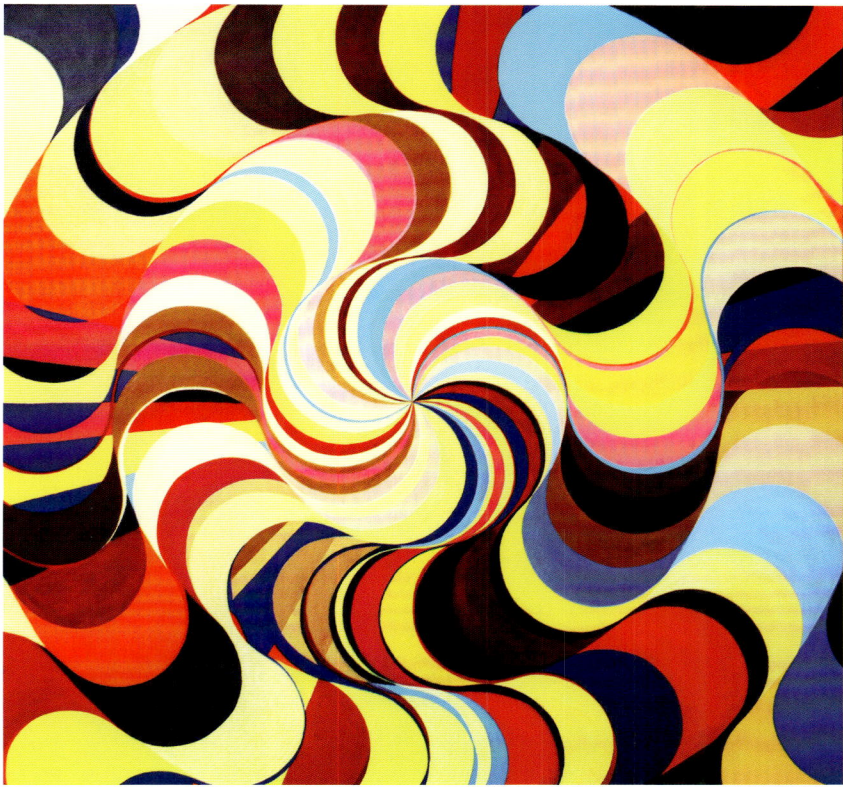

Wheel within a Wheel 2017 (above)
ACRYLIC ON CANVAS, 40 IN X 40 IN, © 2017 BY LORIEN SUÁREZ

Another step in the process of exploration happened when reading Namgyal Rinpoche's book "Unfolding through Art." At first, I was taken aback by the psychological evaluation of artists and their art-making. But, I decided to wait for more clarity before making an overall judgment. There was much that I could readily resonate with as an artist.

As human beings, we strive to become integrated at all levels: sensorial, emotional, intellectual and intuitive. Art-making allows us to discover "the preordained unfolding of [our] being."*** (p. 5) Carl Jung saw the self in its totality represented through the exercise of making a mandala.

Namgyal's book also introduces a series of exercises. The first one is that of a circle and its division into four

equal sections colored in different hues. This mandala represents stability. The second circle has three equal sections each n different colors which moves towards a sense of expansion. The last circle needs to be divided asymmetrically with the added task of bringing these multi-colored pieces towards an arrangement of stability (away from fragmentation.)

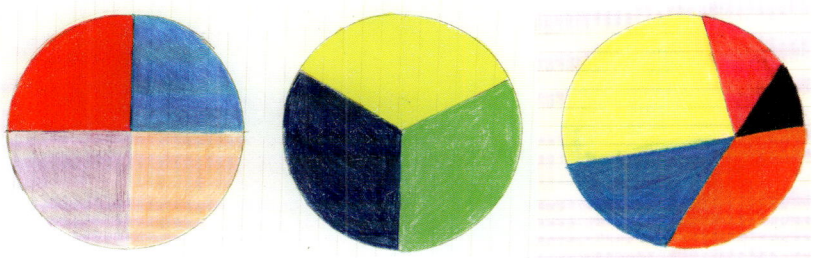

Mandala Exercise, Additional Image 1

The reader discovers whether there's a vulnerability to becoming stagnant from too much stability, or whether they lack stability. Too much expansiveness could potentially lead towards fragmentation. This knowledge is garnered by focusing on the emotions each circle exercise reveals.

What most captured my attention was Namgyal's understanding of geometry and artmaking. While working on an ongoing series of paintings over time, I intuitively came to appreciate a number of the qualities he sets forth in his book on geometric abstract art.

"The precision required to do geometrical work is in itself stabilizing. Some people may not like geometry because its components or aspects are fixed. But geometry represents the precise basic laws upon which the creative flow of the universe is set. Once you know the components, those fixed aspects will come alive. Your interpretation, the details you choose to fill in, will reveal whether your mandala is a living representation of the underlying stability of the universe." (p. 2)

As an example, Namgyal reflects on Mondrian's paintings. His artistic exploration was based on a progressive development. The evolution of Mondrian's work drew from a cultivated knowledgeability of form. His patterns and symbols were distinctively his own.

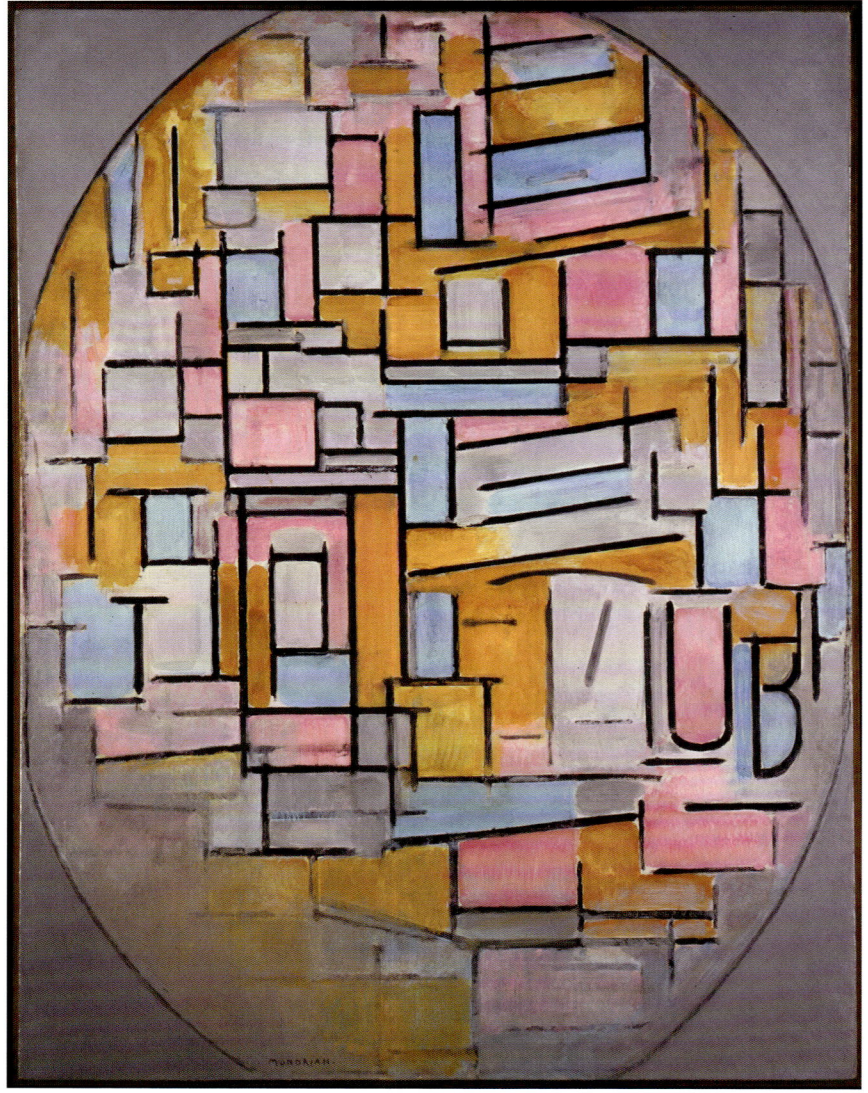

Piet Mondrian, Composition in Oval with Color Planes 2, 1914.

Through numerous progressive exercises, artists experience an evolution in their self-definition. From statements of existence, such as "I am here, I have made my mark," there's an exertion towards mastery. A realization that "I am able to make an impact on my environment" reveals an expansion of the artist's cognizance. (p. 4) Here is the distinguishing testimonial of a Bodhisattva - Namgyal's estimation of an enlightened path.

I discovered the value of truth-telling as a path towards self-discovery and liberation while learning about memoir writing with Mark Matousek. The unveiling of oneself before another nurtures sensitivity and awareness. Mutual understanding grows through this process. There is a community-building quality to these sharing of experiences especially through our stories or paintings as expressions of real life.

Since trust is built through the integrity that is shared by the artist with the audience, a spiritual intimacy becomes possible. Namgyal addresses this quality inherent to the arts that enables individuals to come together. "In every attempt to know, there's a bit of knowing, and knowing is beautiful. Everybody recognizes a masterpiece because the beauty is communicated, it immediately draws the viewer into knowing." (p. 7) This is an empowering, affirming and inspirational meditation for artists.

Seven years ago at MOCA's retrospective of Arshile Gorky in Los Angeles, I appreciated his artistic spirit distilling existential knowledge from the paintings that encompassed his life. The visual experience of the colors, forms, the spaces and movement are unique to his artwork. His earnest artistic engagement amidst everything in the tragic reality of his life stands as a poignant testament of Gorky as a "being of art."

*"Art must remain earnest... I communicate my innermost
perceptions through the art, worldview... I do not paint in
front of but from within nature... Abstract art enables the
artist to perceive beyond the tangible, to extract the infinite
out of the finite. It is the emancipation of the mind. It is an
explosion into unknown areas."*

ARSHILE GORKY

"Unfolding through Art" speaks of art as a stimulus
amongst people for a more expansive and integrated form
of consciousness. Our potential for unity has a hopeful
light in the mystical movements that readily perceive
universal laws and meaning to be found in life.

Art to me is a form of knowledge of the heart. Creative
practice brings forth discoveries that outlive their
creators, serve the evolution of meaningful understanding,
and give birth to a more profound vision of the unfolding of
life.

FOOTNOTES:

** Exhibition: "Personal Structures: Time, Space, Existence," May
13-November 26, 2017, 57th Venice Biennale, hosted by the GAA
Foundation/European Cultural Centre at the Palazzo Bembo*

*** Adapted from "Teilhard for our Times," Copyright 2016 by Cynthia
Bourgeault*

**** "Unfolding through Art", Namgyal Rinpoche, United States: The Open
Path. Copyright 1982. Adapted with permission from Bodhi Publishing,
www.bhodipublishing.org*

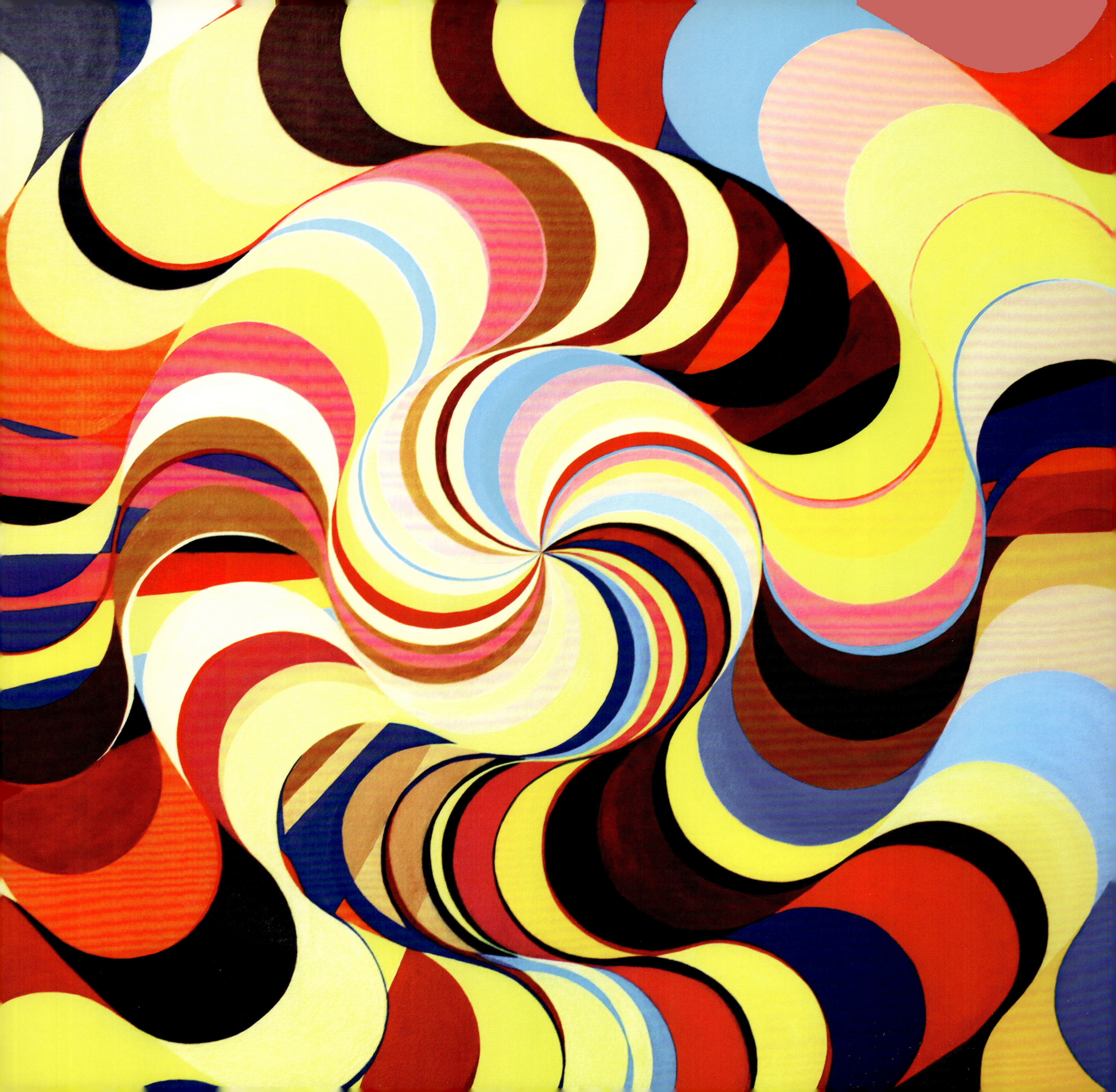

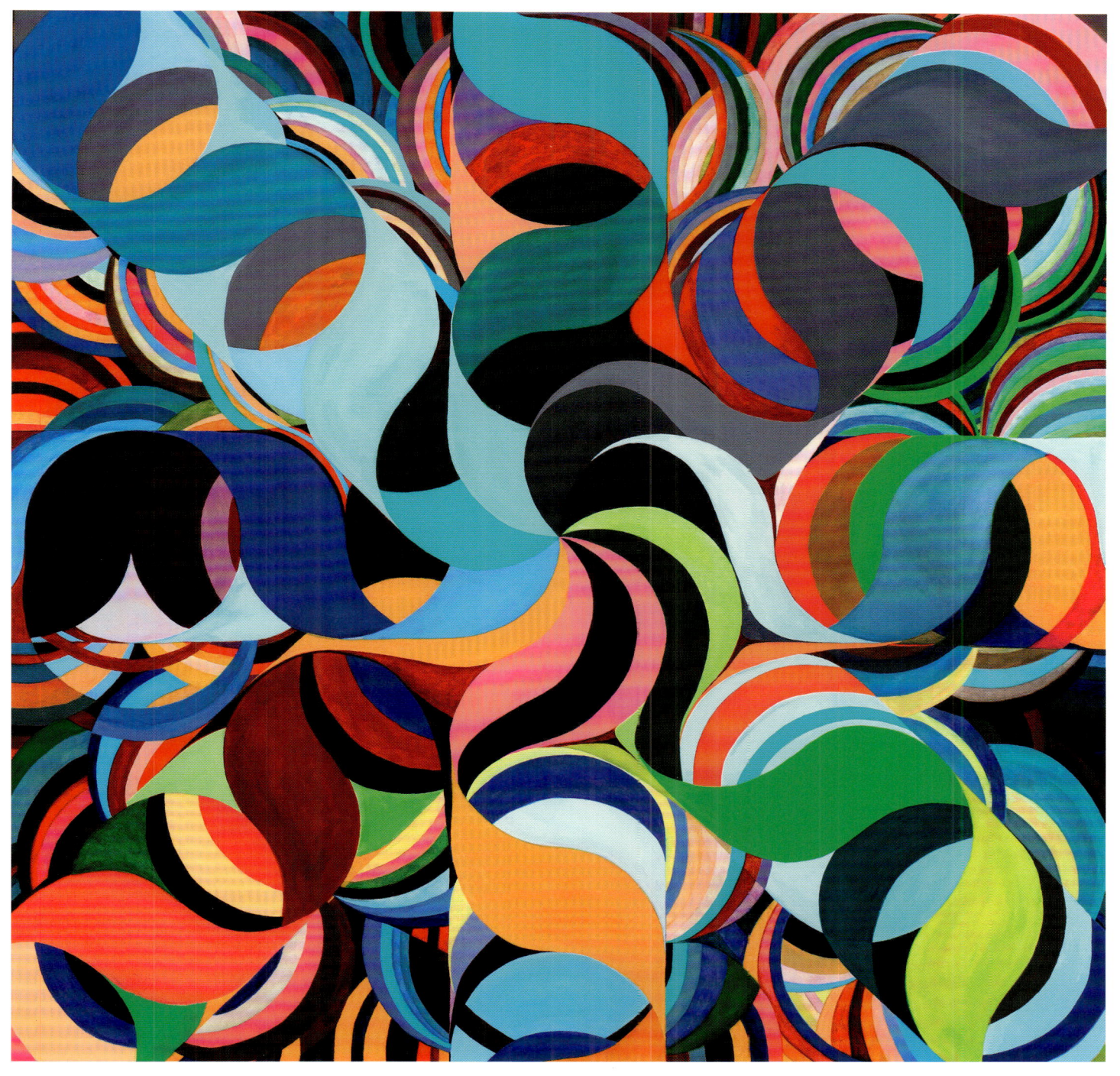

WHEEL WITHIN A WHEEL 114 *(LEFT)*

40 IN X 40 IN
ACRYLIC, 2017

WHEEL WITHIN A WHEEL 116

40 IN X 40 IN
ACRYLIC, 2018

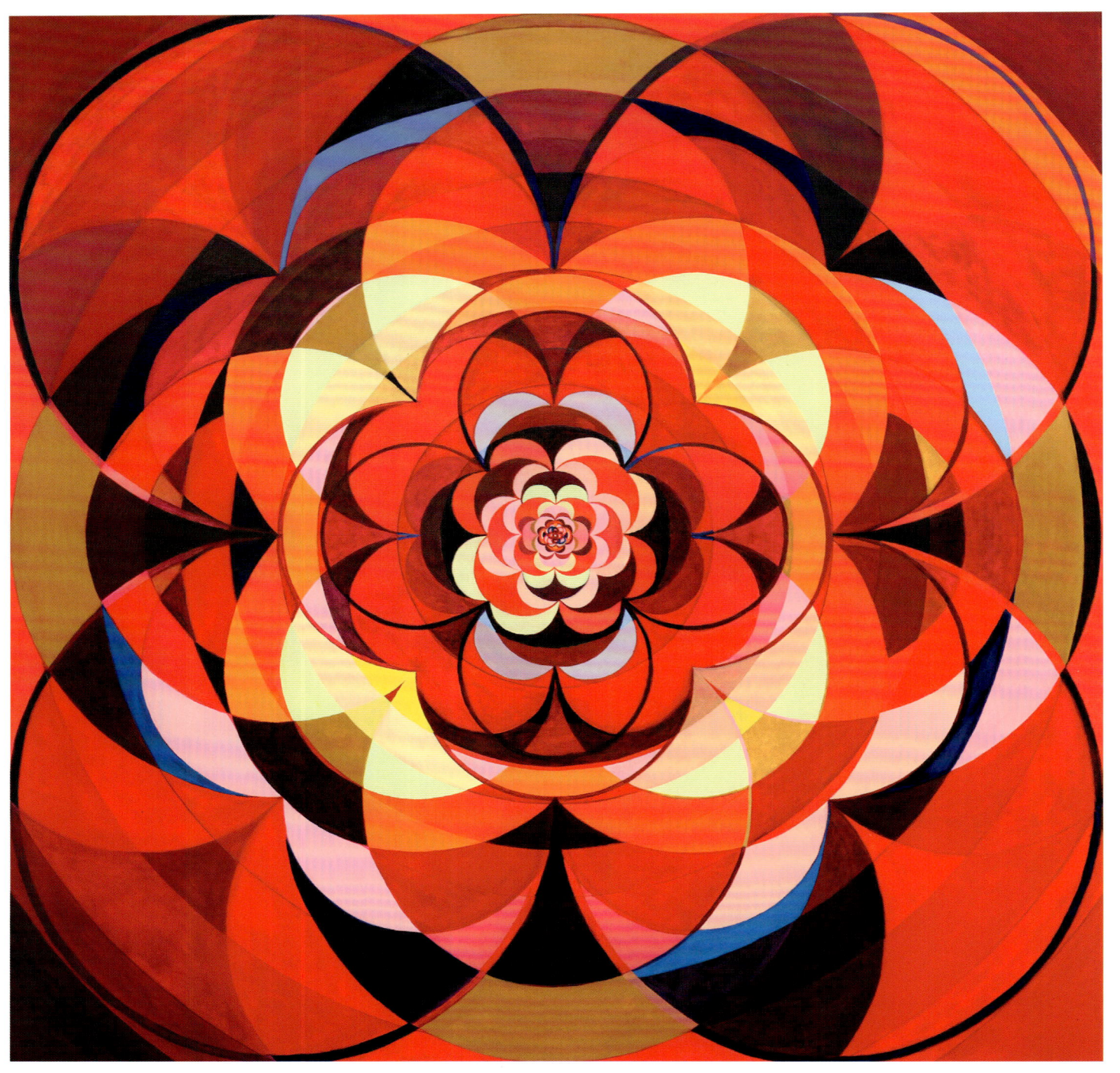

WHEEL WITHIN A WHEEL 117
40 IN X 40 IN
ACRYLIC, 2018

WHEEL WITHIN A WHEEL 118 *(RIGHT)*
40 IN X 40 IN
ACRYLIC, 2018

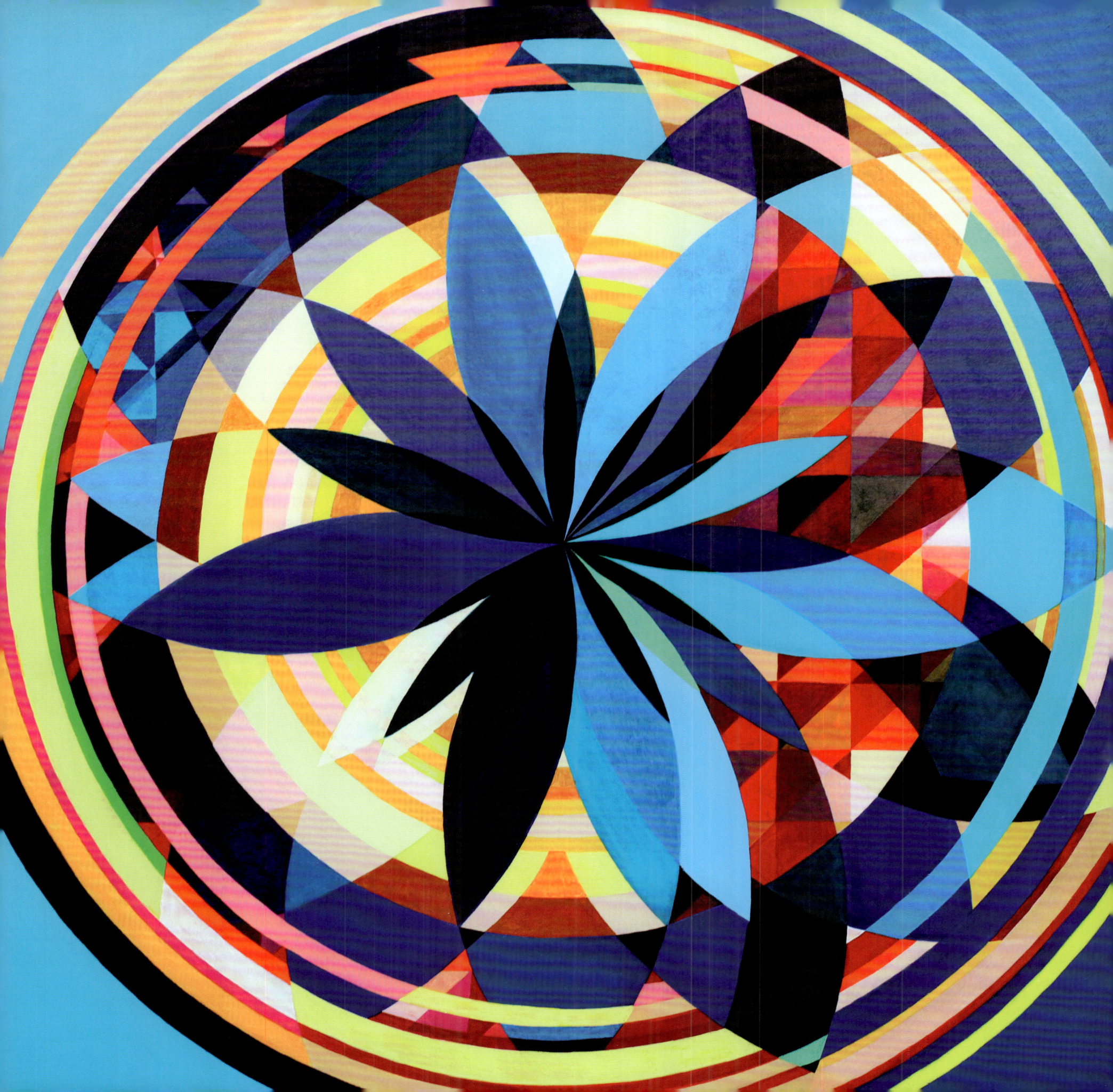

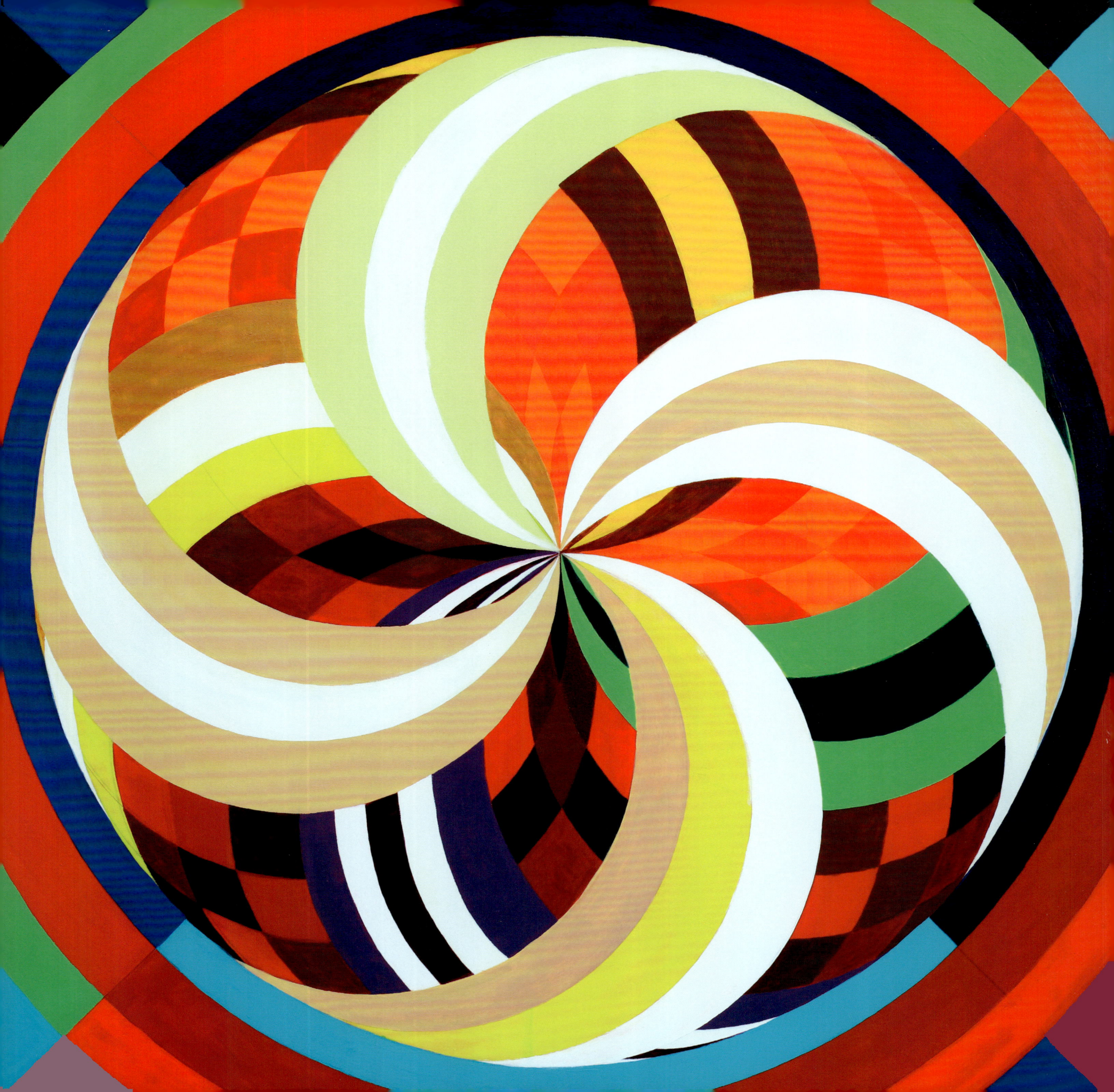

WHEEL WITHIN A WHEEL 119
40 IN X 40 IN
ACRYLIC, 2018

GEOMETRIC BOTANICALS

OBJECTS OF VIRTÚ: CREATIVITY IN USE

MEANINGFUL UTILITY BY LORIEN SUÁREZ-KANERVA

THE THINGS OF THIS WORLD ARE VESSELS, ENTRANCES FOR STORIES; WHEN WE TOUCH THEM OR TUMBLE INTO THEM, WE FALL INTO THEIR LABYRINTHINE RESONANCES.

LYNDA SEXSON

Geometric Botanicals grew from a journey of exploration. Each year more facets about botanical sources such as petals from flowers and bark from trees were discovered. Alongside these plant discoveries, I found new forms of employment of techniques for surface design on textiles as an art form. The journey of exploration led to both a signature style, through a personal language with geometric and botanical forms, and an extension of my creative energy towards utility and practical applications.

Still, it all begins in the garden. Since childhood, I have sought out gardens. I enjoy collecting and tending plants, learning about them, and even experimenting with them. One of the botanical gardens that holds a strong impression from my childhood is the Jardín Botánico de Caracas in

Venezuela. The size of the trees, its vast spaces, along with the extensive and diverse gamut of plant types, that I encountered there, were awe inspiring.

When I moved to Oregon (United States,) I became accustomed to being surrounded with lots of green lush vegetation. All the years of hiking in the forests enhanced my appreciation of plants. So naturally, when I came across David Lee's book *Nature's Palette*, I wanted to undertake the task of working with natural dyes. I fell into its "labyrinthine resonances" and the results were surprising and truly beautiful!

Yet, the mordants needed to fix the dyes to the fabric ultimately made me reconsider and pause. Some of these substances were best not to have around my young son. The project would have to wait for a more appropriate time and workspace setting with the materials.

I still have a dozen or so silk scarves and ties that were dyed with these natural pigments. Many were drawn from eucalyptus trees and garden flowers especially planted for this purpose. Others like Brazilwood and Logwood are still readily available and are well known historically as important dyes in the textile industry. My most memorable dye was that from the Cosmos flower. It is a little yellow-orange wildflower. The dye created from these blooms was the most beautiful gold. I was glad for the chance to work with it at the time to fully appreciate the beauty to be found in botanical pigments!

Along with the exploration of the physical qualities of these botanical dyes, I explored the natural design elements to be found in the geometries that are evident in plants.

These geometric compositions are at the heart of my work and have evolved over many years especially in my work with the *Wheel within a Wheel* series of paintings.

Some of my earliest paintings were abstract idealized flowers. Many were done in my high school years. These continued throughout college, when they began to evolve towards a focus on geometric symmetries.

Through an initial naturalist art workshop, I explored the

portraiture of flowers and fell in love with watercolors! And then, this journey with geometric botanicals evolved towards digital processes, many of which given our technology are more environmentally friendly.

If we consider and care for each object that we keep, we become producers of meaning rather than consumers of goods. **THE BOOK OF HYGGE BY LOUISA THOMSEN BRITS**

My earliest experiences with creating and offering digitally printed scarves for sale took place while I lived in Riverside, California. I would print these using my in-house ink jet printer onto silk and sold these at the Art Museum's Gift Shop. I discovered that my paintings reproduced nicely as textile designs. Each scarf held a different motif based on my paintings and these accessories became useful as objects intended to satisfy a purpose as a fashion accessory. The application of my creative designs on the surface of consumer products allowed for many new means of utility and accessibility.

Along with digitally printed artwork, I also painted with French dyes on silk along with silkscreen printing, gutta resist techniques, stenciling and shibori (or hand knotting) of naturally dyed multicolored scarves.

The process of carving the stencil blocks, the placing of the dyes along the gutta resist lines, creating the silk screens and steaming the dyed silk was in itself a labor of love. The completed scarves and neckties each have their own story of development from start to finish. Along with the design elements, the tactile and visual nature of the materials of these scarves and ties was also relevant and enhanced the appreciation of them.

In our appreciation of a well-turned bowl or delicate watercolor, we participate in its creation. **IBID.**

Some years later, I received an invitation from VIDA to license my artwork and allow them to reproduce my designs digitally onto textile fabrics. They offer artists a means to use their artwork for textile printing of fashion and home accessories. VIDA is a printer on demand and uses environmentally responsible forms of printing. Through literacy programs for their workers, it is also socially responsible. And the workmanship was good. The textile

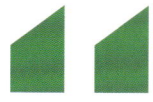

Since childhood, I have sought out gardens. I enjoy collecting and tending plants, learning about them, and even experimenting with them.

accessories are beautiful! With this strong inducement to look at an extension into partnering with a manufacturer of fashion accessories, I became a surface design and textile artist for fashion and home interiors.

A space softened with textiles offers us an entry point into a world of comfort that we can each experience as our own. **IBID.**

Homes and work places can serve as spaces that enrich our souls and nurture our vitality. I've included Louisa Thomsen Brits statements, based on the Danish concept of *Hygge*, since much of my own sense of "*contentment, comfort, and connection*" draws from an artfulness that I've sought to foster in my daily patterns. Through an attentive employment of the "everyday" elements that are to be found in household and personal objects, that hold both practical functions and existential meaning, day to day life can be more readily welcomed as a gift. Social and cultural traditions, like *Hygge*, can serve as signposts with their pragmatic creative wisdom.

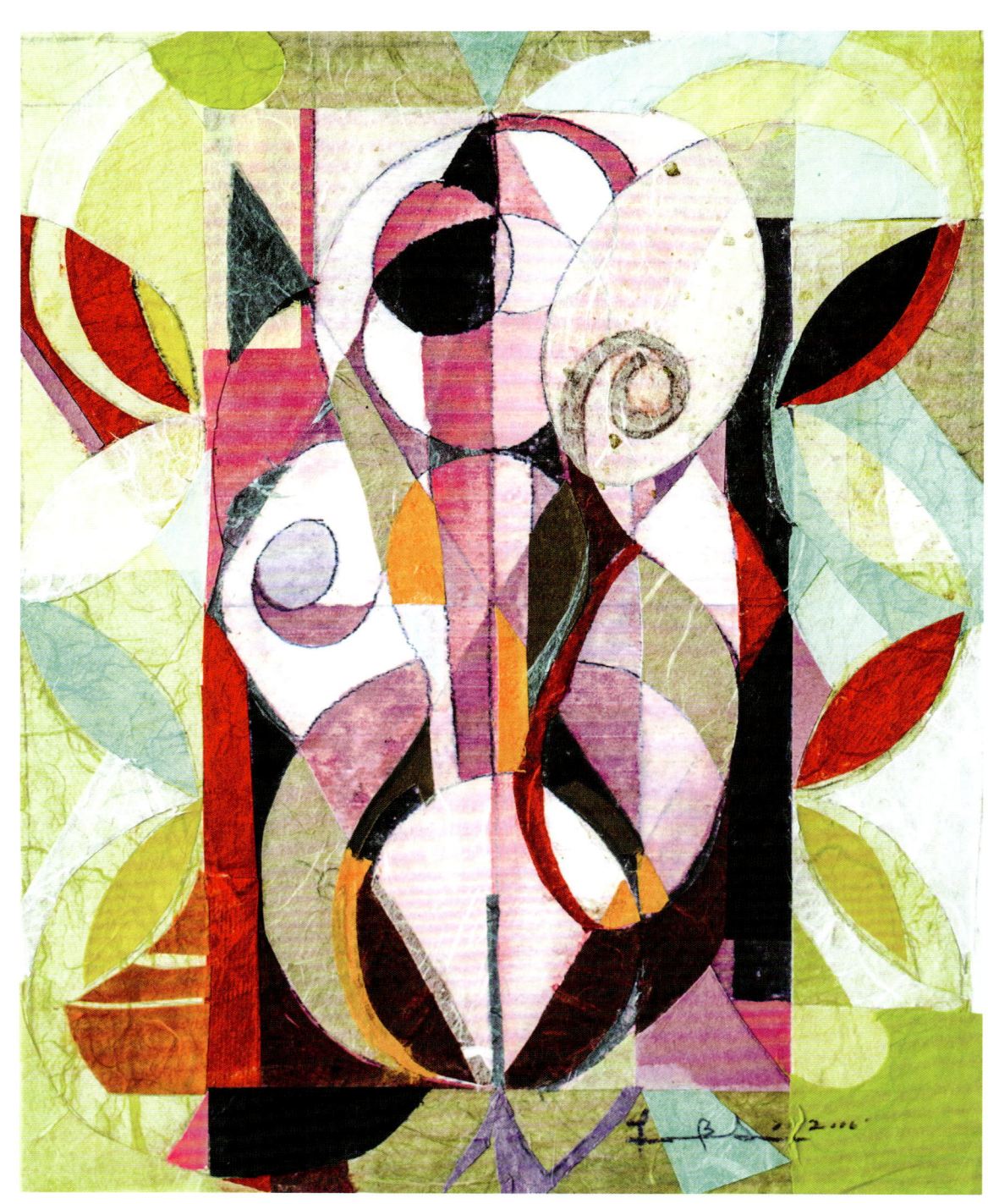

GEOMETRIC BOTANICALS 1

12 IN X 10 IN
COLLAGE, 2009

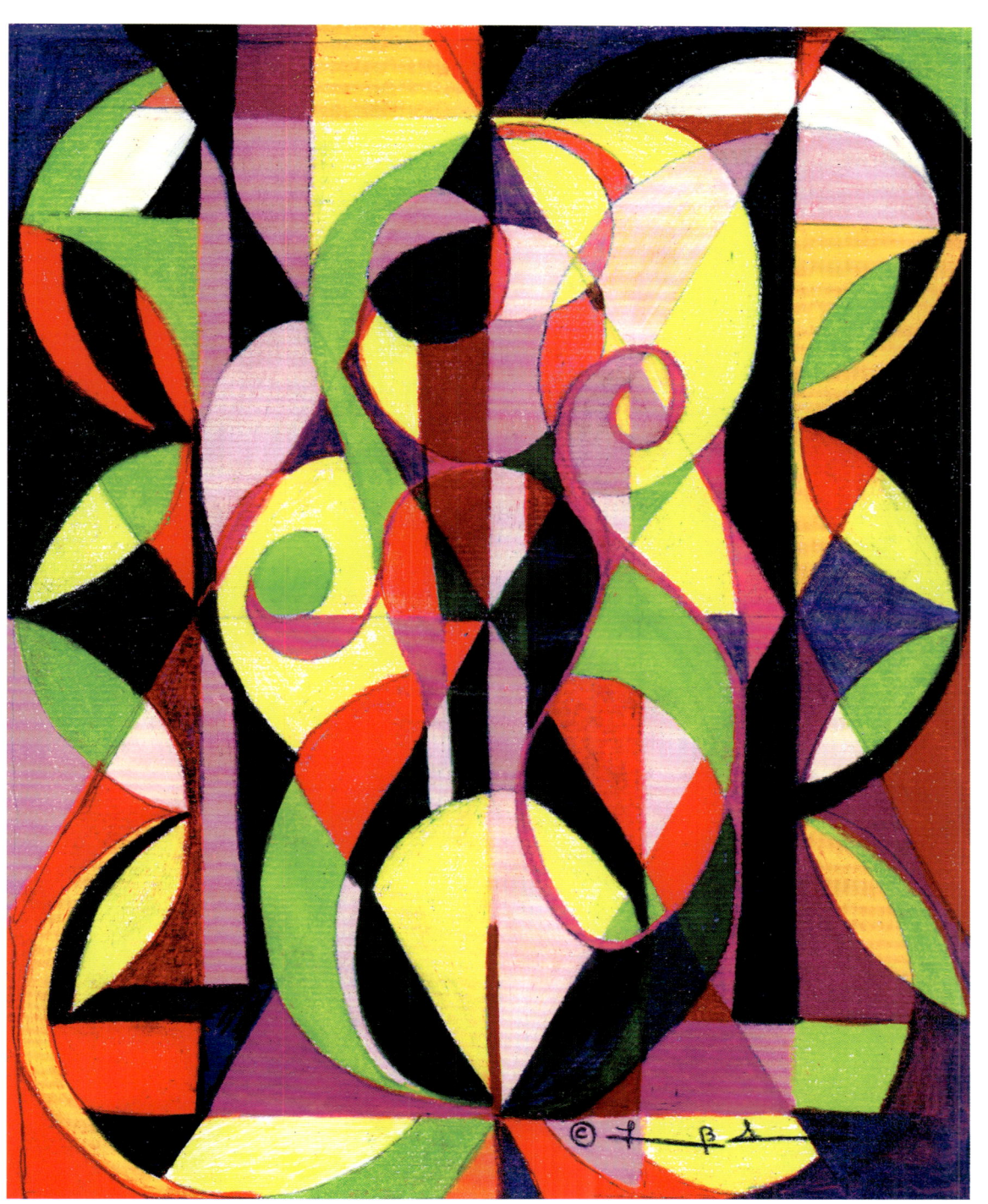

GEOMETRIC BOTANICALS 2
12 IN X 10 IN
PASTELS, 2009

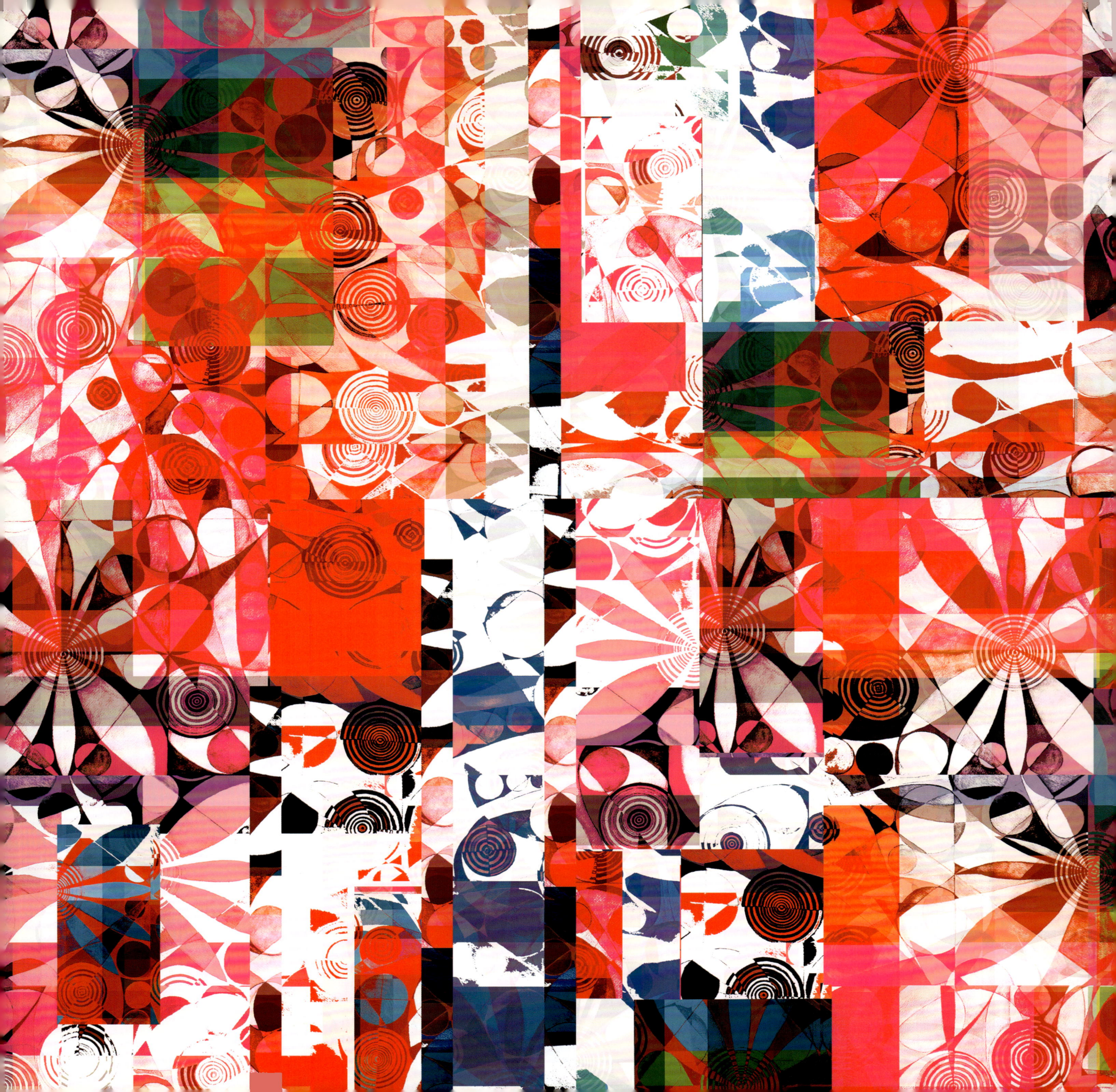

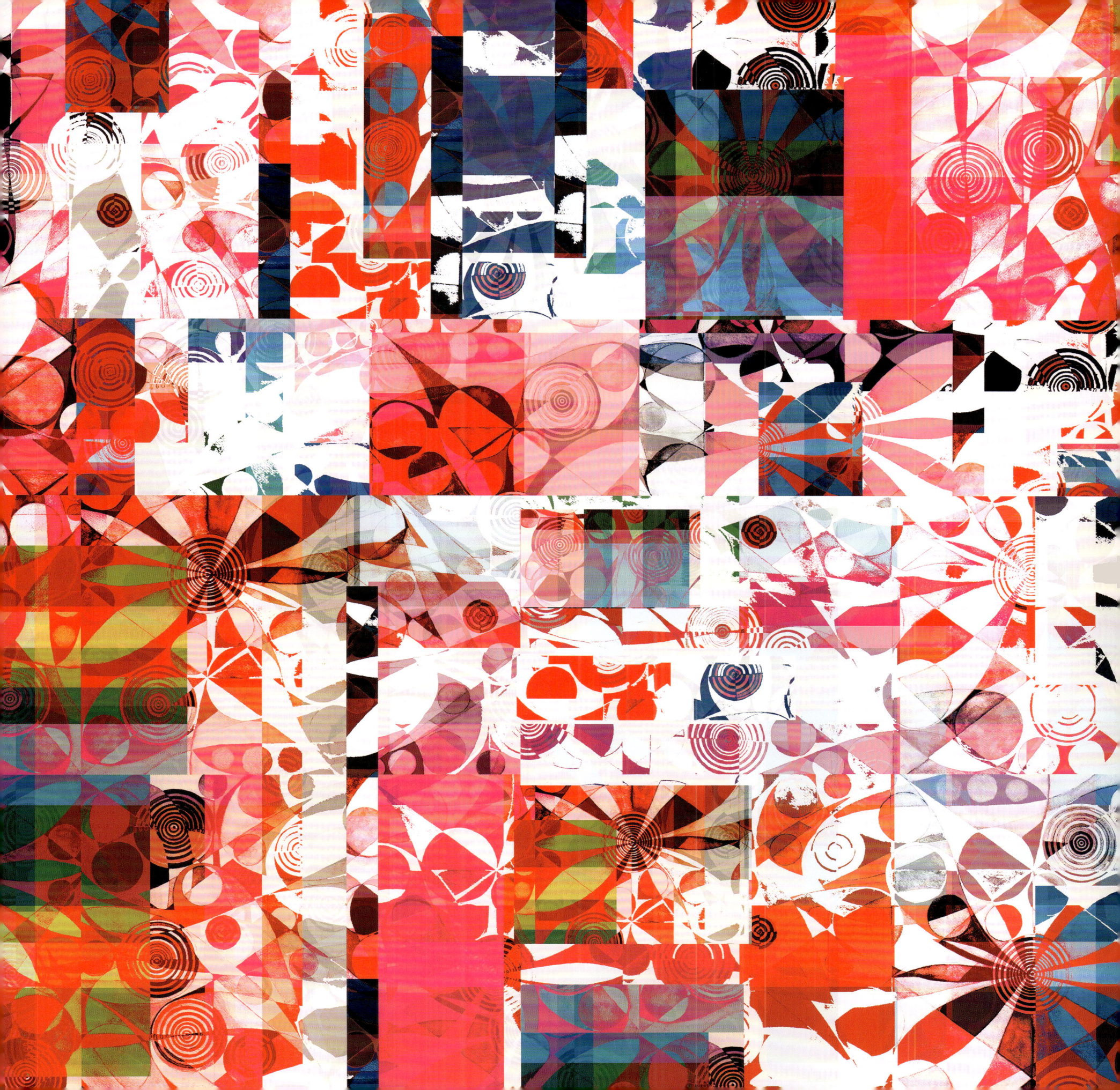

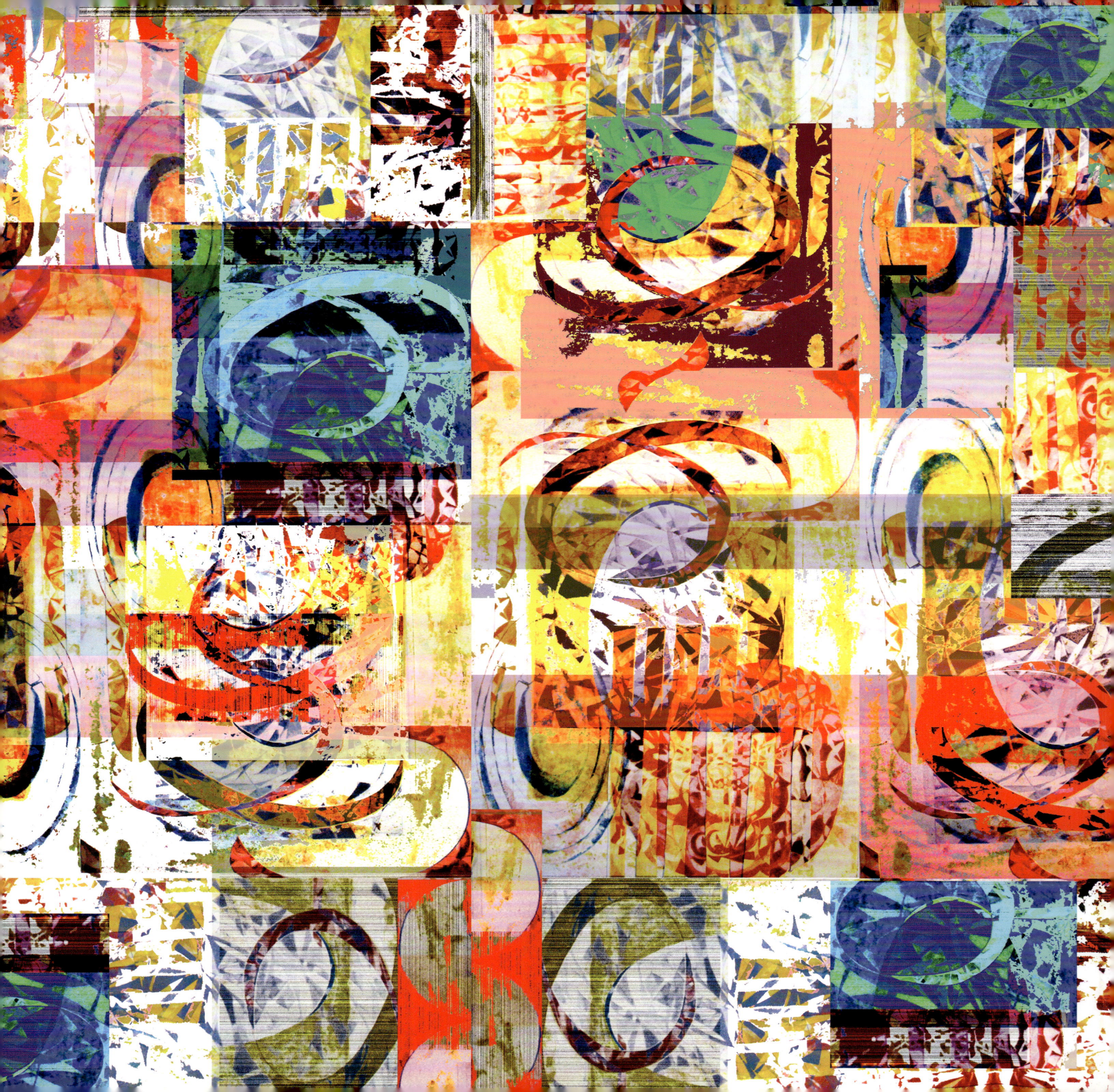

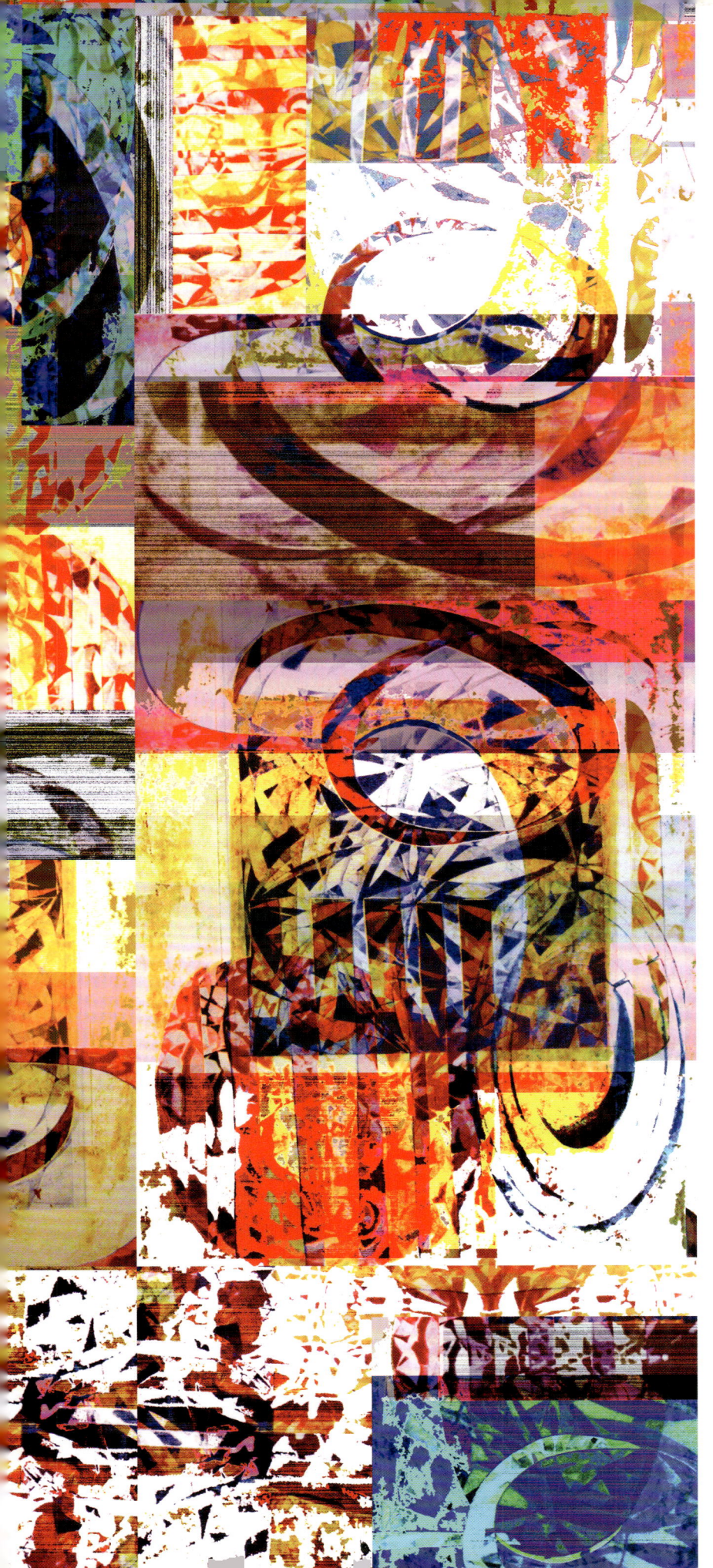

GEOMETRIC BOTANICALS 3 *(PREVIOUS)*

DIGITAL COLLAGE 2016
TEXTILES

GEOMETRIC BOTANICALS 4

DIGITAL COLLAGE 2016
TEXTILES

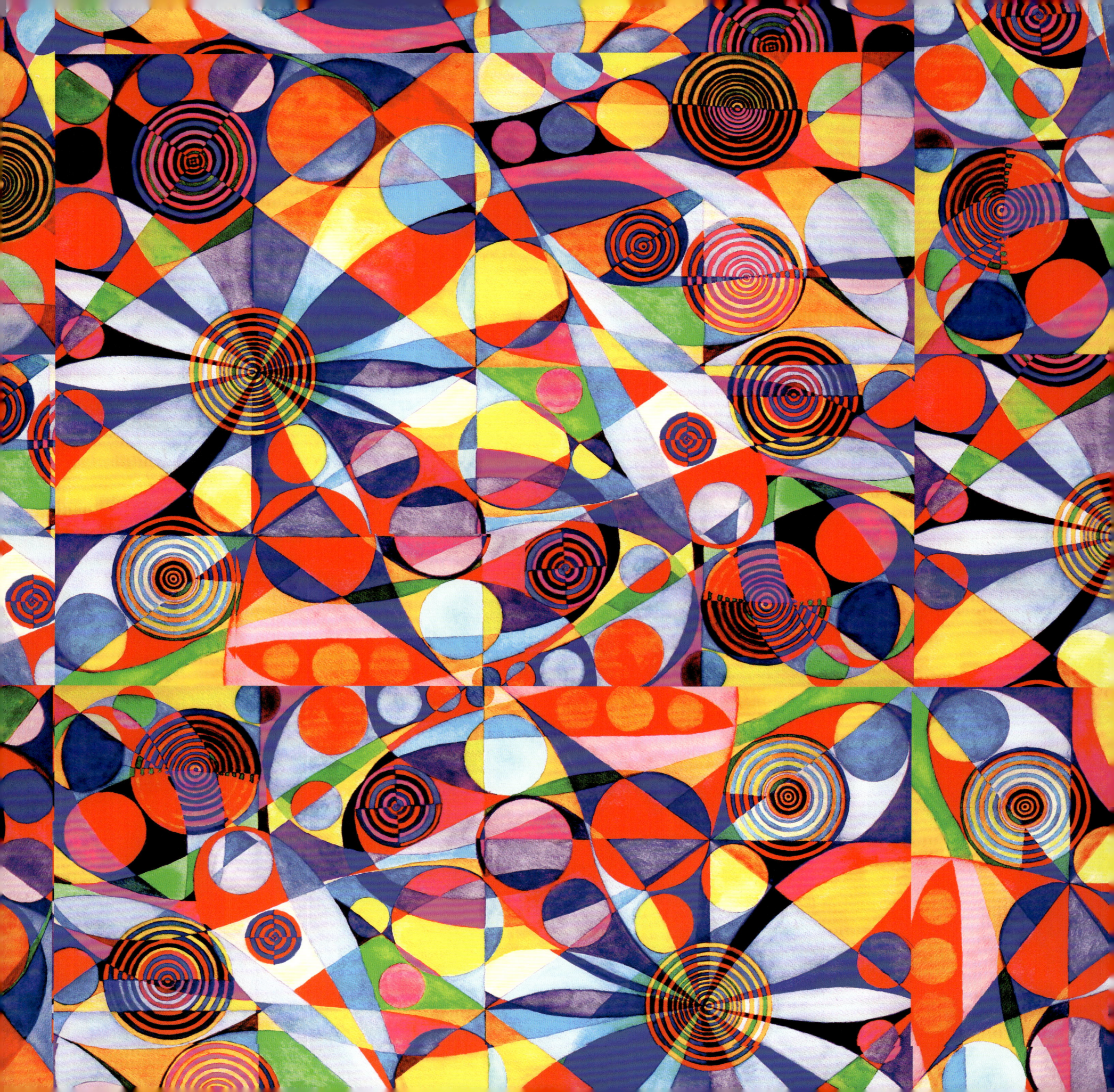

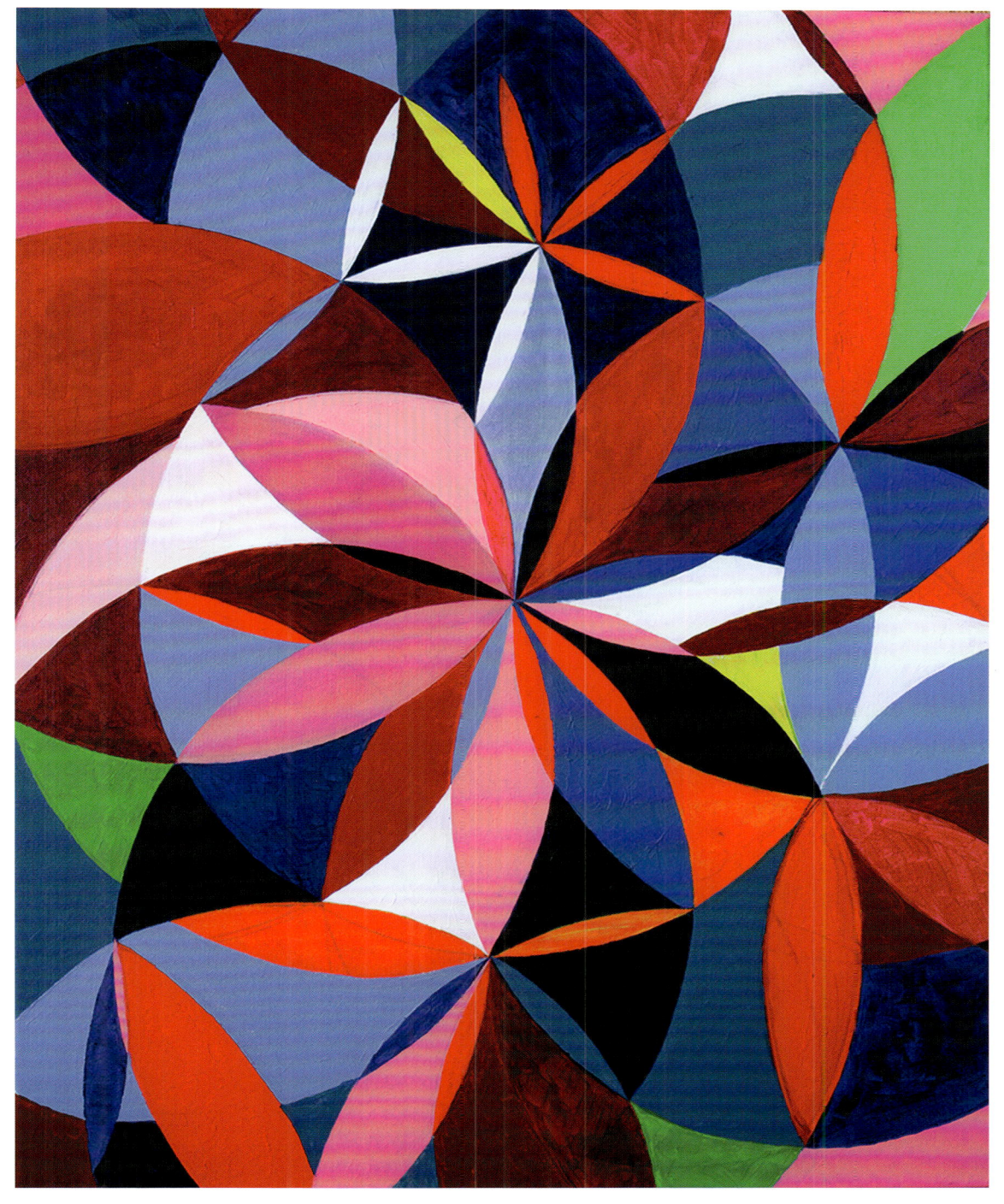

GEOMETRIC BOTANICALS 6 *(LEFT)*

DIGITAL COLLAGE, 2016
TEXTILES

GEOMETRIC BOTANICALS 5

18 IN X 24 IN
ACRYLIC, 2009

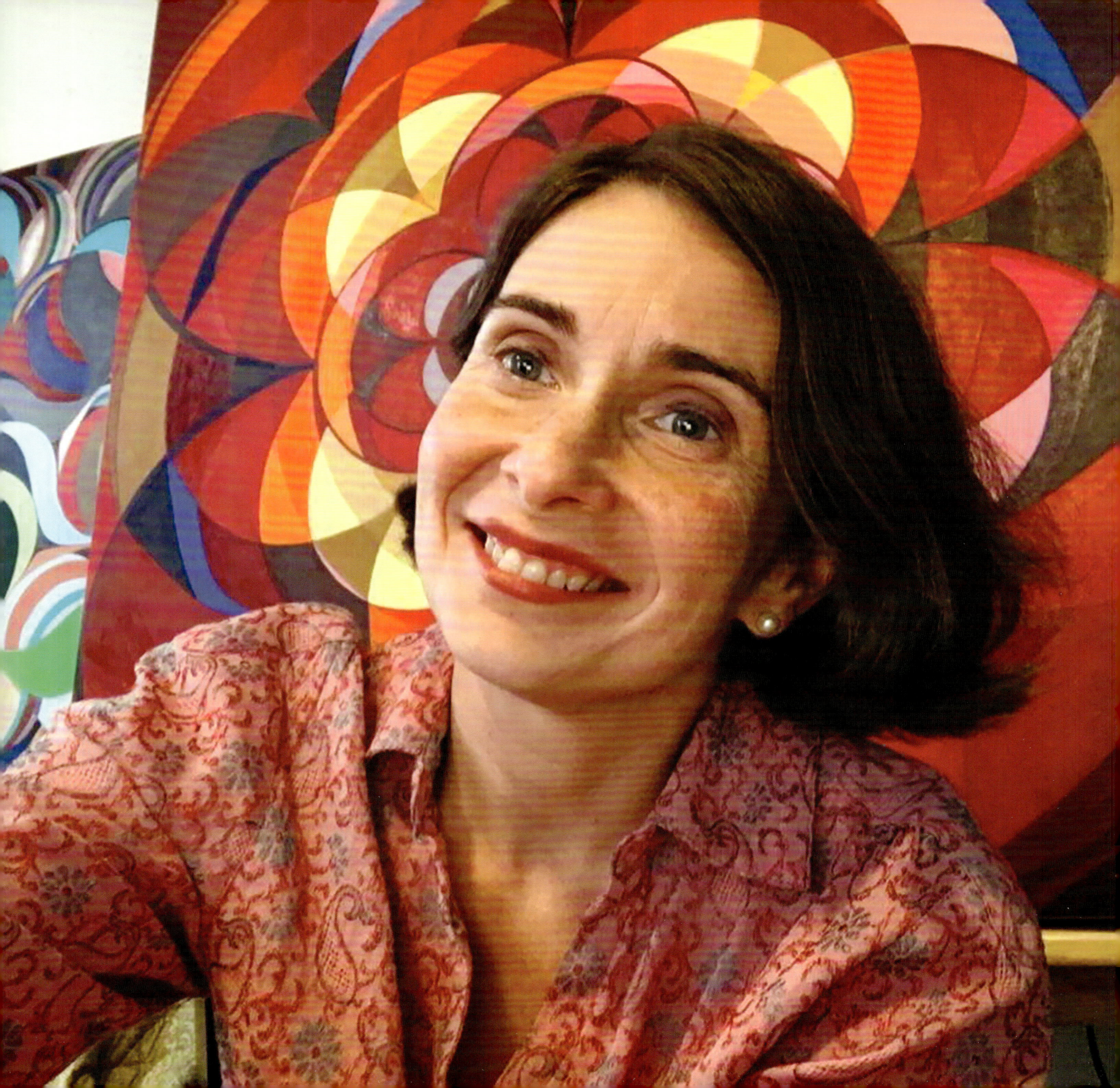

ACKNOWLEDGMENTS

IT IS WITH A PARTICULAR APPRECIATION OF MY FAMILY'S FAITH AND SUPPORT IN MY ARTISTIC PURSUITS THAT I ACKNOWLEDGE HOW I HAVE RECEIVED OVER THE YEARS THEIR BENEVOLENT WISDOM AS MY "KITCHEN CRITICS."

In recognition of Milagros Bello, Peter Frank, John Mendelsohn, Terrence Sanders, Evan Senn and Brittni Winkler for their writing contributions to this book. Each brought through their unique talents and vision an enrichment to the presentation of the artwork.

To Mercedes Samaniego Boneu and Ira Lapidus, whose mentoring presence has followed me through the decades and blessed me with their counsel and influence, as well as the Universities of Salamanca and UC Berkeley, where I had the privilege to study with them.

With appreciation to Leslie Brown for her curated exhibition "Refraction: an Exploration of Light and Color (2008)" where I had the privilege of being included alongside two internationally recognized contemporary artists, Charles Arnoldi and Roland Reiss.

Grateful to Sheila Wolk, Ron Pokrasso and my ex-husband Daniel Foster, who as artists each spoke into my life about the courage, discipline, and craftsmanship, and of the extraordinary respect and appreciation for art that art makers share through their lifetime's dedication to the creative practice.

As a budding seeker on the mystical path, it's with a sign of respect that I acknowledge Richard Rohr, James Finley, Thomas Moore, Cynthia Bourgeault and Mark Matousek. Especially, Cynthia for giving her permission to share from her writings and Mark for his editorial eye on the article "An inside Examination into the Makings of the Process and Practice" that marked my initial foray into the world of writing beyond my academic pursuits.

LORIEN SUÁREZ

WWW.LORIENSUÁREZ.COM
LORIEN@LORIENSUÁREZ.COM

EDUCATION

ESADE Business Graduate Program, Barcelona, Spain 1998 – 2000

KATHOLIEKE UNIVERSITEIT MA in European Studies, Cum Laude, Leuven, Belgium

UNIVERSIDAD DE SALAMANCA History Department, ERASMUS-Acción Jean Monet Graduate Studies, Salamanca, Spain

UNIVERSITY OF CALIFORNIA at Berkeley BA in History, High Honors, Berkeley, California

EXPERIENCE

LORIEN SUAREZ ART STUDIO, Sole Proprietor, Artist, 2001-Present

INTEL CORPORATION, Internship, Corporate Contributions and Academic Relations, Hillsboro, Oregon

INTEL CORPORATION, Internship, Components Research Department, Santa Clara, CA

EXHIBITIONS

60 Americans, Makeshift Museum, Curator Terrence Sanders, Downtown LA, October 22-January 25, 2017

Artists 101 Gallery, Solo Show, Curator Terrence Sanders, Downtown LA, April-May 2016

Untitled Projects, Art Basel Scope Miami, Miami, Florida, December 1-6 2015

Curator's Voice Art Projects Gallery, Curator Dr. Milagros Bello, Miami, Florida

Solo Show: Coalescing Geometries, June 2-30, 2018

Trends, March 10-31, 2018

Currents, February 10-24, 2018

Pinta Miami, *Crossing Cultures*, December 6-10,2017

"New Voices from Latin America," at "Personal Structures: Time-Space-Existence," 57th Venice Biennale collateral event with GAA Foundation, Palazzo Bembo, Venice, Italy. May 13-November 26, 2017.

Optical Shifts, February 11-March 11, 2017

Art Concept Fair, *Modernism and other Languages*, November 20-December 4, 2016

PREMIUM show, November 17, 2016-January 27, 2017

Exposure, August 27-September 24, 2017

Post Kinetics Art, July 23-August 20, 2016

Scope Art Basel Switzerland, June 14-19, 2016

artbocaraton, International Pavilion of the Palm Beaches, Florida Atlantic University, March 2016.

Contra-pose, Curator Milagros Bello, February-March 2016

Miami Art Basel Premium Show, Curator Milagros Bello, December-January 2015

Salon Show, Curator Milagros Bello, September-November 2015

Riverside City College Quad Gallery

Group Show: Ron Pokrasso and Associates, curated by Leslie Brown, Riverside, California 2011-2012

Group Show: Refraction: an Exploration of Light and Color, curated by Leslie Brown, artists: Charles Arnoldi, Roland Reiss and Lorien Suárez, glasswork artists: Michael Hermann, Gina Lunn and John Ruth; Riverside, California 2008

Gallery 128

Group Show: Geometrix II, curated by Gloria Klein, 128 Livington Street, New York, Spring 2009

La Sierra University Brandstater Gallery
Group Show: The Art and Science of Climate Change, curated by Beatriz Mejia Krumbein, Riverside, California 2007

TAG Gallery
Group show: California Open Exhibition, juried by Peter Frank, Santa Monica, California 2007

Riverside Arts Council – Riverside County
Artscape, Winter Exhibition 2006

Riverside Art Museum (RAM)

RAM Art Alliance Outdoor Sculpture-Public Art Project, Giant Orange, 2007

Group show: Monothon, 2007-2009

Group show: Beyond Heritage, curated by Andi Campognone and Peter Frank, 2006

Regional artist showcase for Driven to Abstraction, curated by Andi Campognone and Peter Frank, 2006

Group show: Art Alive, 2005-2006

Museum Artist Members' Show, 2005

Group show: Monothon, 2004

Millard Sheets Gallery
Beyond Heritage, Group show: curated by Andi Campognone and Peter Frank, Pomona, CA, 2006.

Riverside Community Arts Association (RCAA)

Group Show: New Visions: Color, Energy, and Form: Artworks by Jim Huber, Lorier Suárez and Enrique Morales. Riverside, California 2005

Members Gallery Exhibition, Riverside, California 2004-2006

San Diego Art Institute (SDAI)

SDAI Members Show, Juror: Pamela Fong, (Assistant Curator of Collections and Exhibitions, San Diego Museum of Art,) Balboa Park, California 2003

SDAI Multimedia Arts Program Multimedia Art Showcase, Art walk, San Diego, California 2001

Palm Springs Art Museum (PSAM) Artists Council Show, Award: Second Place, Juror: Jeremy Gilbert-Rolfe, Palm Springs, California 2002

Oceanside Museum of Art (OMA) Artist Alliance OMA Show, Oceanside, California 2003

Escondido Municipal Gallery

Group Show: It's a Zoo Out There, Juror: Stephanie Hanor, (Assistant Curator, Museum of Contemporary Art, La Jolla, CA) Escondido, California 2003

Members Gallery Exhibition, Escondido, California 2003

COMMISSIONS, CURATORIAL PROJECTS AND COLLECTIONS

International Association of Boalt Alumni (IABA) UC Berkeley Law School, Boalt Hall, Two Artworks Commissioned, June 2011

Geoform "Geoform is an online scholarly resource, international forum, and curatorial project whose focus is the use of geometric form and structure in contemporary abstract art. The project is edited by Julie Karabenick." http://www.geoform.net

UC Berkeley, Electrical Engineering and Computer Science Department

Painting Wheel within a Wheel 47 commissioned for donation to UC Berkeley, Cory Hall's Alcove commemorating the late Dr. Richard Newton, EECS Professor and Dean of the College of Engineering.

http://www.coe.berkeley.edu/news-center/newton/memories.html